Advance Praise

"To achieve the new Sustainable Development Goals, we must achieve gender equality – and engaging the private sector in this effort is essential. *Gender Lens Investing* lays out the case for why this is more than a moral obligation; it's an economic opportunity investors can't afford to miss."

Kathy Calvin, President & Chief Executive Officer,
United Nations Foundation

"Leading organizations around the world have seen how truly inclusive economic practices lead to increased prosperity for all. Quinlan and VanderBrug detail how and why, and then introduce us to the institutions and investors at the front of this trend. The result is a comprehensive and inspirational read."

Dr. Marcos Eguiguren, Executive Director,
Global Alliance for Banking on Values

"A gender lens makes for better, more informed investment. And investors have an important role in promoting a much needed focus on gender equity in the financial industry and the wider world it affects. Quinlan and VanderBrug help point the way."

David Wood, Director, Initiative for Responsible Investment,
Hauser Institute for Civil Society at Harvard Kennedy School

Global investors increasingly understand that promoting the status of women is not just a moral imperative but a strategic one; it's essential to economic prosperity and to global peace and security. But actions have not matched understanding. Gender Lens *Investing* provides readers with the critical bridge - not only the why but the how – an in depth look at the spectrum of strategies for investing in an inclusive economy.

Melanne Verveer, Former United States Ambassador
for Global Women's Issues

Gender Lens Investing

Gender Lens Investing

UNCOVERING OPPORTUNITIES FOR GROWTH, RETURNS, AND IMPACT

Joseph Quinlan
Jackie VanderBrug

WILEY

Published by John Wiley & Sons, Inc., Hoboken, New Jersey.
Published simultaneously in Canada.

For general information on our other products and services or for technical support, please contact our Customer Care Department within the United States at (800) 762–2974, outside the United States at (317) 572–3993 or fax (317) 572–4002.

Wiley publishes in a variety of print and electronic formats and by print-on-demand. Some material included with standard print versions of this book may not be included in e-books or in print-on-demand. If this book refers to media such as a CD or DVD that is not included in the version you purchased, you may download this material at http://booksupport.wiley.com. For more information about Wiley products, visit www.wiley.com.

Library of Congress Cataloging-in-Publication Data

Names: Quinlan, Joseph P., author. | VanderBrug, Jackie, 1968– author.
Title: Gender lens investing : uncovering opportunities for growth, returns, and impact / Joseph Quinlan, Jackie VanderBrug.
Description: Hoboken, New Jersey : John Wiley & Sons, Inc., [2017] | Includes index.
Identifiers: LCCN 2016027831 | ISBN 9781119182900 (cloth) | ISBN 9781119182894 (epdf) | ISBN 9781119182887 (epub)
Subjects: LCSH: Women—Economic conditions. | Women—Employment. | Women consumers. | Women in development. | Investments–Social aspects.
Classification: LCC HQ1381 .Q476 2017 | DDC 305.42—dc23 LC record available at https://lccn.loc.gov/2016027831

Cover Design: Wiley
Cover Image: © RainforestAustralia/iStockphoto

Printed in the United States of America

10 9 8 7 6 5 4 3 2 1

To mankind's better half—past, present, and future.

—JQ

To gender lens pioneers everywhere—and a world that works for all of us.

—JV

Contents

Prologue

"We must look at the lens through which we see the world,
as well as the world we see, and that the lens itself shapes
how we interpret the world."[1]

—Stephen R. Covey

This book is the result of years of research and analysis, of thoughtful contemplation and discussion, of personal observation and experience. But the idea for the book—the moment when we decided to combine our knowledge and different perspectives on the printed page—came after a joint presentation that was almost a disaster.

We were supposed to meet on several occasions prior to the event to discuss outlooks and approaches, but each attempt proved fruitless. So, the first time we met was on stage. In front of 100 eager audience members. At a Beverly Hills hotel. The topic: Womenomics—or how empowering women can have wide ranging positive social and economic effects. Joe had written widely on the subject for U.S. Trust, the private wealth management arm of Bank of America. Jackie had only recently been hired by U.S. Trust, to build out the firm's impact investing strategy, with a particular focus on an area of expertise of hers: gender.

With no discussion of which points we'd cover, and no idea of how we'd share the spotlight, the old hand and the new hire launched into a rollicking back and forth, quite unlike anything we'd experienced before. With Joe displaying his grasp of facts and figures, and Jackie injecting new angles and subtle counterarguments, we had the audience electrified—and no one had a clue that what was happening on stage was spontaneous. Later, marketing colleagues would dub our performance "The Beverly Hills Hotel Showdown," and remind us to this day that it was one of the best presentations they'd ever seen.

Shortly afterward, we conferred on next steps—and this book is the result.

Why We Wrote This Book

Joe is a global strategist and economist by training, and has long had an interest in womenomics as a driver of global growth and economic development. With a daughter now actively engaged in the workforce, Joe is even more attuned to the gender gaps that exist in the United States. And as a longtime traveler to the emerging markets, he has witnessed the remarkable advancements of women in places like China, Latin America, and parts of Africa—a dynamic, for sure, that remains incomplete. He brings a macroeconomic perspective to women and growth, and firmly believes that in a world struggling to grow, and at a time when many nations face aging populations and shrinking labor forces, countries and companies cannot afford not to fully utilize women as an economic asset.

Trained as a strategy consultant and seasoned as a high-tech executive, Jackie came to the intersection of finance and gender a decade ago. She had helped grow a company through a public offering, then started (and closed) a nonprofit, and was now fully engaged in the emerging impact economy: finding market-based solutions to challenges in education, employment, poverty, and health. Launching a social venture fund while consulting with women's foundations triggered several important questions for her: Why did investors seeking social impact lack the gender lens that philanthropists used? And why were philanthropists avoiding asking more of their investments? What were the possibilities of applying gender analysis across a portfolio? The questions led to research, to product development, and to a seat at the table of an emerging discipline. To her position today as a managing director and investment strategist at U.S. Trust, Jackie brings an entrepreneur's lens of possibility and the experience of reviewing impact investments for a global wealth management platform. She believes that gender equality creates a world that works for all of us.

Gender lens investing—the practice of integrating gender into investment analysis—brings together our expertise and passions. While other books and much of the mainstream conversation speak to growing numbers and influence of women, gender lens investing moves from economic trends to financial strategy.

The time is now for gender lens investing given the mounting case that valuing women drives positive impact, the rising demand for more prudent investments, the maturing field of investable vehicles, and the wave of current cultural zeitgeist.

Women are among the world's greatest underutilized assets, and applying a gender lens allows one to identify companies that recognize this, or uncover the risks of companies that neglect it. A gender lens adds value across the investment community, and the impact reaches far beyond the bounds of portfolios to the economy and society as a whole.

We are far from alone in talking about the role of women in the economy and the enterprises that fuel it. It seems every week brings a new report on women's rising purchasing power, women's heath as the next big investment opportunity, or Japan betting on womenomics to turn the country around. It is no longer a rarity to hear elected officials say, "When women thrive, countries prosper," or to find CEOs holding press conferences committed to "Creating our future with women leaders."

The paradox is that while women are more visible and influential as successful entrepreneurs, corporate executives, and primary family breadwinners, many hurdles remain. Gender-based violence, the absence of women's legal rights, and the persistent wage gap are but a few challenges to be overcome.

We believe there is an unprecedented and underexplored opportunity for investors to productively use their capital using a gender lens.

People are looking for fresh ideas about how to make capitalism work better. Today a growing consensus finds the social costs of global capitalism—financial bubbles in various assets, rising income inequalities, and mounting evidence of damage to the earth's environment—unacceptable. Mainstream investors now see clearly that while the market-based economy often efficiently allocates resources, it is far from perfect.

There is a new type of investor activist emerging. These investors are pushing for greater long-term corporate responsibility. Sure, values and morality matter, but as smart investors they're looking for performance, accountability, and reduction of risk. Institutional investors, hungry for any insights in a rapidly changing world, see that the rise of an increasingly educated, legally empowered class of women affects the future risk and returns of their capital. And individuals, with equal pace, led by women and Millennials, are asking more of their investments. They seek financial returns and social good.

Not only are mainstream investors less resistant to using so-called non-financial measures of performance, many are embracing them as critical to understanding where good financial performance comes from. Just as climate change has become material in investment strategies for all sectors, the critical mass of women in the economy is making gender a material factor.

Few people realize the exciting and varied nature of applying gender considerations to investment decisions. The research base investors demand, coupled with increasing availability of data, has fostered an array of investment vehicles. You will find mainstream exchange traded funds tracking global indices and online loans with no interest. Investors who penned the Women's Empowerment principles are working alongside those newly committed to the power of gender analysis. Skeptics are dipping in toes and advocates are building completely new models. Yes, there is still more discussion than investment, but the field now has a breadth and set of vehicles that deserve to be showcased, invested in, and replicated.

Then there is the matter of the cultural conversations that are taking place on the status of women in society worldwide. Gender lens investing is aligned to today's zeitgeist.

Matthew Arnold, the nineteenth-century English poet and cultural critic who created the term, defines *zeitgeist* as something more than a prevailing worldview at a given time in history. It's a force that influences events. We see gender lens investing at the intersection of so much movement: women's rights, financial innovation and inclusion, entrepreneurial explosions, and corporation reinvention for the twenty-first century. How do we know this is a part of today's zeitgeist?

Sheryl Sandberg's *Lean In* ignited a conversation in bathrooms and boardrooms—and especially resonated with her target audience, younger professional women charting their careers. Sandberg's call to "lean in" also elicited some critical reactions from women who felt that "leaning in" was perilous without supportive systems and structures. Corporations have responded to the outcry and, with the leadership of women's scholars like Sylvia Ann Hewlett and her team at the Center for Talent Innovation, things are shifting: Many executives, entrepreneurs, and investors, and others you will meet in this book have begun a journey to gain the competitive advantage offered by including women.

The overwhelming resonance among women of Anne Marie Slaughter's article in *The Atlantic*, "Why Women Still Can't Have It

All," led her to reverse her pledge not to write more on the topic, producing the book, *Unfinished Business: Men, Women, Family.*[2]

Slaughter, whose life's work includes mother, wife, tenured professor, international lawyer, Director of Policy and Planning at the State Department, and now president and CEO of New America, picked up the early voice and arguments for structural and cultural changes in the workplace to accommodate and support modern family life. These were also well-articulated by Madeleine Kunin in her book, *The New Feminist Agenda: Defining the Next Revolution for Women.* Kunin, a former U.S. ambassador and governor of Vermont, reflected on her disappointment in the pace of change in women's roles and called for a new coalition of "Feminists for Families." Michael Kimmel, professor of sociology, brought feminism for men into the mainstream. And the husband and wife journalist team of Nicholas Kristoff and Sheryl WuDunn wrote *Half the Sky* to communicate together their worldview of the heartbreak of gender inequalities in many countries to an audience far beyond the feminist vanguard, and galvanized middle school children, ladies who lunch, and mid-career executives to stand with women around the world.

The time is now for a conversation about how investments—the trillions of dollars that fuel our global economy—impact and are impacted by these forces.

Who This Book Is For

We write as investors, for investors. Of course, investors are a very heterogeneous group. Many more individuals are investors than self-identify with the label: A Millennial with a new 401(k). A hedge fund manager heading into her second decade. Board members of the world's largest pension funds and of nonprofits raising their first endowment. Family offices stewarding assets for four and five generations with varying priorities. Cashed-out entrepreneurs with newly created wealth. Angel investors doing due diligence on a portfolio of startups. A municipal bond team reviewing new offerings.

We believe gender matters to all of you.

More now than ever before. And even more in the coming years.

We also know that investors come to this topic from dramatically different life and investment experiences, as well as vastly varying knowledge of gender dynamics and theory. To us, the diversity of interest and backgrounds creates remarkable dialogue and possibilities for action.

Professional investors steeped in the invisible hand of the markets bring skepticism—as they rightfully do to all things—that a gender lens could add any value. They seek models with track records, isolating signals and understanding every factor possible. After all, efficient markets should overcome any biases and move capital to the best opportunities. A similar amount of skepticism comes from those grounded in women's rights, economic empowerment, or gender-focused philanthropy. The distrust of the capital markets runs deep and the investing jargon can be mystifying and off-putting. We seek to bridge this spectrum, demystifying the process of using a gender lens, illustrating where it currently adds value, and highlighting some of the future opportunities.

Investors will find a cohesive historical narrative, a compelling collection of data, and set of practices from which to build. This is not, as you will see, a fad of the moment or a politically correct compendium. Rather it is like moving tectonic plates, reshaping our planet. These forces have been changing and will continue to change how investors' fortunes will be made and lost. We've compiled some new data, but also aggressively collected that of vastly different organizations to paint a picture of essential global trends. And we move beyond the simplistic mode of "counting women" to reveal where real value could be unleashed and to tell stories of those who are already using the data to inform their investing practices. As you read, we hope you see how gender is additive to, not replacing, traditional methods of investment analysis.

We hope to provide encouragement to gender equality advocates to continue becoming part of the movement for improving investing techniques. We recognize that investing is another tool in your toolbox; it in no way replaces philanthropy and advocacy. But your voice, expertise, and experience will change the investment conversation. And we suggest that, given its power, the activation of investment capital is necessary for the change you seek. Fortunately, three in ten women say they want to invest for gender equality while only eight percent have. That gap represents a huge unmet need, and capital waiting to be activated.

We write also for entrepreneurs and corporate executives, those looking for opportunities and those curious how gender lens investors might evaluate them. This book is for academics whose work we cite and for those newly curious about investor mindsets. If we could pull all readers into a room, we'd celebrate it as the gender capitalism ecosystem. And, as gender lens innovators in one area, asset class, geographic region, or industry sector are often heads down in their own work, they may miss diversity of the entire ecosystem, despite their best intentions. We try to provide that bird's-eye perspective across the ecosystem.

A Few Things to Clarify

Writing about gender lens investing can be challenging. The paradox of women's rising power and women's historical and current disadvantages, for one, defies simple explanations. As we wrote and edited we could hear the critique of experts who know the complexity of identifying and addressing gender bias. We have tried our best to write intelligently and without bias about gender complexity. That being said, two real human beings with their own experiences and lenses are writing this book; we hope that we are forgiven if we do a little wrong in oversimplifying the complex gender landscape to do a lot of right advancing this field.

We have restricted our lens to gender for this book, although we know that gender operates in relationship to other identities such as race, class, ability, and sexual orientation. Some investors have begun to engage in analyzing these intersections, and we think there is much to be learned in this area.

And since we've broached intersectionality (and its related discussions of oppression and discrimination) we want to clarify that investments will not single-handedly address global challenges (gender inequality among them). In fact, investors of all types are most effective when acting in concert with the civil society and governmental sectors. We believe gender equality is a moral imperative. The fact that it is economically compelling just adds to the attraction.

This is a big tent book. We see the gender lens investing ecosystem broadly and find the intersections of various motivations, approaches, and asset types essential. You won't find an exhaustive treatment of any sector, country, or investment approach. The number of fund managers with new vehicles and executives with great stories defied our ability to fully present them all. Different investors will find different parts more or less relevant, but we believe the patterns, meta-themes, and contexts (asset classes, sectors, and geographies) translate for the wide range of readers.

For all its promise, at less than five years old, gender lens investing is a fairly nascent space in the world of investing—indeed, mainstreaming it is one of the reasons we're writing this book. As such, by the time this goes to print, there will surely be new information released that would have fit nicely within these pages. Every week a new study comes out with relevant data that refines our knowledge and refuels our quest to learn more. We hope that this book provides context for, and interest in, that new information as it comes out.

The Chapters

The chapters in this book shine different lights on the wide variety gender lens investing strategies and the diverse contexts and motivations for choosing a particular approach. It is no accident that gender lens investing itself embraces diversity or that it is flexible.

The book moves in an arc from macro to micro to field. We begin with three chapters that depict our worldview of womenomics and provide an essential (and often missing) bridge between womenomics and gender lens investing. The rest of the chapters cover investing approaches and the state of the field and play.

We start at the 65,000 foot level in Chapter 1, where we outline and discuss the subject of womenomics and related metrics that matter. We chose ten key metrics to present a short and quantitative perspective on how women have emerged as key drivers of economic growth and development. We also discuss the gender gaps that exist today at considerable costs to nations and companies.

Chapter 2 explores the role of women in the developed nations, notably the United States but also Europe and Japan. That women have been key contributors to economic growth in the past—a fact largely unrecognized and unappreciated by policymakers and investors—becomes very clear to the reader. Also quite evident: When it comes to gender equality, much more work needs to be done.

Chapter 3 turns to women in the developing nations. We highlight their importance in driving growth in Asia, the Middle East, Africa and elsewhere. In many developing nations, however, women still confront a number of barriers to education and employment and violations of such basic rights as the right to vote, work, and own land. We compare and contrast the role and influence of women in China with women in India and reflect on the positions of women at the crossroads of promise and peril in each country.

Chapter 4 digs into the concept and construct of gender lens investing. The chapter is a primer on one of the most exciting and explosive fields of investing and a reminder that basic definitions of gender and sex are not synonymous—they add to one's understanding of how the field was defined and is evolving. We discuss the key drivers of gender lens investing, introduce some of the pioneers, and highlight some of the ways gender lens investing is being used to generate market and social returns.

Chapter 5 examines the problem of access to capital for women. While women entrepreneurs are hugely important to the future of any economy, gaining and attracting risk capital remains a herculean task for women relative to men. This is true despite the multiple economic and social benefits associated with more female entrepreneurs—think more capital reinvested in families and communities, more innovation, and higher returns and relative outperformance.

Chapter 6 goes inside the organization and examines gender inclusion as a determinant of growth for companies. We also explore the evolving approaches to combating gender bias and the opportunities from boards through senior management and into supply chains. Empowering women cuts across all functions within a firm, and the use of a gender lens helps investors decode which companies are serious by leveraging all talent across all activities and which ones are not.

In Chapter 7, we widen the lens a little and examine the ways in which industrial designers, R&D researchers, and corporate marketers can integrate gender knowledge into their designing, innovating, and selling of products. Although women represent one of the largest and wealthiest cohorts in the world, it is remarkable how complacent and unsuccessful companies have been in creating goods and services to meet the distinctive needs of women. When gendered knowledge is introduced the level of innovation increases and the risk of failure drops. As one of our colleagues said, "Don't forget, it is not just about counting women." Indeed, it's about valuing women and their roles as professionals, as parents, and as customers.

In Chapter 8, we get specific and discuss the various funds and instruments leading the charge in gender lens investing. A relative new field just a few years ago, there are now at least fifty vehicles for investors to invest their capital in women and women-related funds. The field has exploded over the past two years, with more and more investors demanding gender-specific investment approaches. We name names—people, places, and products to give the reader a sense of who is playing but we don't advise or endorse any particular investment strategy.

Chapter 9 looks to the future, outlining megatrends that will influence the adaption of gender analysis by investors. These include the global commitment to the U.N. Sustainable Development Goals, the role of big data in the world of gender lens investing, and the growth—or not—of professional women investors in the ecosystem flywheel of human talent and financial capital.

The practice of gender lens investing remains new, with much yet to be discovered. But it isn't hard to imagine its reach. The global purchasing power of women is in excess of $15 trillion, with more upside at stake. Global challenges from sustainable energy to safety and security cry out for the most bold and innovative teams and solutions. The challenge for those entrusted with deploying capital is to identify the companies that understand the profit-determining and competition-enhancing dynamics of the full participation of men and women.

That is an opportunity we can't afford to squander.

—Jackie VanderBrug and Joe Quinlan
October 2016

Notes

1. *The 7 Habits of Highly Effective People: Powerful Lessons in Personal Change,* by Stephen R. Covey
2. "Why Women Still Can't Have It All," *The Atlantic Monthly,* by Anne Marie Slaughter, July/August 2012. www.theatlantic.com/magazine/archive/2012/07/why-women-still-cant-have-it-all/309020/; and *Unfinished Business: Women, Men, Work and Family* (New York: Penguin Random House, September 2015).

Acknowledgments

There would be no book on gender lens investing without the support of Chris Hyzy, friend, colleague, and chief investment officer for the Global Wealth & Investment Management division of Bank of America.

We are indebted to many others at Bank of America, including Angela Ameruoso, Michelle Buckley, Kimberly O'Neil, Andrew Vasylyuk, Ehiwario Efeyini, Harald Gunderson, Joe Curtin, Emily Howes, Ian Prior, Surya Kolluri, and Kim Paris. Ann Limberg, Deanne Steele, Gillian Howell, Claire Costello, Andrea Sullivan, Pam Seagle, Tanya Satter, Robyn Polansky, and Sue Burton-Kirdahy have passionately supported the use of a gender lens across the firm. And special thanks to Joe's traveling partner, Jeff Tiger, as well as Lisa Carnoy for her support over the past year. Susan Danger, head of the American Chamber of Commerce to the European Union, and one of Europe's top female executives, was also very supportive during the project.

We would also like to express a huge debt of gratitude to Lauren Sanfilippo, a rising star on Wall Street, for her tireless work in rooting out data, exhibits, footnotes, and other materials. In many ways—notably with her sense of humor—Lauren was a critical partner in the book's completion.

We would not have finished, nor would the narrative have been digestible, without the ongoing guidance of Ann Graham, who partnered with us through the journey. Ann midwifed the book, bringing her broad background in finance, development, and business strategy, her relentless optimism, and her willingness to respond at any hour. Her commitment to the transformative potential of *Gender Lens Investing* saw us through many a rough patch.

A very special thanks to Tula Batanchiev at John Wiley & Sons for taking a chance on us, for enthusiastically seeing the potential for a book on how gender matters to investors, and for so ably assisting us throughout the process. Among that assistance was matching us with Julie Kerr, our development editor. Julie's unwavering support, insightful pen, and willingness to edit chapters out of order and over weekends made her an indispensable part of our team. In addition, we were very fortunate to work with Sharmila Srinivasan of Wiley, India.

We are also deeply grateful for the remarkable professionals and friends who from the early days of the field of gender lens investing encouraged, supported, and collaborated with us: Sarah Kaplan, Joy Anderson, Suzanne Biegel, Jennifer Pryce, Fran Segull, Anna Snider, Catherine Gill, Jacki Zehner, Betsy Dietel, Louisamaria Ruiz Carlile, Kathleen McQuiggan, and Mara Bolis. You all have pioneered this work, feeling its potential and creating the research, networks, and products to bring it to life.

Thanks to Jackie's Aspen Fellows "Flat Stanleys" group, who shared the relevance of this work to their firms and their lives; Ambassador Swanee Hunt for the late-night conversation on the "Blinding Obvious"; Ambassador Melanne Verveer for finding space at CGI; and Kevin Jones and Rosa Lee Harden, who early on saw gender as a lens for social investors.

We are also indebted to the talented Ritu Yadav and Jennifer John, who combed through early drafts for the essence of ideas that mattered; Mark Newberg, Sarah Kaplan, Jan Piercy and Mara Bolis, who provided detailed comments on chapters; and Jonathan Lewis for the constant encouragement and commiserating on authors' neurosis and eating habits.

When it mattered most, Sandi Maro Hunt, associate director of the Wharton Social Impact Initiative, brought her passion for and knowledge of the field and made our ideas clearer. Our colleague, Arun Kumar, burned the midnight oil offering invaluable analysis and global perspective.

The SRI, impact, and gender lens investing communities are vibrant, expanding, and generous. We benefited from countless interactions, panels, and papers. Many people selflessly shared their time, insights, and experiences, including: Najada Kumbuli, Sharon Vosmek, Abigal Noble, Andrea Turner Moffitt, CJ Juareaz, Cindy Padnos, Ed Powers, Ellen Remmer, Geri Stengel, Henriette Kolb, Inez Murray, Jenny Klugman, Joe Keefe, Kristin Hull, Laurie Spengler, Linda Scott, Mary Ellen Iskenderian, Nina Weissberg, Peter Roberts, Sally Beck, Lauren Embrey, Sue Miers, Terri McCully, Victoria Budson, Londa Schiebinger, Tracy Palandjian, Katherine

Lucey, Tina Arreaza, Yasmina Zaidman, Kristi Mitchem, Joanna Nash, Debbie McCoy, Ross Baird, Rachel Whittaker, Alexa Von Tobel, Janet McKinley, Kelly Northridge, Natasha Lamb, Ron Cordes, Marty Cordes, Stephanie Cordes, Eric Stephenson, Shadi Mehraein, Rebeca Hwang, Christina Brodbeck, Susan Duffy, Patricia Foley Hinnen, Stephanie Gripne, Bonny Moellenbrock, Lisa Woll, Larke Riemer, David Sand, Abigail Ingalls, Christopher Day, David Wood, Patricia Dinneen, Monica Brand, Daniel Epstein, Teju Ravilochan, Tara Kenney, Cathy Clark, and Ruth Shaber.

Finally, we are deeply indebted to our families for all the support during this project. To PJ, Corrie, and the kids; Sarah and Will; Brian; Kimheak and Matt; and my trusted partner, Karen—thanks for your unwavering patience, support, and keen sense for when and when not to ask about "the book."

Mom and Dad, Mike and Renee—you encouraged, understood, and showed up to help with childcare, wine, and more; Anika and Schuyler (who both published before me), you asked great questions and exhibited amazing patience; and Bradford—who can sense the future before I see it, your support, belief, and love mean everything to me.

About the Authors

Joseph Quinlan

Joseph Quinlan is managing director and head of Market & Thematic Strategy for the Global Wealth & Investment Management (GWIM) division of Bank of America. In this role, Joe leads a team responsible for global market analysis and thematic research in support of asset allocation and portfolio construction among portfolio managers and other investment associates. Joe began his career with Merrill Lynch and worked for nearly ten years as a global economist for Morgan Stanley. He lectures on finance and global economics at Fordham University and regularly lectures at various universities around the world, including Wuhan University in China, where he is a visiting professor. In 1998, he was nominated as an Eisenhower Fellow. Currently, he is a Senior Fellow at the Paul H. Nitze School of Advanced International Studies of Johns Hopkins University, Washington DC, and a Senior Fellow at the German Marshal Fund, Washington, DC.

Jackie VanderBrug

Jackie VanderBrug is managing director and sustainable platform lead for the Global Wealth & Investment Management (GWIM) division of Bank of America, where she co-chairs the Impact Investing Council. Since supporting the founding of Net Impact in 1993, Jackie's passion has led her to the intersection of business, innovation, and social good. As managing director at Criterion Ventures, she was instrumental in the establishment of the pioneering social investing fund, Good Capital. She led Business Development at iBasis, growing the global VOiP firm through a successful IPO, and cofounded Work in Progress, a nonprofit social enterprise. Her understanding of the interrelated aspects of social change was formed as a domestic policy analyst for the U.S. Congress, and she gained strategy skills as a management consultant for CSC Index.

Jackie is an Aspen Fellow and serves on the board of the trustees of the Donations and Advisory Boards for the CASE Initiative on Impact Investing and Oxfam's Women in Small Enterprise initiative. She was named one of the fifty most influential women in private wealth management by Private Asset Management in 2016.

CHAPTER 1

Womenomics and the Measures That Matter

> "All economies have savings and productivity gains if women have access to the job market. It's not just a moral, philosophical or equal-opportunity matter. It's also an economic cause. It just makes economic sense."[1]
> —Christine Lagarde, Managing Director,
> The International Monetary Fund

Say the word *womenomics* to a crowded room of investors and the typical reactions include snarky bemusement to utter bewilderment. Rolling of eyes and tilting of heads toward the ceiling—you bet. There are invariably some mumblings of "women-what?" since a majority of investors (men and women) have neither heard of the term nor ever contemplated women as an economic cohort with significant financial or commercial relevance.

They're not alone. Although the debate over gender equality has raged for decades in the United States, women and their potential contribution to economic growth remains a novel concept. Even the practitioners of the Dismal Science have yet to fully grasp the economic importance of women. Open up any standard economic textbook and you will see a chapter on fiscal and monetary policies, trade, foreign exchange, investment, and other traditional metrics of economic growth. Good luck, however, finding that chapter on gender—it's not there because sex-disaggregated data and gender-driven growth remain outside the economic mainstream, notwithstanding the accumulating evidence that the greater the participation of women in the formal economy, the greater the upside potential for real growth.

Quantifying womenomics is no easy task since statistics on all aspects of the subject remain relatively sparse and incomplete. Analyzing significant gender dynamics is not just about economics: Various political, social, and cultural dimensions come into play as well. The quest for more and better data is a crucial one. Evidence from research and experience from practice are both necessary tools to build this field. To that end, within this chapter we provide a brief overview on ten measurable developments that explain and portray the rising economic influence of women. These measures—while not all encompassing—offer a starting place, and will be referred to and analyzed in greater detail throughout the book. As a footnote, when we refer to the "formal" economy, we are talking about participation in the "paid" economy, an important distinction for women since a great deal of female economic participation is unpaid work versus paid.

Starting with the basics and the first of the metrics, the **female labor force participation rate** is one of the most fundamental metrics of womenomics, but perhaps one of the most important as well. The greater the number of women participating in the formal economy with paid jobs, the greater the opportunity and upside for economic growth. When more women enter the workforce, the nation's productive capacity increases, boosting the potential for more output, income and spending, as well as investment and trade. To this point, and discussed further in Chapter 2, America's expanding middle class and economic prosperity over most of the postwar era was due in large part to the steady increase in working women in the United States economy. And around the world, notably in China for instance, one of the most important macroeconomic trends is the inclusion of women into the formal economy and the attendant boost in growth. But much work needs to be done since the playing field in both developed and developing nations remains tilted against women at a significant cost to both women and their economies. As the McKinsey Global Institute notes, if women's participation rates were the same as men around the world, it would add up to $28 trillion, or 26 percent, to annual global GDP by 2025.[2]

The **rising educational levels of women** is another major change of the past few decades, and a trend just as prevalent in the developed nations as developing countries. Data and studies show that in many parts of the world girls now outperform boys academically, and more women are getting college degrees than men. Women are more actively involved in the formal economy today because they are better educated, skilled, and qualified for virtually any job in any sector. Among women ages 25 and over in the United States, the percentage of women with a college degree nearly tripled from 1970 to 2015. In 2014, the number of female graduates with bachelor's degrees was nearly 10 percent higher than males.[3] Meanwhile, the same trends are unfolding around the world—in Europe, the Middle East, and Asia in particular, where women at all levels of higher education are excelling and participating in education at a higher level than men.

Next, due in part to the rising educational levels of women, the **incomes, purchasing power, and investable wealth of women** have climbed steadily over the past few decades, giving women more independence and decision-making power. In our opinion, the power of the purchase represents one of the most powerful and promising metrics of womenomics. Expanding on the groundbreaking data and analysis of Michael Silverstein and Kate Sayre, we estimate the global purchasing power of women totaled roughly $15 trillion in 2015. That is a figure some 40 percent larger than the Chinese economy, and larger than every other economy in the world except the United States (see Figure 1.1).[4] Think about that—in a world struggling to grow, women could be a potential new growth engine. Meanwhile, globally, women control upward of $20 trillion in wealth—a staggering sum of capital that speaks to the financial influence of women. In the United States alone, women control just over half of the nation's personal wealth or investable assets, or $14 trillion. By 2020, this nest-egg is expected to total $22 trillion as women earn and save more, and become recipients of a massive transfer of wealth from their spouses.[5]

Despite the rise in the educational attainment of women, **the gender earnings gap**—another key metric—between male and female workers remains a key sticking point and barrier to gender-led growth. Women working full time in the United States, for instance, earned 79 percent of what men did in 2014, according to the 2014 Census Bureau comparison of the median earnings of full-time, year-round workers. African-American women in the United States earn just 63 cents and Hispanic women 56 cents to males.[6] And what is true in the United States is true around the world—where, on average, women earn 16 percent less than men.

Women are not only paid less than men, they do much more **unpaid work** than men. This metric certainly matters because

(Trillions of $)

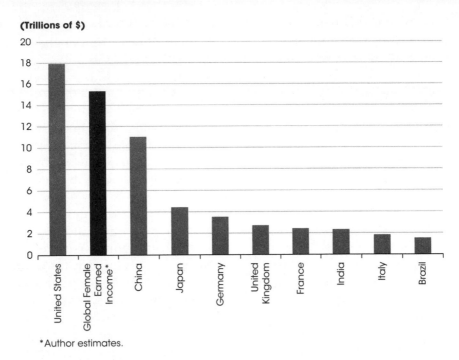

*Author estimates.

Figure 1.1   Women vs. the world's largest economies: Global female earned income, 2015.
Sources: BCG; IMF. Data as of July 2016.

the OECD defines unpaid work as both "an important aspect of economic activity and an indispensable factor contributing to the well-being of individuals, their families and societies." This includes cooking, fetching water, house cleaning, getting kids to and from school, grocery shopping, and caring for children, elderly relatives, and family members who are sick.

In 2016, Melinda Gates ignited a frenzy of news and social media by declaring "time-poverty" to be a universal gender problem. In her half of the annual Gates Foundation letter, she said, "I'm sorry to say…Unless things change, girls today will spend hundreds of thousands more hours than boys doing unpaid work simply because society assumes it's their responsibility."[7] Thanks to the uneven and unequal distribution of responsibilities at home, women and girls spend two to ten times more time and effort on unpaid care work than men. On a global basis, women spend an average of 4.5 hours per day doing unpaid work; men spend less than half as much time.

Quantifying this dynamic, the OECD estimates that unpaid "care" work equates to a staggering $10 trillion annually in lost output.[8] That is another equivalent to the size of China's economy.

Non-traditional Measures of Womenomics

All the womenomics data just cited are traditional—and essential—for measuring economic growth. But there are other, emerging metrics that underscore the underlying economic potential of women. Widening the lens, women are more than just workers, consumers, and caretakers—they are also entrepreneurs, engineers, senior executives, scientists and public servants. And their numbers are growing. Even if the playing field is not level yet, women are a force in determining the fate of countries in the global economy.

The **number of women entrepreneurs** is a key metric since women are just as much creators of businesses as men. Even with the challenges of access to capital, the 2014 Global Entrepreneurship Monitor (GEM) found 200 million women starting or running businesses all over the world, and 128 million operating established (in place over three and a half years) businesses.[9] That is 328 million women impacting the global economy—and this survey counts only 83 of the 189 countries recognized by the World Bank. These entrepreneurs span the spectrum of industry, and include hair salon owners, high-tech visionaries, and everything in between, all making critical economic contributions.

Women started nearly 40 percent of the new firms in the United States in 2014. Meanwhile, a Barclays Bank psychological study of 2000 entrepreneurs and employees in the United States, United Kingdom, Germany, and Singapore consider the questions of what an entrepreneur is—and how this changes by industry, geography, age, and gender. By gender, across regions and industries, 47 percent of women entrepreneurs said they were "extremely interested in starting a new business within the next three years" versus 18 percent of men.[10]

Evidence continues to mount that **corporate gender diversity** helps drive superior corporate results, and is therefore included in our ten measurable developments that matter. By *diversity*, we are not just talking about the number of women on corporate boards. We are referring to the spectrum of women's representation in a firm and the entire pipeline of women, of all races and ethnic groups, which it drives. More women on boards is great, but looking to this metric alone does not suffice for positive impact on women or on bottom lines. Firms that effectively deploy women across disciplines and functions within the firm, creating a diverse and dynamic gender pipeline, have produced better performance.

Bolstering this point, a 2015 Peterson Institute analysis of gender diversity in management and profitability—based on a global survey of close to 22,000 public companies in 91 countries—showed a repeated and significant "correlation between women at the C-suite level and firm profitability."[11] A profitable firm with 30 percent women in leadership positions could add more than 6 percentage points to its net margin compared with similar firms with no female leaders, according to the report. While this is correlation and not causation, the report indicates that gender diversity could have a positive impact on profit.

Despite the evidence, however, much work needs to be done. Although management pipelines vary considerably by industry, region, and company, the higher in the hierarchy one goes the smaller the number of women in line to fill leadership roles. At the top, the number of women named as CEOs declined sharply in 2015. Indeed, according to a survey conducted by Strategy&, only one of the 87 new CEOs named to lead a publicly traded firm in the United States and Canada in 2015 was a woman. Globally, women made up only 10 out of 359 of the newly appointed CEOs.[12]

Another measurable development that matters: **paid family leave** and **work–life balance programs** for employees who are of childbearing age. Rarely do investors think of this metric as pertinent to the health of a nation or a company, but at a time when many nations, including the United States, are experiencing rapidly aging populations, shrinking labor forces, and a drop-off in both male and female labor force participation rates, it's even more imperative to keep working moms (and dads) formally engaged in the economy through top-notch public child-care facilities, suitable family leave benefits, and pre- and after-school programs. Family leave and other employee support programs, in other words, are significant factors influencing the women's labor force participation rate. And it's worth emphasizing again, the higher the rate of female participation in the economy, the greater the growth potential of the economy.

Only glacially, however, is this message sinking in in the United States. Child care, paid leave, and workplace flexibility are not a strong suit of the U.S. government and many corporations, and therefore represent an Achilles Heel to the long-term growth potential of the country. The United States is one of the few nations in the world that does not mandate paid maternity leave. Our policies and practices are aligned with a small list of countries, including Papua New Guinea—one of the least developed nations in the world. This "motherhood penalty" not only hurts females and their households, it also penalizes the U.S. economy in general. Companies, of course, suffer as well, but are belatedly waking up to the fact that a better work/family balance is critical to their long-term success and survival. Paid leave and workplace flexibility programs designed to meet the needs of men and women are becoming more of the norm in many forward-looking firms where the war for talent is heating up.

Women in politics matters because the more women participate in the political decision-making process, the more diverse the debate. The inclusion of women increases bipartisanship and advocacy for issues like family leave and special education for children. Politico.com, weighing in on the 104 women in Congress, notes that women politicians in America "have long been viewed—and sold to voters (and donors)—as distinctly different from men, more grounded and tuned in to the real-life health and welfare needs of women, children, and families; more collaborative and cooperative … Women of color in particular, and African-American women especially, were known as advocates for a wide range of marginalized communities."[13]

A World Bank survey of women in parliaments around the world notes that "women are more likely to act in a bipartisan manner and are more likely to surface new ideas and bring new issues to the policy table. Increasing the number of women in our parliaments can have a positive impact on government transparency and result in policy outcomes more inclusive of the whole population."[14]

All of the above makes democratic institutions stronger and sturdier, and given the current political rancor in the United States, any elements that increase bipartisanship would be surely welcomed by investors. Yet despite the case for it, "female political representation tells a sad tale of underachievement," as pointedly stated by the World Bank.[15] While women political leaders around the world have doubled since 2005, political participation of women remains relatively low worldwide. Presently there are more than 175 heads of state worldwide, and women account for just 18 of those posts or just over 10 percent, according to the United Nations. And while the World Bank's review of 84 countries shows the share of women in parliaments has increased in the last 15 years, the share was still less than a quarter—about 22 percent—in 2015.[16]

Finally, **women and technology** is a sector shift with game-changing potential for women and the global economy. But first the bad news—more men than women have access to the Internet around the world, putting millions of women at a disadvantage in a host of activities, including banking, looking for work, networking, creating business contacts, trading, receiving microfinancing, and studying online. Over two billion women have never logged on to the Internet, with the bulk of these women in developing nations. Now the more encouraging news: The number of women with access to the Internet or ownership of a smartphone continues to rise, notably among Millennials. True, there are many social and cultural norms to overcome yet, as we discuss in Chapter 3, but as women around the world become more connected and engaged in the global digital economy, the upside for the world economy is tremendous. An Intel analysis says that making the Internet accessible to 600 million women and girls (40 percent of them from developing countries) could generate an estimated additional $13 to $18 billion in annual GDP across 144 developing nations.[17] This would also, hopefully, encourage more girls and women to pursue careers in STEM (science, technology, engineering, and math), where women are overwhelmingly underrepresented. The share of young women earning computer science degrees in the United States has dropped from 38 percent in 1985 to just 18 percent today.[18] This translates into less available female workers in critical and high-paying jobs like civil engineering, computer programming, industrial engineering, and mechanical engineering. If you combine women with technology—and its time-saving and productivity-enhancing capabilities—real growth could potentially accelerate, income inequalities would most likely narrow, providing a vastly improved future for all.

Social Progress and the Fairer Sex

Our ten womenomics metrics, which underpin the chapters that follow, are hardly exhaustive. Nor is our analysis unique, although we think it's essential to list macroeconomic indicators that respond to what Karl Marx once said: "Social progress can be measured exactly by the social position of the fair sex."

Different initiatives to create better measures of social progress and well-being are gaining credibility alongside the traditional economic indicators that have been used for decades. Riane Eisler's Caring Economy Campaign, Michael Porter's Social Progress Index, the Institute for Economies and Peace's annual World Peace Index, and the Omidyar Foundation's Property Rights Index are just a few of the new initiatives exploring how to measure social and economic progress together. We acknowledge the importance of these types of indicators and talk about them in other chapters, but the list we have chosen supports a strong framework and sharpens our lens on the promise and peril of women as economic drivers of growth, cultural change, and social progress.

Progress toward the *Oxford English Dictionary* definition of gender equality—"the state in which access to rights or opportunities is unaffected by gender"—differs by region, country, and within countries significantly. Much work remains before many countries, the United States included, come close to anything resembling gender equality.

Much work also needs to be done in better defining the metrics and measurements of womenomics. Our ten areas of measurement are just a start but have proven to be engaging enough to enlighten a room of investors about the economic potential of women and their overwhelming relevance to investment strategy. So returning to our room full of investors, typically by the time we get done explaining the economic benefits of more women fully engaged in the labor force—when it sinks in that women are outperforming men in education; when it dawns on the crowd that women are not paid equally but are nevertheless a potent consuming and wealthy cohort no company can ignore; when it becomes clear that America's family-leave policies are some of the most archaic in the world and an underlying threat to our global competitiveness; when it clicks that women are creators of businesses, enhancers of corporate performance, capable political leaders, and savvy technology users—well, by then, minds are racing and eyes have stopped rolling, and the skepticism surrounding womenomics is less palpable. Questions about strategies and approaches for such changes still exist among listeners, for sure, but, at the conclusion of our talks, most folks walk out of the room with a better understanding of what womenomics is and how gender lens investing can enhance gender equality and equity, and generate financial returns that will turn their heads.

Our Top 10 Metrics

1. Female labor force participation rate
2. Educational attainment
3. Women's income and wealth
4. Gender pay gap
5. Unpaid work
6. Women entrepreneurs
7. Corporate gender diversity
8. Paid family leave
9. Women in politics
10. Women and technology

Notes

1. "IMF's Lagarde: Women in Workforce Key to Healthy Economies," NPR (March 28, 2014). www.npr.org/2014/03/28/294715846/imfs-lagarde-women-in-workforce-key-to-healthy-economies.
2. Jonathan Woetzel et al., "The Power of Parity: How Advancing Women's Equality Can Add $12 Trillion to Global Growth," McKinsey Global Institute (September 2015). www.mckinsey.com/global-themes/employment-and-growth/how-advancing-womens-equality-can-add-12-trillion-to-global-growth.
3. U.S. Department of Commerce, Census Bureau, American Community Survey (ACS), 2014. Table 104.50. Persons age 25 and over who hold a bachelor's or higher degree, by sex, race/ethnicity, age group, and field of bachelor's degree: 2014. Data as of December 2015.
4. Michael J. Silverstein and Kate Sayre, "The Female Economy," *The Harvard Business Review* (September 2009).
5. Heather R. Ettinger and Eileen M. O'Connor, "Women of Wealth: Why Does Financial Services Industry Still Not Hear Them?" *Family Wealth Advisors Council* (2012).
6. U.S. Census Bureau, 2014 American Community Survey, median annual earnings of full-time, year round workers, ages 16 and older.
7. Melinda and Bill Gates, Gates 2016 Annual Letter, "If You Could Have One Superpower What Would It Be?" (February 22, 2016). www.gatesnotes.com/2016-Annual-Letter.
8. Gaelle Ferrant, Luca Maria Pesando, and Keiko Nowacka, "Unpaid Care Work: The Missing Link in the Analysis of Gender Gaps in Labour Outcomes," OECD Development Centre (December 2014). www.oecd.org/dev/development-gender/Unpaid_care_work.pdf.

9. Donna Kelley, Candida Brush, Patricia Greene, Mike Herrington, Abdul Ali, and Penny Kew, "GEM 2014 Women's Report, GEM: Special Report Women's Entrepreneurship" (November 17, 2015).

10. *The Psychology of Entrepreneurship: A Data Driven Study into the Psychology of New Business Creation* (Barclay's Bank and the Psychometric Centre, University of Cambridge, June 2015), p. 2. www.home.barclays/content/dam/barclayspublic/images/news-newsite/2015/06/Barclays%20report%2020150616v1 final.pdf.

11. Marcus Noland, Tyler Moran, and Barbara Kotschwar, "Is Gender Diversity Profitable? Evidence from a Global Survey," Peterson Institute for International Economics (February 2016). piie.com/publications/working-papers/gender-diversity-profitable-evidence-global-survey.

12. Strategy&, "2015 CEO Success Study" (May 2016). www.strategyand.pwc.com/ceosuccess.

13. Judith Warner, "104 Women in Congress: Does It Matter?" *Politico* (January 2015). www.politico.com/magazine/story/2015/01/104-women-in-congress-does-it-matter-113903#ixzz48J3cbJUy.

14. Frances Rosenbluth, Joshua Kalla, and Dawn Teele, "The Female Political Career," The World Bank (January 13, 2015). www.womeninparliaments.org/wp-content/uploads/2015/01/Final_13012015_The-Female-Political-Career.pdf.

15. Ibid.

16. Ibid.

17. "Women and the Web: Bridging the Internet Gap and Creating New Global Opportunities in Low and Middle Income Countries," Intel Corporation and Dahlberg Global Development Advisors (2012), p. 2. dalberg.com/documents/Women_Web.pdf.

18. National Student Clearinghouse Research Center. Table 1A: Degree Counts by Field of Study and Gender. Data as of graduation year 2014, Bachelor's graduates.

CHAPTER 2

It's the Women, Stupid

> "Essentially all of the income gains that middle-class American families have experienced since 1970 are due to the rise in women's earnings."[1]
>
> —Economic Report of the President, 2015

James Carville, political strategist for Bill Clinton's presidential bid in 1992, famously coined the phrase, "It's the economy, stupid," a campaign rallying cry that focused the election on the ailing U.S. economy and the attendant need for political change.

In the same vein, "It's the women, stupid" challenges investors to look beyond the battle of the sexes and recognize that women are distinct economic forces in the world. The expression speaks to the fact that women everywhere are increasingly defining the social, political, and economic agendas of nations and the future of the planet. This book isn't making a case for this as the *right* thing; we're focusing on what makes it, inarguably, the *smart* thing.

Revitalizing economic activity is needed everywhere in the world. Almost a decade after the Wall Street financial crisis of 2008 brought the global economy to its knees, the countries that account for most of the world's GDP are still struggling to stand upright. Despite unprecedented levels of cheap liquidity from central banks, and multiple fiscal and monetary measures to promote growth in economies large and small, the global economy's recovery remains fragile. The standard pro-growth policies are not working.

Post-crisis annual U.S. GDP growth has been the weakest in seven decades, leaving millions of U.S. citizens frustrated and angry about their economic lot in life, while triggering rising political populism

13

both at home and abroad. Overseas, Japan's economy barely has a pulse, while the performance of countries in sclerotic Europe has been pitiful, with the region stumbling from one crisis to another. Of the fabled BRIC cohort—Brazil, Russia, India, China—half of the membership—Brazil and Russia—is in recession at mid-decade. Not even the economic superpower-in-waiting, China, has been spared. Annual growth rates in China have been cut in half since the financial crisis.

Add it all up, and the world economy, at best, seems stuck in neutral. Yet policy makers continue to prescribe the same prescriptions of the past, which begs the following question: Rather than continuing to rely on central banks to print more money with little long-term economic consequences, why not adopt gender-driven growth policies built around the needs and capabilities of women, the world's greatest underutilized resource? Why not? Because, as Heidi Crebo-Rediker, the first person (and woman) to hold the post of chief economist at the U.S. State Department, observed, "The narrative of women as drivers of economic growth remains a difficult sell, often eliciting defensive comments from senior economic policy-makers."[2]

Or consider these scenarios: What would happen if countries did more to encourage childbearing-age working women to stay in the workforce after they have children? What if there was more support for women entrepreneurs who face gender bias, making it easier for them to succeed? What if companies and educational institutions work harder, and together, to prepare young women for careers in science and technology fields and to attract them to these fields? What if everyone agrees we need to correct gender imbalances, and find better ways to accelerate progress?

What would happen if all of the above transpired? Remember from Chapter 1, the McKinsey Global Institute's "full potential" prediction of $28 trillion added to global GDP by 2025 if "women participated in the economy identically to men." Alternatively, McKinsey's "best-in-region" scenario in which "all countries match the progress toward gender parity of the fastest-improving country in their region" would add as much as $12 trillion in annual 2025 GDP, equivalent in size to the current GDP of Germany, Japan, and the United Kingdom combined. This is twice the likely growth in global GDP contributed by female workers between 2014 and 2025, in McKinsey's third "business-as-usual scenario."[3] Estimates from the International Monetary Fund (IMF) and Organization for Economic Cooperation and Development (OECD) are just as tantalizing: if female labor force participation rates rose to equivalent male levels in the United States, GDP would be increased by 5 percent. The increase in Japan would be even greater, 9 percent, and absolutely stunning in a country like Egypt where it would increase by 34 percent.[4] Based on OECD models, closing the gender gap in labor market participation could add 12 percent to the OECD GDP over the next fifteen years. Some nations, like Italy for instance, would see an increase of 20 percent or more in GDP over the same time period.[5] Both the IMF and OECD have become more vocal about promoting gender-driven growth policies, although member states have yet to grasp the full importance of womenomics. Too few governments get that women are a crucial economic input to growth, and fail to understand that the more nations raise their female labor force participation rates, the more women are included and engaged in the economy, the better the prospects for long-term growth and innovation.

How the U.S. Economy Stands on Women's Shoulders

The U.S. economy has stood on the shoulders of women through two world wars, the oil shocks of the 1970s, and several recessions. Whatever the challenge or crisis, American women have been part of the solution, and a critical pillar of support underpinning the economic ascent of America in the last half of the twentieth century. This happened despite legal, religious, and educational conventions that inhibited American women from fully participating in the paid, professional workforce.

Before World War II, few married women worked outside the home. For women who supported themselves the choices were limited. When mobilizing for war, however, the United States cast aside its conventions, and women eagerly went to work. In the 1940s, women took jobs on assembly lines and shop floors. The pay was better than jobs they were used to doing, and women eagerly jumped into factories as men left the workforce to fight the war. Women helped manufacture virtually everything—uniforms, parachutes, munitions, tanks, and aircraft. Rosie the Riveter and Tillie the Toiler became icons of American industrial might as women welded ships, assembled B-25 bombers, and riveted together tanks, trucks, and other heavy machinery.

Women also became train conductors and postal carriers, drove ambulances, fought fires, and served in the armed forces. From 1939 to 1945, the female labor force surged from 12 million to nearly 19 million. Impressively, U.S. industrial production doubled between 1939 and 1945, a surge in output that would never have happened had women stayed home.[6]

When the war ended, many women gave up their jobs—often involuntarily. Most started families and returned to being home-makers and let their husbands be the breadwinners. Several million women did continue working, mostly in clerical and low-paying service jobs, because they were single, or liked the independence that came with a paycheck. But in 1950, only one-third of American women had a paid job. Only 15 percent held managerial roles in companies.

By the 1960s, women still made up only one-third of the work-force (see Figure 2.1), but women's expectations were changing. They were no longer sure being a housewife and mother was enough. They wanted careers, and better jobs, but opportunities were limited and the earnings gap wide. In 1960, for every dollar a man earned, a woman earned just 59 cents.[7] Women were paid less for the same job simply because they were women. Newspaper classified ads for positions might say the job was either for men or women.

When young unmarried women gained access to the first birth control pill in the 1970s, everything changed. As *New York Times* columnist and author Gail Collins writes in her book, *When Every-thing Changed, The Amazing Journey of American Women from 1960 to Present*, "Once young women had confidence that they could make it through training and the early years in their profession without get-ting pregnant, their attitude toward careers that required a long-term commitment changed."[8]

Along with the sexual revolution, the passage of a number of federal anti-discrimination laws, beginning in the early 1960s, fundamentally altered the role of women in the U.S. economy. This included the Equal Pay Act of 1963, which created basic labor standards requiring employers to pay women and men the same wages when performing similar jobs. One year later Congress passed the Civil Rights Act of 1964, with Title VII banning employment

Percent of Civilian Labor Force, Population Age 16+

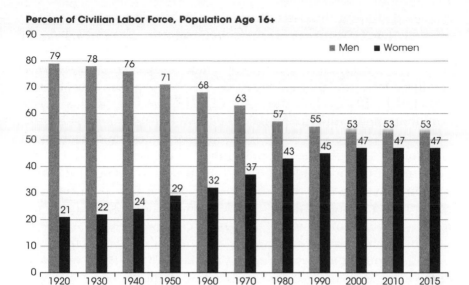

Figure 2.1a   U.S. labor force participation by gender over the decades.
Sources: Bureau of Labor Statistics, Current Population Survey. Data through 2015.

Percent of Population Age 16+

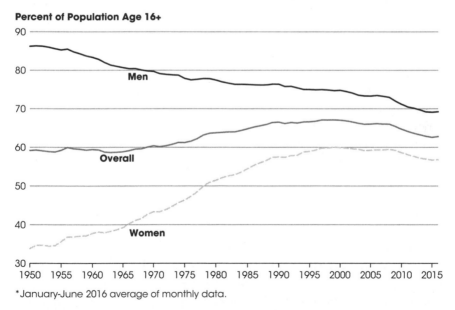

*January-June 2016 average of monthly data.

Figure 2.1b   Labor force participation by gender, 1950-2016.
Sources: Bureau of Labor Statistics, Current Population Survey.

discrimination on the basis of sex, race, color, national origin, and religion. The Civil Rights Act was followed by the affirmative action, anti-discrimination Executive Order 11246 in 1965, which applied to federal government contractors. The foundational laws were reinforced with the passage of the Education Amendments of 1972, the Pregnancy Discrimination Act of 1978, the Civil Rights Act of 1991, and the Family and Medical Leave Act of 1993.

In 1960, there were only two women senators and 11 women among the 435 members of the House of Representatives. Of 307 Federal district judges at the time, only two were women.[9] Though women's faces, in general, were missing on the U.S. political landscape, their energy, expertise, and fervor were not absent, as the few women in place fought vocally for their fellow women.

Although mostly men crafted and cast their votes for long-overdue protections for women, it was Martha Griffiths, a representative from Michigan, and a rare woman in the House, who was a leading voice for the 1960s gender-based civil rights legislation. First elected to Congress in 1954, she was a champion of these issues until she retired in 1975.[10]

The laws passed provided protection and more rights for women, and helped over the decades to boost women's presence not only in politics but also in the formal economy. Legislation subsequently helped raise the labor force participation rate, advanced the educational achievements of women, increased women's earning, and increased the workforce participation rate of working mothers. Landmark legislation unleashed womenomic power over the second half of the twentieth century—a fact that should be not lost (although it often is) on today's policymakers in the United States and elsewhere.

In addition to pro-womenomics policies, women's effect on the U.S. economy was borne out by necessity. When the world's top oil producers decided to jack up the price of oil in the early 1970s, the price spike and subsequent surge in inflation crushed family incomes across the United States, notably the incomes of traditional households where the father worked and mother stayed at home. The oil shock and ensuing recession drove millions of women into the labor force as the middle class of that time struggled to shore up family finances and preserve their lifestyles.

Stay-at-home moms entered the labor market in record numbers, with the working ranks of women swelling over the balance of the 1970s. In 1978, the participation rate breached 50 percent for the first time in U.S. history and as the 1980s began, three out of five families had at least two household members in the labor force.[11] In 1982, another milestone was reached with more women than men earning bachelor degrees, a trend that has only become more pronounced since then (see Figure 2.2). In the 2012–13 academic year, over 57 percent of graduates earning a B.A. were women, nearly 60 percent of masters, and 51 percent of doctorate degrees. And that's not all. In the same year, women accounted for a significant share of degrees in medicine (48.0 percent), law (48.1 percent), pharmacy (61.6 percent), and veterinary medicine (77.3 percent).[12] These figures are remarkable on their own but are even more impressive considering how many top all-male universities did not admit women until the late 1970s. When Supreme Court Justice Sonia Sotomayor graduated from Princeton University in 1976, her class was only the fourth to include women.[13] Columbia was the last Ivy League school to go co-ed in 1987.[14]

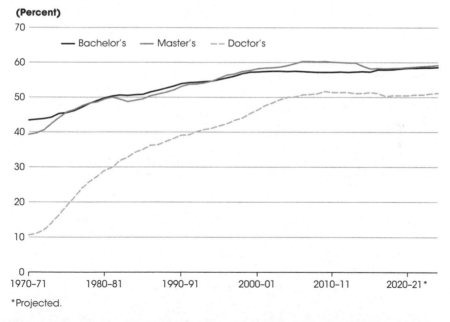

Figure 2.2   Share of U.S. post-secondary degrees received by women.
Source: National Center for Education Statistics. *Digest of Education Statistics: 2014.* Data as of April 28, 2016.

Economic growth and educating girls and women are inextricably linked. This is a global theme of this book, backed up by data from multiple sources and studies that show the strong correlation between women's educational attainment, labor force participation rates, earning power, and contribution to GDP growth. To this point, the U.S. economy is $2 trillion, or 13.5 percent, larger than it would have been without women's increased participation in the labor force and hours worked since 1970, according to the Economic Report of the President.[15] Looking forward, the OECD estimates that closing the gender gap completely in labor participation rates in the United States would raise U.S. GDP by about 10 percent by 2030.[16]

Women as Drivers of Growth

Whether or not the United States ever fully unlocks the potential of its female working population remains unclear. More certain is the underlying economic power and promise of women when viewed separately as consumers, entrepreneurs, and investors.

Women consumers

The annual collective purchasing power of women around the world is estimated at a staggering $15 trillion. U.S. females account for roughly 20 percent of that total, or $3 trillion, which means the purchasing power of American women is greater than the aggregate output of nations like France, Brazil, Italy, and India. Today, 43 percent of the wealthiest people in the United States are women, and, as the Census Bureau notes, the number of U.S. women with six-figure incomes is rising at more than three times the rate of men who earn that much.[17] Even with the gender wage gap, women of all ages are now earning more than their mothers ever dreamed of, a dynamic many companies and investors have yet to grasp.

The fact that women account for 80 percent of consumer purchases in America suggests they're the ones deciding the size of homes, the models of cars, the choice of electronics, clothing, health care, furniture, and family vacations.[18] Whether it is discretionary or nondiscretionary spending, or large or small-ticket items, women increasingly set the pace. And women do more than buy for themselves. They also buy for others—for their kids, siblings, parents, and friends—exponentially increasing their economic impact.

Women's spending habits and aspirations have an outsized influence on markets. Entire industries are being reshaped and redefined by the growing wealth, needs, and desires of women. Despite this, however, it is remarkable how slow companies have been in marketing to women. It is understandable, though. Men still outnumber women in executive roles, both in function and frontline roles, in many large companies. And it has been shown that male-top-heavy companies are slow in hiring and promoting women.

The American automotive manufacturing industry is a case in point. This is an industry where women now buy nearly 40 percent of the more than 16 million cars and trucks sold in the U.S. each year.[19] That's a lot of vehicles but it is just the tip of the iceberg. Women also influence 80 to 85 percent of car purchases and now spend $300 billion a year on cars and maintenance.[20] More women than men have a driver's license. And yet walk into any automobile showroom or body shop in the United States, and you will be hard pressed to find a woman salesperson or mechanic.

In auto sales, women make up less than 15 percent of the salespeople at 20,000-plus auto dealerships around the United States, and less than 3 percent of dealerships are owned by women, according to Anne Fleming, founder of Women-Drivers.com, a market research and publishing business she started to educate auto executives and dealers about women and their cars. In body shops, women are nearly as rare as white rhinos. In 2014, women made up 1.6 percent of automotive body and related repairers and 1.4 percent of automotive service technicians and mechanics.[21] Women account for only 3 percent of the U.S. automobile executive ranks, with Mary Barra, the chief executive officer of General Motors, the most high-profile exception. But Barra has the same challenge as her male colleagues: According to GM surveys, 74 percent of women feel that they're misunderstood by car manufacturers.[22]

Belinda Parmar, a business consultant to the industry on gender, says, "Supercar makers are like teenage boys at a high school dance… They don't have a clue how to speak to women."[23] That includes the male engineers who design cars as much as it does salespeople and repair guys. Tesla's Elon Musk is trying to change things by pulling women into the early stages of designing the firm's new SUV-minivan Model X, a smart move considering that women account for roughly half of total SUV sales in the United States. Tesla is also tuned into women's interest in the environment, and talking the benefits of Tesla's electric cars.[24]

The sports equipment business is another industry where women are poised to determine the winners and losers of the future. For more and more women, fitness and fashion have converged, triggering an explosion in active wear or "athleisure." The upshot: Women's athletic apparel has emerged as one of the fastest growing segments of sportswear over the past few years, helping to boost overall U.S. sportswear sales by a staggering 37.8 percent between 2010 and 2015.[25] Today, the active-wear or sportswear market is in excess of $100 billion in the United States, up from $71 billion in 2009, according to figures from Morgan Stanley.[26] Globally, we are talking about an industry that is approaching $300 billion in sales, with plenty of upside given the convergence of the health and wellness and fashion markets in the United States, Europe, Latin America, Asia, and, notably, China.

Dick's Sporting Goods, a one-time bait-and-tackle shop turned bulky sports merchandiser for virtually everything a man likes, is in the process of reinventing itself yet again for women. It is shifting from sports gear toward athleisure wear, footwear, and related accessories designed for women while boosting ecommerce options for time-impoverished women with plenty of money. The firm recently launched Chelsea Collective stores in northern Virginia and Pittsburgh, billed as "fitness and lifestyle boutiques," with complimentary services like a free running stride analysis, and free alterations on clothing and bra fittings. The floor plans in Dick's traditional retail outlets have changed, too—with more apparel and footwear front and center and sports gear staples in the background.

Already the largest sporting-goods company in the world, Nike wants to be even larger and is banking on women to be a critical component of the company's future growth. How critical? Well, the company expects its women business to roughly double by 2020, rising to $11 billion from $5.7 billion in 2015, an aggressive goal by any measurement.

Women entrepreneurs

While businesses of all types are seizing the day in women's markets of all kinds, women entrepreneurs and women-owned companies are making their own mark as well. Between 1997 and 2015, the overall number of U.S. businesses expanded by 51 percent, and the number of women-owned firms soared by 74 percent— a rate 1.5 times the national average. As of 2015, it was estimated that there were over 9.4 million women-owned businesses in the United States, generating nearly $1.5 trillion in revenues and employing more than 7.9 million people.[27] This is an impressive record given how many startups fail.

In 2009, the Center for Women-Owned Businesses developed the first model of its kind to measure the economic impacts on output, income, and employment of women-owned businesses in the United States. Its finding: $2.8 trillion dollars and 23 million jobs are generated annually by majority-women-owned firms, proving, as the study reported, "women-owned firms are not a small, niche market but are a major contributor and player in the overall economy."[28] The data is being used to make the case for better support for women seeking to grow businesses they have started, with raising capital among the most difficult tasks for women.

Women investors

Finally, in terms of investable assets, U.S. women now control almost half of the estates valued over $5 million, and they stand to inherit some 70 percent of the $41 trillion to be inherited over the next four decades in the largest intergenerational transfer of wealth the world

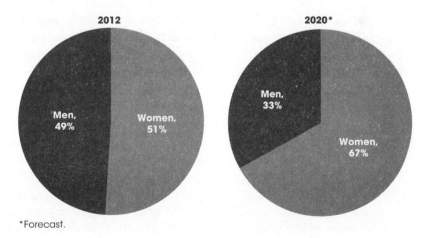

*Forecast.

Figure 2.3   Men vs. women: Who controls U.S. wealth?
Source: CFA Institute.

has ever seen. By 2020, roughly two-thirds of the private wealth in the United States will be held by women.[29]

Yet with American women on the cusp of receiving one of the largest financial transfers in modern economic history, only 3 percent of U.S. mutual funds are managed by women.[30] If a survey showed that, hypothetically, even only 20 percent of American women with investable assets wanted a woman over a man to manage their money, would the financial services industry be ready? Of course, this is a personal choice that will vary widely, but it is certainly a question that companies that manage women's money should be asking (see Figure 2.3).

Minding the Gaps That Matter

Remember the President's Economic Report quoted at the beginning of the chapter? "All of the income gains that middle-class American families have experienced since 1970 are due to the rise in women's earnings." That is a stunning figure, and reflects the fact that America's women's workforce has never been so well educated, and the human capital of educated women so valuable. Not unexpectedly, then, this has given a big boost to what women are paid. Between 1979 and 2015, annual weekly earnings of women rose by 4 percent on a compound annual average basis versus 3.2 percent for men, a growth differential that has somewhat narrowed the gender pay gap.[31]

Still, the median income of American women working full time in 2014 was 79 percent men's income.[32] In other words, a woman makes 79 cents for every dollar a man makes. Compare that to 59 cents for every dollar in 1960 that looks like progress. With this current wage gap, on average, women have to work at least an extra month to earn what men did by the end of the previous year. What's more, when it comes to full compensation, most women working in lower-paying occupations do not get employer-sponsored health and retirement benefits, paid leave, or sick days, so the wage gap is even wider than the numbers suggest.

"The cumulative effect of closing the wage differential would be huge," says Evelyn Murphy, a resident scholar at the Women's Studies Research Center at Brandeis University and former Lieutenant Governor of Massachusetts. Adds Murphy, "The turnover effect could be extremely important in terms of products purchased and jobs created. The purchasing power effect would span all pay scales but the real consumer stimulus is closing of the pay gap for middle and lower-income women."

And this is not just a problem for low-income earners—the gap exists among high-income earners as well. For instance, a 2015 *Bloomberg* survey of the post-MBA pay gap between women and men from 2007 through 2009 was noticeable but not sizable ($98,000 for women and $105,000 for men). By 2014, however, the gap among the same group was quite large, with the median salary of men ($175,000) well ahead of women's ($140,000). In other words, women from some of the top business schools in the nation were making 80 cents on the dollar relative to males—in line with the national average, but nonetheless less than men.[33]

Clearly, the gap remains—and the debate over the causes and consequences of gender pay continues. Even the baseline figures are hotly debated number. For instance, the U.S. Census Bureau said women made 79 cents on the dollar in 2014, based on median annual earnings of $39,621 for women and $50,383 for men.[34] However, the figures from the Bureau of Labor Statistics (BLS) are slightly different. The BLS reported weekly earnings of women working full-time were 83 cents of those of males in 2014; based on hourly wages, the gap becomes even smaller—15 cents. Any way you cut it, in other words, there is a gap between women's and men's wages.

There's no shortage of explanations why men earn more money than women. Discrimination, stereotypes, limited job options, fewer hours worked, less work experience, women who don't ask for raises or "lean in." They are all valid. But the biological fact is women are more likely than men to spend time away from the labor force because they bear children. Those women who wait to go back to work until their kids are older create holes in their resumes and gaps in their professional development. They lose seniority and they forfeit raises.

That motherhood comes with a pay penalty has been corroborated by many studies, but one by Cornell University professors Shelley J. Correll, Stephen Benard, and In Paik stands out. Women with identical qualifications were asked to evaluate a pair of job applications. The only difference among the women was that one group were mothers and the women in the other group were not. The study showed the mothers were judged to be "significantly less competent and committed than women without children." Mothers were also held to higher standard for promotion and they experienced harsher punctuality standards. The mothers considered less likely to be promoted to management were offered a starting salary more than 7 percent less than the offer to non-mothers.[35]

An economy not fully deploying its human capital—both men and women—is an economy operating below capacity, inhibiting its ability to compete, drive growth, spark innovation, reduce poverty, and increase equality. There is, in other words, a significant economic cost to women being paid less in full-time jobs, opting out of the labor force, or choosing to work fewer hours. This cost: less output, less investment, and less incomes for families.

The second gap of concern is government family benefits, which, in general, is a uniquely American problem. The United States is one of the few governments in the world that does not guarantee some form of paid leave to workers when they become parents.[36] However, a few states have enacted paid leave.

Under federal law, employees can take up to 12 weeks of unpaid leave when a child is born. However, the guaranteed time off (without pay) only applies to businesses with more than 50 employees, leaving millions of workers toiling for small firms—the backbone of the U.S. economy—without any statutory leave. The 1993 Family and Medical Leave Act was intended as a small step to fill the leave gap, but the Act placed so many conditions on workers' eligibility that fewer than 20 percent of new mothers qualify. Most industrialized nations have offered workers paid maternity leave since the 1970s. Nearly half the nations followed by the ILO provide maternity leave and paternity leave is paid in 90 percent of these nations.

Though not widely recognized, the lack of childcare policies, paid leave, and workplace flexibility in the U.S. labor force is an Achilles Heel to the U.S. growth story. The female participation rate in the United States has stalled and declined over the past few years due in part to unfriendly family policies in the public and private sector. The labor force participation rate of working women between ages 16 and 64 years old was 67.2 percent in the middle of 2016 from the pre–financial crisis levels of 2009 (69 percent) and from 2000 levels (nearly 71 percent). In 1990, the United States had the sixth highest female labor force participation rate among the twenty-two members of the OECD. By 2010, the ranking slipped to 17 and even further to 21 in 2015.[37] Some of this decline reflects that more women and men have retired, but unfriendly family policies are also to blame.

Another gender gap lies with STEM—or science, technology, engineering, and math. While turbo-charged change is the norm of the information technology sector, there's nothing speedy about the progression of women in tech industries. Male-oriented structures, routines, cultures, and biases of many technology firms remain in entrenched at a time when America's innovative edge in STEM is being eroded by foreign competition.

All of this leaves the United States with a glaring and dangerous deficiency: At a time when U.S. innovative capabilities are being eroded by the lack of government funding and increased competition from the likes of India and China, a critical resource—women—is missing (Figure 2.4).

Research by the Center for Talent Innovation reported that U.S. women working in the fields of science, engineering, and technology are 45 percent more likely than their male peers to leave the

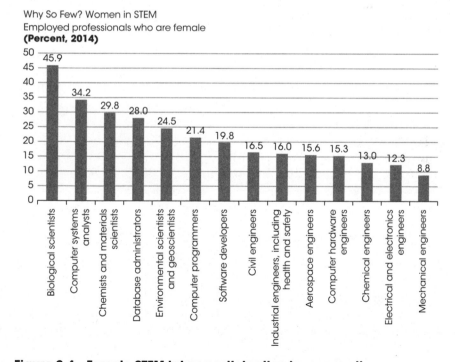

Why So Few? Women in STEM
Employed professionals who are female
(Percent, 2014)

Figure 2.4   Female STEM labor participation by occupation.
Source. U.S. Department of Labor, Bureau of Labor Statistics. Data as of February 12, 2015

industry out of frustration with the "lab-coat culture" of science, the "hard-hat culture" of engineering, and the "geek workplace culture" of technology.[38] The "lab-coat culture" glorifies extreme hours and penalizes men and women with families who need more time out of the lab. The engineering "hard-hat culture" describes how women dress modestly to avoid "cat calls" from male colleagues, and tech's "geek workplace culture" is compared to "a super-competitive fraternity of arrogant nerds." These may be stereotypes and exceptions certainly exist, but the data point to very real challenges for women that these cultures are at least partly to blame for.

Posts on STEMfeminist.com—which documents accounts of discrimination and harassment against women—speak volumes about this culture. It is full of stories of women scientists being mistaken for secretaries; of women succeeding in the math class because they are "eye candy" for the department; and of male colleagues addressing everyone in the room except the women. All of the above is another way of saying that when it comes to women and the sciences, the mindset and culture needs to be radically altered—or blown up and pieced back together again.

Japan's Gamble on Womenomics

If there is one world leader who understands the economic importance of women, it's Shinzō Abe, the prime minister of Japan.

In addition to presiding over an economy that has gone nowhere in over two decades, the Japanese leader is sitting atop a demographic timebomb. Japan's population and workforce are shrinking at one of the fastest rates in the world. By 2035, one-third of all Japanese will be 65 or older. The old-age dependency ratio—or the number of elderly as compared to the working age population—is already at 36 percent, and set to soar over the next few decades. Meanwhile, between now and 2060, Japan's total population is projected to shrink by 30 percent, sapping the one-time Asian economic powerhouse of its vitality and strength.[39] In rural Japan, entire villages are evaporating. Schools have closed, shops and homes have been boarded up, and empty buildings blight the landscape. With increased budget deficits and debts, and these challenging shifts in workforce as the backdrop, if there was ever a nation that needed to utilize every resource available to them—women included—it's Japan.

Enter Mr. Abe, prime minister since 2012. To breathe life into Japan's morbid economy, Abe has placed a massive bet on women, making greater female labor participation in Japan a core growth strategy.

Goldman Sachs estimates that if Japan's gender employment gap was reduced (or if female employment rates matched those of males), some 7.1 million workers would be added to the workforce, boosting, in the process, Japan's GDP by as much as 12.5 percent.[40] Meanwhile, the International Monetary Fund estimates that increasing the female labor force participation rate in Japan would add another 0.25 percent to growth each year and raise income per capita by 4 percent.[41] OECD estimates are just as telling: Closing the gender gap in Japan would add nearly 20 percent to GDP over fifteen years. If it were narrowed by 50 percent, just over 11 percent would be added to GDP over the same time period.[42] That would likely be a remarkable boost to growth for a nation dying for a shot in the arm.

Mr. Abe wants and needs women to "shine" in Japan, knowing full well that past circumstances and policies—low pay, less training, and few career tracks for women, along with long hours, inflexible work practices, and male-centric business cultures—have marginalized the economic contribution of women in Japan and contributed to the nation's "lost decades."

To break these barriers for women—or begin to, at least—the Abe government has embraced women as the key driver of economic growth like no other government in the world. The goal is to raise the number of employed women ages 25 to 44 by at least 5 percent by 2020. Mr. Abe is also pressing companies to boost the number of women in leadership and management roles by 30 percent between now and 2020. Women fill only 6.2 percent of management positions in Japan, versus 34 percent in the United Kingdom and 44 percent in the United States.[43] He also wants publicly traded companies in Japan to have at least one female executive board member.

To make all of this happen, the government has adopted family-friendly policies. Four hundred thousand new spaces in nursery schools have been created to reduce waiting lists; parental leave programs have become more generous; and assistance for retraining moms hoping to reenter the workforce has been made available to target the roughly 70 percent of Japanese women who quit work after having their first child.[44]

Thus far the results are mixed. The good news: Japan's female labor force expanded by 230,000 women between 2012 and 2014, after falling modestly over the previous five years. Meanwhile, the country's overall female labor participation rate rose to a record high of 66 percent in 2014, up from 59.6 percent in 2000.[45] There is now a higher percentage of working-age females employed in Japan than either the United States or Europe.

Yet for all the cheerleading about womenomics and Abe, the execution of the programs has run into stumbling blocks that highlight the importance of cultural norms, and the lack of prudent implementation and measurement of policies. In 2014, the Labor Ministry set aside 120 million yen for a subsidy program for firms that promote women, but not a single firm applied in the first seventeen months of its existence. Meanwhile, a large share of the new jobs reported represent part-time work while the gender gap in pay remains quite large. Women in Japan earn on average 71 percent of their male counterparts. This is one of the largest gaps among the developed nations and a major constraint on the government's push to drive growth through higher female participation in the economy. Women in STEM also remain quite low in Japan. Among OECD nations, Japan has one of the lowest percentages of women in Science and Technology, at just 12 percent of the total.[46] According to Japan's Ministry of Education, Culture, Sports, Science, and Technology, women account for only 14 percent of the science and engineering students at Japanese universities, even though they represent 43 percent of college students over all, excluding medical and agricultural schools. In the humanities, they make up 66 percent.[47]

Japan's gender-specific policies are one of Japan's last and best chances to restart growth and to avert a slide into economic oblivion. Will it work? It's too early to tell. In order for Japan to remain globally competitive, the nation must do a better job—among other things—of boosting the female participation rate in computer science, engineering, and other technology-related activities. Japan, like many other nations, needs more women in the hard sciences. And it must get more women working across the board.

Trends in Europe Echo America's

The trends among college-educated women across Europe largely mirror the United States. More women entering the labor force over the past few decades have undergraduate and graduate degrees. Like the United States, more European women than men now graduate from college each year. In 2010–2011, for instance, women outnumbered men 55 percent to 45 percent at the university level in the United Kingdom.[48] Belgium, France, Spain, Sweden, and many European nations are following the same path. Women graduates are entering fields such as education, health care, social sciences, business, and law, which in turn is raising women's pay and overall productivity among the full workforce.

Well-educated women are being paid more, but women, on average, still earned 16 percent less than men in 2013.[49] The most equitable nations when it comes to gender pay are the Nordic nations like Sweden, Norway, and Denmark, while Italy, France, Spain, and Greece are the laggards.

But despite the earnings gap, the female purchasing power of the European Union (EU) is quite formidable, and on par with the United States, tallying an estimated $3 trillion in 2014.[50] As an aside, the figures include the United Kingdom, which voted to leave the European Union in 2016. Minus the U.K., the figure—over $2.7 trillion—is a staggering sum, and when combined with U.S. figures, the female spending power of the United States and Europe is in excess of $6 trillion.[51] That represents one of the largest markets in the world. Only the economies of the United States and China are larger. Any company ignoring or ignorant of this market dynamic confronts a rocky future.

The OECD estimates a narrowing of the gap between male and female employment since 1995 has accounted for a quarter of Europe's annual GDP growth.[52] Narrowing the gap more and faster would mean a lot for Europe over the next few years. Among OECD countries, the bulk of which are European, the workforce participation rate of women was just 63 percent in 2014, below the U.S. average, while the figure for men was nearly 80 percent.[53] This is a sizable gender gap that, if closed, would be a tremendous boost to growth in the region. In fact, the OECD estimates nearly 12 percent would be added to the OECD GDP over fifteen years if the female male employment gulf somehow disappeared.

By country, OECD estimates show that closing the male–female labor market participation gap completely would add 11.2 percent to GDP in Germany, 9.4 percent in France, and 22.5 percent in Italy in fifteen years.[54] That is an astounding jump in output so desperately needed by these nations.

Or consider Greece, Europe's most extreme economic outlier and whose female participation rate—59 percent—is among the lowest in Europe.[55] In addition to its soaring debt levels, uncompetitive industries, and creaky infrastructures, the underutilization of women is yet another self-inflicted drag on growth. Sadly, amid all the financial and economic conditions piled on Greece by its creditors in 2015 when negotiating yet another bailout package, not one had anything to do with the increased participation of women in the economy. As a key missed opportunity and lack of acknowledgment of the facts around women in the workforce, the nation's creditors did not discuss that Greece adopt policies to help employ women. How is Greece ever going to pay back its mountain of debt if a significant share of its labor force is unengaged in the formal economy?

Greece needs to think like Japan when contemplating the economic role of gender. Or it could look to Eastern Europe, where female participation rates in nations like Russia and Poland are above the average for Europe in general. In Russia's case, the loss of so many men in World War II made women's participation in the economy essential. As a percentage of the total, women hold more senior jobs in Russia, Poland, Lithuania, and Estonia than the average of the European Union.

Other models for Greece to follow: Norway, Sweden Switzerland, and Denmark, which have some of the highest female labor force participation rates in the world and, coincidentally, some of the highest standards of living on earth. These nations have been at the forefront of adopting family-friendly policies that are highly supportive of keeping both moms and dads engaged and gainfully employed.

What magic have these nations wrought? When it comes to specific policies, we are not talking rocket science—just common sense: high-quality, all-day, affordable day care for children; free universal preschooling; generous and supportive parental leave policies; more flexible work options; the elimination of tax disincentives that penalize a second income; flexible policies to help with elder care. Such initiatives have kept women economically active, with the female participate rate in Norway, Sweden, Denmark, and Switzerland in excess of 75 percent in 2015, a remarkable figure and one that compares to a global average of 55 percent.[56]

While true that such initiatives for gender equality come with a cost and are associated with Europe's much-maligned corporate welfare system, U.S. policy makers would be wrong to dismiss womenomic initiatives. An even greater cost lies with women having no realistic option but staying at home, pushed out of the labor force all together, and robbing the economy of a critical input to future growth. When it comes to decisions about work life and home life, men and women should be resourced and compensated in such a way that they can have a truly balanced discussion about what's best for themselves, their careers, and their families and not be put in a situation where pay gap and unrealistic policies all but force women to opt out. A recent IMF paper on Finland and Norway—celebrated for their emphasis on gender equality—shows that publicly-funded parental leave and childcare facilities have increased the number of working women and raised the fertility rate, too, something Japan in particular could learn from.

As policy makers in the United States, Europe, and Japan struggle to generate growth and plan for the future, they would do well to revisit the role of women in the economy—one of the world's best resources for growth.

Notes

1. *Economic Report of the President*, Chapter 4; page 157, February 2015.
2. Heidi Crebo-Rediker, *Pushing Forward Gender-Driven Growth* (June 24, 2013). www.state.gov/e/oce/rls/2013/211088.htm.
3. Jonathan Woetzel et al., *The Power of Parity: How Advancing Women's Equality Can Add $12 Trillion to Global Growth*, McKinsey Global Institute (September 2015).
4. Katrin Elborgh-Woytek et al., *Women, Work, and the Economy: Macroeconomic Gains from Gender Equity*, International Monetary Fund (September 2013).
5. *Closing the Gender Gap: Act Now*, OECD (December 17, 2012).
6. *Labor Force Change: A Century of Change 1950–2050* (Washington, DC: Bureau of Labor Statistics, May 2002).
7. *Fifty Years After the Equal Pay Act*, The White House, National Equal Pay Task Force, June 2013.

8. Gail Collins, *When Everything Changed: The Amazing Journey of American Women from 1960 to Present* (New York: Bay Back Books, October 2009), p. 203.

9. *American Women Report of the President's Commission on the Status of Women*, U.S. Department of Labor, October 28, 1963.

10. "A Changing of the Guard: Traditionalists, Feminists, and the New Face of Women in Congress, 1955–1976." history.house.gov/Exhibitions-and-Publications/WIC/Historical-Essays/Changing-Guard/Introduction/.

11. Sar A. Levitan and Richard S. Belous, *What's Happening to the American Family?* (Johns Hopkins University Press, 1981).

12. U.S. Department of Education, National Center for Education Statistics Table 324.50. Degrees conferred by postsecondary institutions in selected professional field, by sex of student, *Digest of Education Statistics 2013*.

13. C. J. Prince, *Women Power*, BofA Merrill Lynch Global Research 2015.

14. Shira Boss-Bicak, "25 Years of Coeducation," *Columbia College Today* (July/August 2009). www.college.columbia.edu/cct/jul_aug09/features1.

15. *Economic Report of the President*, Chapter 4, p. 158. February 2015. Note: Using the Current Population Survey from 1970 to 2013, CEA calculated the increase in hours worked by women and assumed that the average product of labor was unchanged.

16. Katrin Elborgh-Woytek et al., *Women, Work and the Economy: Macroeconomic Gains from Gender Equity*, IMF Discussion Note (September 17, 2013).

17. Carmen DeNavas-Walt, Bernadette D. Proctor, and Jessica C. Smith, *Income, Poverty, and Health Insurance Coverage in the United States: 2012* (Washington, DC: U.S. Census Bureau, September 2013).

18. Judith Warner, "The Women's Leadership Gap," *Center for American Progress* (March 7, 2014).

19. "A Tension for America's Auto World: Winning Women behind the Wheel," *The Washington Post* (January 13, 2015).

20. Alliance of Automobile Manufacturers, "Women and Autos: The Engine of the Auto Economy" (January 30, 2013).

21. Bureau of Labor Statistics, *Women in the Labor Force: A Databook*, "Table 11: Employed people, by detailed occupation and gender" (Washington, DC: Bureau of Labor Statistics, December 2015).

22. "Car Sellers Refine Pitch to Women," *The Wall Street Journal* (August 20, 2014).

23. Agnieszka Flak, "Supercar Makers Neglect Women at Their Peril," Reuters (May 19, 2015).

24. Dana Hull, "Tesla Asked Women What They Wanted and Came Up with Model X SUV," Bloomberg (September 18, 2015).
25. Euromonitor International, *Sportswear in the U.S.* (May 2016).
26. Morgan Stanley Research, "Global Athletic Wear" (October 12, 2015).
27. *The 2015 State of Women-Owned Businesses Report,* American Express OPEN (May 2015).
28. *The Economic Impact of Women-Owned Businesses in the United States,* Center for Women's Business Research (October 2009).
29. Heather R. Ettinger and Eileen M. O'Connor, "Women of Wealth: Why Does Financial Services Industry Still Not Hear Them?" Family Wealth Advisors Council (2012).
30. *Fund Managers by Gender,* Morningstar Research Report (June 2015).
31. *Highlights of Women's Earnings in 2014* (Washington, DC: U.S. Bureau of Labor Statistics, November 2015).
32. *Current Population Survey Annual Social and Economic Supplement* (Washington, DC: U.S. Census Bureau, 2014).
33. Suat Ozsoy, "The Pay Gap That Haunts MBAs," *Bloomberg Businessweek* (October 27, 2015).
34. *Current Population Survey Annual Social and Economic Supplement,* (Washington, DC: U.S. Census Bureau, 2014).
35. Shelley J. Correll, Stephen Benard, and In Paik, *Getting a Job: Is There a Motherhood Penalty?* Vol. 112, No. 5 (Chicago: The University of Chicago, AJS, March 2007).
36. Guy Ryder, *Maternity and Paternity at Work: Law and Practice across the World* (ILO, 2014).
37. OECD stat, data as of 2015.
38. Sylvia Ann Hewlett, "What's Holding Women Back in Science and Technology Industries," *Harvard Business Review* (March 13, 2014).
39. *Womenomics 4.0: Time to Walk the Talk,* Goldman Sachs (May 30, 2014).
40. Ibid.
41. Katrin Elborgh-Woytek et al., *Women, Work and the Economy: Macroeconomic Gains from Gender Equity,* IMF Discussion Note (September 17, 2013).
42. "Closing the Gender Gap: Act Now," OECD (December 17, 2012).
43. "Top Paid Nikkei 225 Female Leader Shows Japan Gender Hurdles," Bloomberg, (August 18, 2014).
44. Demetri Sevastopulo, "Abe Pushes 'Womenomics' to Shake Up Japan's Workforce Dynamic," *Financial Times* (December 7, 2014).
45. "Global Employment Trends for Women 2012," International Labour Organization (December 11, 2012).
46. OECD Economic Surveys: Japan, Organization for Economic Cooperation and Development, April 2015. http://www.oecd.org/eco/surveys/Japan-2015-overview.pdf.

47. Miki Tanikawa, "Japan's 'Science Women' Seek an Identity," *New York Times* (June 16, 2013).
48. OECD, *Education at a Glance 2014: OECD Indicators* (October 2014).
49. Eurostat dataset (March 15, 2015).
50. "The Case for Investing in Europe," *AmCham EU* (June 24, 2015).
51. Ibid.
52. *Gender and Sustainable Development: Maximizing the Economic, Social and Environmental Role of Women*, OECD.
53. Ibid.
54. *Achieving Stronger Growth by Promoting a More Gender-Balanced Economy*, OECD, ILO, IMF, World Bank, August 15, 2014.
55. OECD dataset, "Labor force participation rate, ages 15–64, percentage," 2014.
56. Ibid.

CHAPTER 3

Womenomics Goes Global

"Gender balance isn't a battle between men and women ... This is best understood in countries where the modern world is seen as a threat. Men there know—better than most—that gender equality is the dividing line between modernity and its deniers."

—Avivah Wittenberg-Cox, November 2015[1]

The economic influence and game-changing potential of women extends well beyond the United States and other developed nations. It is global in nature. In a majority of developing nations, China in particular, women have become influential drivers of economic activity and the key to future growth. It is finally dawning on many nations—but not all, for sure—that empowering and encouraging women to participate in the economy are among the best ways to promote growth, boost productivity, offset shrinking labor forces in some nations, and reduce poverty.

Meanwhile, smart, global and forward-looking companies are working hard to tap this long-ignored growth dynamic. Around the world and across various industries, many firms are busy crafting strategies to leverage the talents of women, while simultaneously designing products and services for this new consuming cohort. It is finally dawning on both states and companies that allowing and enabling women to fully engage in the economy is one of the best options available for promoting global growth and prosperity for all parties. It's that simple—yet that hard.

Despite progress in various parts of the world, treatment of girls and women remains downright primitive. Many nations have yet to empower and engage women in the formal economy, and continue to embrace discriminatory norms and practices that compromise the economic contribution and safety of women and girls. Most of these states are found in the developing nations, where growth and development remains challenging. In this universe, the underutilization of women remains quite real. Here, women stand at the crossroads of promise and peril.

Getting the Basics Right

Progress has been made. Across the developing world, women are healthier and living longer, better educated, and becoming more embedded in the formal economy. Women of child-bearing age are having fewer children, and their children (boys and girls) in turn are healthier and better educated than previous generations. And, remember, the women of the developing nations also possess some serious spending power. By our estimates, their collective female purchasing power totaled $8.3 trillion in 2015, a sum greater than comparable figures in both the United States and Europe. China accounts for the bulk of this total but even when the Middle Kingdom is excluded, the spending power of women in developing countries is around $4.4 trillion. This purchasing power is something no company or investor can ignore. What changes have underpinned these dynamics?

The key to more income begins with education, and across the globe, the gender gap in education continues to narrow. While less than half of children ages 6 to 11 years old were enrolled in primary school in 1960, today the figure is closer to 90 percent.[2] According to the World Bank, two-thirds of all nations in the world have reached gender parity in primary school enrollment, and in one-third of the countries, girls outnumber boys in secondary education.[3] And similar to the United States, more women than men now attend universities in a majority of developing nations thanks to a sevenfold increase in women's tertiary enrollment since 1970 (versus fourfold among men).[4]

More educated girls means more women entering the formal economy, with the labor force participation of women expanding dramatically over the past few decades in a number of nations

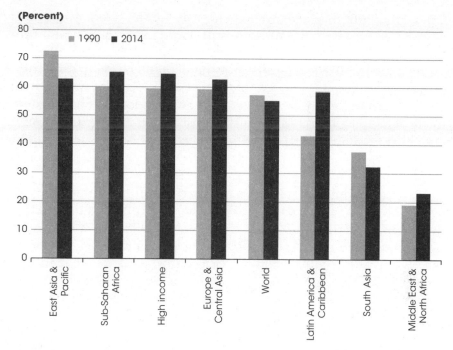

Figure 3.1   Female labor participation rates, by region.
Source: ILO.

(see Figure 3.1). Attaining higher levels of education has additional benefits beyond the potential of future earnings and resultant purchasing power. Educated women, for instance, have fewer children, and often get married later, allowing for family planning that includes their points of view and goals. The better educated the woman, the lower the risk of maternal mortality, a key cause of death among women in the developing nations. Better nutrition and diets are associated with more education as well, which by extension means better health for women and their families.[5]

The United Nation says, "When you educate a girl, you educate a nation." However, similar to trends in the developed nations, rising educational attainment does not necessarily equate to equality in pay and employment. Nor does it directly translate into reduced hours of unpaid work for girls and women or basic legal and human rights. This is a no-brainer, but something so obvious and commonsensical can also be hard to communicate. Melinda Gates, with her daughter Jenn, lived with a family in Tanzania in 2014. The family had a boy and a girl about the same age as Jenn Gates. After a late dinner, all the women cleaned up. "We were still doing dishes late at night in the dirt under the moonlight at 10:30 at night," Gates recalled in an interview with NPR. "And when my daughter finally came out with a headlamp on her head, the thing that this girl most wanted— and she was quite shy—was my daughter's headlamp. She needed the headlamp light to study after she finished the dishes. She doesn't even start her homework until after 10:30, whereas I saw her brother doing it when it was around 4 or 5 o'clock in the afternoon," said Gates.[6]

Adding complexity to this issue, there is nothing homogeneous or standardized when it comes to the economic role of women in the developing nations. Their plight and potential varies dramatically by region and country. Labor force participation rates, for instance, are 65 percent in Sub-Saharan Africa, as low as 23 percent in the Middle East and North Africa, and as high as 68 percent in East Asia. In Jordan, less than 17 percent of the nation's women are counted as part of the labor force; in Saudi Arabia the figure is roughly 21 percent and less than 26 percent in Egypt.[7]

Wars, droughts, famines, deeply ingrained levels of corruption, broken institutions—there's a laundry list of reasons why the poor nations of the world remain poor. But in many cases, grinding poverty goes hand in hand with the harsh and often brutal treatment of girls and women. We may be living in the twenty-first century, but in many parts of the world women are still forbidden to work, leave their home, drive a car, own land, open a checking account, and have a phone.

The World Bank's *Women, Business and the Law* report showed that women face gender-based job restrictions in 100 of the 173 economies included in the 2016 report. In 18 of these economies, husbands can legally prevent their wives from working. Many countries have official restrictions related to job qualifications and requirements; beyond that, there are myriad cultural challenges also faced by women in getting jobs. Meanwhile, in nearly two dozen nations, married women are not allowed to pass citizenship on to their children while fathers can.[8]

When nations deny women basic rights—whether it is applying for a passport, making decisions for the household, or just leaving the home alone—economic growth is stunted. The country's vitality is suppressed because women are oppressed by customs and government policies that sustain the status quo. In these conditions, millions of women are disengaged from the formal economy because they spend a majority of their time doing work just to subsist. Rural women spend two to nine hours a day doing menial tasks like gathering wood, fetching water, collecting fuel, tilling the fields, cooking, and caring for young and old. These are important daily activities but add nothing to the overall growth and productivity of a country. Many girls, rather than being in school, are tasked with these chores until they are adults, and therefore are short-changed of the life-long benefits of education.

The fate of one group of girls—child brides—is even crueler. In countries where child marriage is common, many parents see child marriage as the only way to care for their daughter since many feel incapable of providing food and education to all their children. Today, one in seven girls in developing nations (excluding China) will be married before the age of 15; one-third of girls in developing nations will be married by age 18. In Bangladesh, even though child marriage is illegal, 65 percent of Bangladeshi girls marry before the age of 18, most forced to marry by their parents. The United Nations estimates 67 million women worldwide aged 20 to 24 in 2010 were married before they turned 18. Sadly, this number could rise as high as 140 million by 2020 if current trends continue.[9]

What happens after these young girls are married? Nothing good. Human Rights Watch studies show child marriages are highly correlated with health dangers to young mothers with early pregnancies, and go hand in hand with low education levels, grinding poverty, HIV, and spousal abuse.[10] It's a cycle of despair documented for decades by the international organizations that collect data on poverty.

While the statistics are shocking, a single photo overpowers a thousand data points. Photographer Allison Joyce's Instagram image of "the saddest bride I have ever seen," first picked up by the *Washington Post*, and then on media all over the Internet, shows a 15-year-old Bangladeshi girl on her wedding day. The teen bride kneels beside her husband to be, a man twice her age. Both are dressed in resplendent ceremonial garb, but their facial expressions are drawn and grim. "It's tradition for the bride to look shy and coy during the wedding," Joyce wrote in an email. "But I noticed this sadness and unspoken fear and uncertainty even when she was in her room with her friends before the ceremony or at the parlor with her sister (who was also married around the same age)."[11] In its 2015 report on the status of women, the UN calls child marriage "a fundamental violation of human rights that limits girls' opportunities for education and development and exposes them to domestic violence and social isolation."[12]

In some of the poorest nations in the world, the lack of toilets and running water in schools also means girls entering puberty (and beginning their menstrual cycle) find it difficult to stay in school. In the absence of the most basic modern sanitation facilities, girls have to wait hours to relieve themselves and endure the psychological angst of dealing with menstruation in a public place. To avoid the embarrassment and humiliation, girls opt out of school and stay home, which is the first irreversible step toward a life with dramatically limited opportunity. UNICEF estimates that one in ten school-age African girls will either skip school during menstruation or drop out entirely due to the absence of separate facilities for boys and girls and decent facilities for both.

In India, 640 million men and women—nearly half the country's population—still defecate in the open, according to the World Health Organization. Close to 70 percent of households (rural and urban) do not have toilets in their households. The risk is high for young girls and women of being sexually assaulted when they use public bathrooms. Two Japanese companies—Lixil Corporation and Toto LTD—have created low-cost, waterless toilets to address the needs of the emerging markets, and the Japanese government supports them.[13] But India needs the government to be more involved. As Nitya Jacob, who leads policy for the Indian branch of the international charity WaterAid, told the *Associated Press*, "There is a kind of a feeling among politicians that if we ignore the problem it will go away."[14] India's Prime Minster Narendra Modi promised to deliver more than 1 million toilets when he was elected in 2014, but even though they have been planned or built, studies show that the majority are not being used, especially in the rural communities because the toilets are not connected to clean water and sewers—a reminder that well-executed implementation and culture-shifting education is also needed to change people's habits.[15]

When the Law Is Against Women

Restrictions on women were rarely cited as a source of stunted economic growth by previous generations of (mostly male) development economists. The World Bank's Women, Business and the Law project, launched in 2009, was the first to collect data on laws, regulations, and policies that systematically undervalue and deny women economic choices and human rights. The data collected are used to evaluate seven indicators of women's rights and well-being: access to financial institutions, property rights, ability to get a job, incentives to work, "going to court," which includes legal representation, the ability to build credit, and protections from violence. Within these categories the report tracks legislation on issues such as nondiscriminatory access to credit, care leave for sick relatives, the legal age of marriage, and protection orders for victims of domestic violence. The report details how a lack of legal rights is often associated with fewer girls attending secondary school relative to boys, fewer women working or running businesses, and a wider gender wage gap, among other issues.

As the United States continues to refine its laws against discrimination, 155 of 173 countries in World Bank's 2016 report have at least one law that differentiates rights of women and men, and discriminates against women. In 100 countries, women face gender-based job restrictions. Forty-six countries have no laws specifically protecting women from domestic violence.

The Womenomic Difference Between India and China

India and China are the two most populous countries on earth—1.39 billion people in China and 1.27 billion in India. Together, they account for 36.4 percent of the total world population of 7.2 billion as of 2014.[16]

India is a democracy and was one of the first democracies to be led by a woman. China is ruled by a small male-dominated cohort representing the Communist Party. China is strong in manufacturing and trade, while India lags in both. China's economy is relatively open; India's is closed. Women consumers play a greater role in driving growth in China than in India. All of this comes back to the progression from education to earnings, plus the legal and social factors that make women-led economic growth possible. What helps separate China from India: the role of women in the economy.

Take China first. Many factors account for the nation's remarkably rapid rise as a global economic power. Chief among them: a low-cost, skilled labor force, open trade policies, and liberal government incentives that have attracted billions of dollars in foreign investment. These catalysts are well known to most investors. Less known, or understood, is the big part women in China have played in the nation's economic miracle, as workers and consumers. The ubiquitous "Made in China" label is courtesy of the young Chinese female workers who migrated in droves from the rural areas to coastal cities over the past three decades. Millions of Chinese women took to the factory floors beginning in the 1980s, sewing everything from shirts, jackets, and footwear to assembling radios, televisions, computers, and tablets purchased around the world. China's exports soared over the past few decades, and this transformed the country from an economic backwater in the late 1970s to the world's top exporter of goods by 2012. Against this backdrop, and absent the mass migration of young female workers to China's factories, the rise of China might not have otherwise occurred—or would have transpired at a much slower pace. Women are the unsung heroes of China's economic success; they are also China's future.

A woman we will call Fan, for reasons of privacy, is among the millions of young Chinese women who will help determine China's economic future. Fan is an enthusiastic 24-year-old with a Master's degree in Finance from a top U.S. university. While her relatives spent their productive years on the shop floor, Fan used her math skills to attend one of the best universities in China before heading to the United States for graduate studies. She now lives in Shanghai and works for a large Chinese bank, but she could easily pass for a newly minted Wall Street banker on the streets of lower Manhattan.

Fan is the first in her family to earn a university degree. She is also the first in her family to own a cell phone, a computer, and to have traveled overseas. She has a good income, and spends what she earns on things she considers essentials—cosmetics, clothes, footwear, and electronics. She is not afraid to use her credit card to buy extras—nutritional supplements or several pairs of running shoes.

Her parents, in contrast, are more likely to save than spend. They don't trust credit cards or buying anything online. They have traveled around China, but have never left the mainland. They wish Fan would think about getting married, fearing she will become a "leftover woman." (In China, a woman who is considered "leftover" is typically over the age of 27 and is deemed old, undesirable, and unwanted by Chinese society for waiting so long to be married.) But Fan, like many other women urban dwellers, is not interested in marriage or worried about being unmarried. She is more focused on traveling, enjoying the good life, and advancing her career.

Now multiply Fan by over 33 million women, which is the number of young single women in China, according to figures from the Hong Kong research firm, CLSA.[17] This cohort is far different from previous generations of women—they are better educated, more tech savvy, more global in nature, and prefer to work in an office, not a factory. They are well positioned to benefit from China's shifting growth model—away from manufacturing and toward more service-based industries and Internet-based activities.

Fan and her contemporaries are also urbanites, not rural dwellers. They are more independent and confident thanks to their educational achievements. While only nine million women had received any type of higher education in China in 1996, the figure stood at 52 million in 2012—a near-sixfold increase. In 2009, women accounted for more than half of all college students in China for the first time ever. A year later, in 2010, the number of women college graduates working toward a Master's degree surpassed men while the share of women working on Ph.D. programs has also soared over the past decade.

More female university graduates is just what the mainland needs since China's factories of the future will need fewer nimble fingers to sew shirts and sneakers and more workers who are computer literate, familiar with data processing and the Internet, and can operate sophisticated computerized manufacturing equipment. The digitization and automation of factories also reduces the physical demands of manufacturing in industries such as automobiles and textiles. The door is open to a new generation of educated digital natives in factories where women have been underrepresented. Advances in manufacturing also increase the promise of mass customized design and production, which women want.[18] This is certainly what Padmasree Warrior is thinking about as the new U.S. CEO and global chief development officer at NextEV, a Chinese startup that's building an electric car to compete with Tesla.

How Women Will Make Electric Cars in China

PriceWaterhouseCoopers forecasts that roughly two-thirds of automotive industry growth until 2020 will come from the "developing Asia-Pacific" region, including 40 percent from China alone. Padmasree Warrior, the former chief technology officer at Motorola and then Cisco, is hoping they're right.

In 2015, Warrior left Cisco to join NextEV—an electric car company started by three Chinese Internet entrepreneurs—as its CEO and global director of development. In an interview with *Fortune* magazine, she says EV will "apply technology to solve fundamental problems"—climate change and global pollution, among them. NextEV's edge over Tesla, she says, will be the "user experience." Warrior drives a red Tesla Model S—"and will keep it until I build my own car."

She has never worked in the car business, or for a startup. But she has worked at the top of engineering-driven companies for decades. Born in 1961 in Vijayawada, India, she made her way to the United States to study at Cornell University and then returned to the Indian Institute of Technology.

NextEV, which is headquartered in Shanghai, will sell its first cars in China, in just the kind of digital factory of the future that is inviting for women workers. Warrior is based in San Jose, California, where the startup has an 85,000-square-foot research and development center. It also has operations in Hong Kong, London, and Munich. At the top of her LinkedIn page, Warrior enthusiastically posts, "We're Hiring," and includes a link to send a resume, and a pitch to appeal to future women customers and employees:

> "We aim to shape a joyful lifestyle for everyone who touches the things we create. Making the ownership of a car easy, stress-free and exquisitely aspirational once more, we are a company dedicated to becoming a user enterprise—shared by all in the mobile social era, and whose vehicle owners feel nothing but pure delight."

Women now account for 44 percent of China's labor force, one of the highest percentages—not only among the developing nations but anywhere in the world. China's female labor force participation rate of roughly 70 percent is more in line with Western nations, the United States included. In business, a quarter of

China's entrepreneurs are women. And when it comes to generating new-found wealth, no country does it better than China, a nation with more self-made female billionaires than any other country in the world. According to the rich list compiled by China's Hurun Report, eight out of ten of the world's richest self-made businesswomen come from China. Two-thirds of those women are billionaires.[19]

Zhou Qunfei is one of them. Dubbed the "touch screen queen," Qunfei founded Lens, a company that makes touchscreens for mobile devices and has made her one of China's newest women billionaires. Raised by her blind father in rural Hunan province, she quit school at age 16 and moved to Shenzhen, and started out working on an assembly line making watch lenses for a $1 a day. After starting her own company in 1993 with about $3,000, she eventually won a contract from Motorola to make screens for the Razr, a popular Motorola cell phone model introduced in 2004. Lens was listed on Shenzhen's ChiNext board in March 2015, raising Qunfei's net worth to $7.8 billion—that represents some serious purchasing power.[20]

By our estimates, the purchasing power of Chinese women was a staggering $3.9 trillion in 2015—a number greater than the spending of American and European women, respectively. Whether self-made or inherited wealth, Chinese women are drivers of global sales of cars, cosmetics, travel, entertainment, clothing, footwear, and digital devices. In the luxury category, China's first homegrown haute couturier, Guo Pei, profiled in the *New Yorker*, captures the energy of the ancient and modern China. "Changing your look every season to please a fickle customer isn't how I work. I aim to create heirlooms," says Pei.[21] Wealthy Chinese women now spend more than $27 billion on personal luxury goods, and smart Western firms have become more embedded in the local markets.[22] Maserati, the Italian sports car brand, reports that 30 percent of its buyers in China are women, while the comparable figures in the United States and Europe are less than 5 percent.[23]

The incomes of these upwardly mobile Chinese women have more than tripled since 2000. L'Oreal, the French cosmetics giant, has built its own research center in China. Not surprisingly, Chinese women want skin products and cosmetics that are different from what Western women like. To tap into this massive new market and make the most of the infusion of educated women with career ambitions, multinationals like General Electric are hiring local women to run their Chinese operations.

In the end, while circumstances are hardly perfect in China, and the nation's one-child policy did result in the deaths of an unknown number of girls, the country has done a far better job than India in developing and leveraging the talent and human capital of women—and the economic outcomes speak for themselves. India, regrettably, has not invested in its women, and this has undermined the nation's economic potential for decades.

Let's start with the basics in India—literacy. Only two-thirds of Indian girls and women are literate; over 300 million women in India can't read or write at all.[24] Compare this to China, where 93 percent of women are literate, meaning they are equipped to obtain a secondary school education, which leads to university and in turn leads to greater job potential and opportunities, rising incomes, and a promising future. Without fundamental reading and writing skills, these women are unable to attend school, much less get a job outside of the home that could elevate them and their families economically. More women than men in India work in low-productivity jobs; for example, 75 percent of women living in rural areas are employed in agriculture versus 59 percent for men. Women in India do almost ten times the amount of unpaid care work that men do. This compares with Chinese women in rural households who do about three and four times the amount of unpaid care work as men do.[25] Three-quarters of this unpaid work by rural women in India are the routine household chores that are necessary because of poor basic services such as sanitation, clean water, and clean sources of cooking fuel. Walking miles for water and other resources is a necessity for India's rural poor, but it is not contributing to India's measureable growth and productivity or a better future for most of the population.

Internet access is another indicator of how women in India are left out of opportunities for growth. According to a 2015 market research study by the Internet and Mobile Association of India and the Indian Market Research Bureau, India had 402 million Internet users as of December 2015, with a projected 371 mobile users by June 2016. This makes India the second largest Internet user base in the world, after China and ahead of the United States. The number of mobile Internet users in India could reach between 700 million and

900 million by 2025.[26] Currently, though, India's men far outnumber women on the Internet. In mobile, the difference among urban users is 62 percent men versus 38 percent women. In rural India, where almost all Internet use is via mobile devices, the gap is even starker: 88 percent men and 12 percent women.[27]

India's cultural expectations hold back women who want to be more independent and more productive in the economy (Figure 3.2). This is true in all socioeconomic groups. The World-wide Web Foundation calls the Internet "a game-changer for India's marginalized women".[28] While that is certainly true of the Internet's potential, women using the Internet does not go down well in many parts of the country, even though India boasts one of the most tech-savvy workforces in the world.[29]

Meanwhile, a woman going off to work is frowned upon in tra-ditional rural homes. A woman's job is taking care of her children, husband, and the elderly, and a variety of other tasks. In some cases, the workload is so heavy that it takes more than one wife to get every-thing done in a day—a practice that remains even though polygamy

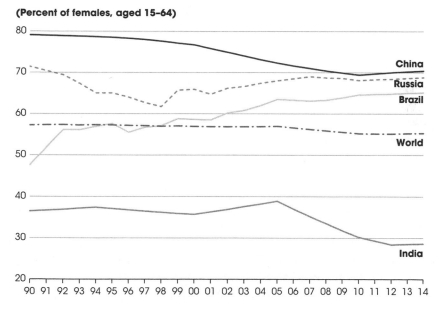

Figure 3.2 India and its peers: Labor force participation rates.

Source: ILO. Data as of 2015.

is outlawed in India. In the drought-stricken village of Denganmal in western India, "water wives" have become the answer. In an interview with Reuters, local villager Sakharam Bhagat explains his dilemma: "I had to have someone to bring us water, and marrying again was the only option. My first wife was busy with the kids. When my second wife fell sick and was unable to fetch water, I married a third." Bhagat says "marrying for water has been the norm here from many years."[30] Also of note, the international press coverage of India is putting the spotlight on sexual assault, which is also a major symptom of India's gender-driven economic development dilemma.

Even in modernization, India's hierarchical and gender traditions remain strong and limiting for women. As Anuranjita Kumar, Citigroup's chief human resources officer for South Asia, told Bloomberg, "That whole notion that 'my job is secondary to my husband' is carried by the women themselves, a mindset we fight here every day."[31] To counter this mindset, like Japan's initiatives, India's companies (domestic and foreign) are trying out programs like "Bring Your Mother-in-Law to Work" day, "Take Your Baby on Your Business Trip," and longer paid maternity leaves and subsidized day care.

As a result of these and other factors, India has long lagged behind China's growth and development due to women's labor force participation. India's female workforce participation rates peaked at 39 percent in 2005 and fell to 29 percent as of 2014, according to World Bank.[32] Those statistics are a stark contrast to the over 70 percent of women in China participating in the labor force, and are a staggering missed opportunity for India and the multimillions living in poverty. But India has not lost to China yet. Change is afoot. There is much it can do.

Citigroup's Anuranjita Kumar tries to stimulate "a sense of hunger" in the young professionals she works with so they won't leave, and she is hopeful attitudes are changing. "The optimist in me sees that the landscape is changing, but the pace could be faster," she says.[33] Today, many young women in India's largest cities are better educated, getting married at a later age, planning to have fewer children, and are connected to the Internet. While more than 25 million girls in 2010 were married before the age of 18, the median age at first marriage among young women is climbing. Critically, educational attainment levels among women in India are also rising, portending a better future for millions of girls, assuming their parents and communities encourage and help them stay in school. In India's largest cities, Mumbai and New Delhi, it's not uncommon to see mothers standing with their children in uniforms and packs on their back, waiting for the school bus outside tin-roofed shacks. Just around the corner well-educated, well-dressed women are on their way to jobs in banks, advertising agencies, and India's diversified conglomerates. In the global epicenter of call centers—Bangalore—thousands of young women workers take to the phones each day, helping thousands of customers reboot their computers, pay their bills, and make reservations.

If India were able to achieve parity between employment rates for men and women, according to McKinsey projections, the gross domestic product in 2025 would be an astounding 60 percent higher than if women's work status remained at current levels.[34] India as a nation will not come close to reaching this potential unless the government and society come to view and treat women differently.

Positively, women CEOs in India—like Chanda Kochhar of ICICI Bank, India's biggest private lender—and high-profile corporate women outside India—like Padmasree Warrior and Indra Nooyi, the CEO of PepsiCo—are powerful models. Nooyi and Kochhar are both known for speaking about their roles as CEOs, daughters, wives, mothers.[35] With any luck, many more girls and women will follow in their footsteps inside the country and abroad.

While women will play a key part in determining India's future, the same can be said of the Middle East, North Africa and Sub-Saharan Africa, where women's rights and privileges, while still limited in many cases, are gradually improving. Many women in these regions still confront legal, religious, and other cultural constraints, although more women are now fully engaged in the formal economy—as small business owners, teachers, doctors, and various other occupations. Accordingly, the potential upside for many nations in Middle East and Africa is significant. The future of the Middle East, for instance, does not have to lie with oil—it could pivot on the talents of women and their potential contribution to growth and development. In many African nations, women remain under-utilized, although thanks to rising educational levels and the use of technology, notably cell phones, females are becoming important drivers of growth. Africa's future economic prospects will be shaped by women, with Rwanda as a prime example. The nation ranks sixth overall in the World Economic Forum's 2013 *Global Gender*

Gap, an annual report that quantifies the degree of gender-based disparities among states. Rwanda's 2003 constitution enshrined women's participation—as voters and candidates—as a part of its gender-based growth policies. As a consequence, roughly 60 percent of the nation's parliament is composed of women, which is one of the highest ratios in the world.[36] Education has been another priority, with the nation achieving 100 percent gender parity in primary and secondary school enrollment. This has helped boost the female labor force participation rate to a stunning 88 percent, although many of these jobs are in agriculture and low-end service activities. Rwanda has become one of Africa's most dynamic economies, and it serves as a case study for how more women fully engaged in the economy and politics can transform a country.

Women Crossing the Digital Divide

If women are ever going to reach their full potential in the developing nations, the digital gender gap must narrow. When girls and women have computers, and even more so, mobile phones, it opens their world and their prospects for a better education, a better job, and a sustainable income.

A mobile phone empowers a woman to start a business and better manage her health and her family's health. It also provides more protection and security when women are traveling. It gives women a voice to speak out on the conditions that hold women back and to participate in the growing number of initiatives—many of them on the Internet—that support girls and women rising. Because women have less time and mobility relative to men (in both developed and developing nations), women stand to benefit the most when they are connected to the Internet and have access to mobile phones.

The digital divide between men and women in developing countries today is a gulf, not a gap. The Intel study of the digital divide in developing countries shows women are nearly 25 percent less likely to be online than men.[37] In addition, women in developing nations are 21 percent less likely to own a mobile phone than men, with figures even less promising in Africa (23 percent), the Middle East (24 percent), and South Asia (37 percent).[38]

This is an enormous missed opportunity for countries to strengthen and modernize economies and improve many people's lives in the process. Income-generating opportunities are lost;

women become marginalized at a much faster rate; and benefits of greater connectivity that allows for greater education, expressions, social participation, and entertainment are lost.

The Intel study suggests that women themselves may stand in their own way. No doubt driven by a culture that has told them so, for example, one in five women in India and Egypt participating in Intel's study in 2013 said they believed that the Internet was not "appropriate" for them. They further said they did not have the money to go online, and visiting cybercafés was frowned upon. Yet, "without the Internet, we are blind fools," is how one Indian user of the Internet put it.

Blind fools, indeed. And at a terrible personal cost and a great cost for countries and companies. The Intel report estimates that if the number of female Internet users reached 1.2 billion users, the estimated boost in output in the developing nations would be in the range of $13 billion to $18 billion. For Intel, that surge would equal about a $50 billion to $70 billion spike in new platform sales, data plans, and network access. The Internet at the fingertips of women around the world represents one of the best chances of boosting global growth and driving greater gender equality.

In the end, there is little doubt that life is getting better for millions of women around the world. More girls are in school. More women are working. Women have never been more important to a global economy that continues to struggle and recover from the Great Recession of 2008–2009. However, despite these steps forward, there are too many nations moving too slowly when it comes to closing the gender gaps in employment opportunity, income, and respect. Other nations remain frozen in time, clinging to traditions and customs that so obviously handicap women and economic growth and prosperity. Notwithstanding a number of hurdles, the force of women in the economy will only gather steam as time goes on, emerging, in the process, as one of the most important macro trends of our times.

As important, the market-driven opportunities for companies to solve social problems are being recognized by more and more forward-looking enterprises, from multinational companies to startups, many of them founded, led, and driven by women. Many investors have yet to grasp this dynamic. Neither have many companies. But as the chapters that follow show, we believe they will soon.

Notes

1. "Gender at Work Is Not a Women's Issue," *Harvard Business Review* (November 17, 2015). hbr.org/2015/11/gender-at-work-is-not-a-womens-issue.
2. UNESCO (United Nations Educational, Scientific and Cultural Organization) *Statistical Yearbook 1970–1971*, United Nations, p. 97.
3. Gender Equality and Development report, 2012. siteresources.worldbank.org/INTWDR2012/Resources/7778105-1299699968583/7786210-1315936222006/Complete-Report.pdf.
4. Ibid.
5. UN Women's Health Facts and Figures on Women's Empowerment (updated April 2015). www.unwomen.org/en/what-we-do/economic-empowerment/facts-and-figures.
6. David Brancaccio, "Melinda Gates on Balancing the Burden of Unpaid Work," Marketplace (March 23, 2016). www.marketplace.org/2016/03/21/world/melinda-gates.
7. The World Bank, Labor force participation rate, female (% of female population ages 15–64) (modeled ILO estimate), 2014. data.worldbank.org/indicator/SL.TLF.CACT.ZS/countries/SL.TLF.CACT.ZS.
8. The World Bank, *Women, Business and the Law 2016* (Washington, DC: The International Bank for Reconstruction and Development/The World Bank, 2015).
9. United Nations Population Fund, "Marrying Too Young: End Child Marriage," 2012.
10. "Child Marriage," Human Rights Watch. www.hrw.org/topic/womens-rights/child-marriage.
11. Nick Kirkpatrick, "The 'Saddest Bride I Have Ever Seen': Child Marriage Is as Popular as Ever in Bangladesh," *The Washington Post* (August 28, 2015).
12. United Nations, *The World's Women 2015 Trend and Statistics.*
13. "Japan Pinpoints Toilet Technology as a Way to Improve Quality of Life for Women," by Eleanor Warnock, *Wall Street Journal*, August 29, 2015. blogs.wsj.com/japanrealtime/2015/08/29/japan-pinpoints-toilet-technology-as-a-way-to-improve-quality-of-life-for-women/.
14. "Billions Have No Access to Toilets," Associated Press (July 1 2015). www.theguardian.com/society/2015/jul/01/billions-have-no-access-to-toilets-says-world-health-organisation-report.
15. Rhitu Chatterjee, "In India, Access to Toilets Remains a Huge Problem," Public Radio International (May 12, 2016). www.pri.org/stories/2016-05-12/india-access-toilets-remains-huge-problem-worst-all-women-and-girls.

16. United Nations, World Population Prospects: Key Findings and Advanced Tables 2015 Revision (July 29, 2015). https://esa.un.org/unpd/wpp/publications/files/key_findings_wpp_2015.pdf.
17. Credit Lyonnais Securities Asia (CLSA) and AXA Investment Managers, *Market Thinking*, "Mr. and Mrs. China Still Daring to Dream," February 29, 2016. https://www.axa-im.com/en/news-archive/-/news/market-thinking-29th-february-2016-a-view-from-the-equity-market/maximized/2wOz.
18. "Women's Work: Driving the Economy," *Equity Research: Fortnightly Thoughts*, Goldman Sachs Global Investment Research, April 25, 2013. www.goldmansachs.com/our-thinking/investing-in-women/research-articles/womens-work.pdf.
19. Josh Horwitz, "China Is Home to Two-Thirds of the World's Self-Made Female Billionaires," *Quartz* (October 21, 2015). qz.com/529508/china-is-home-to-two-thirds-of-the-worlds-self-made-female-billionaires/.
20. Ibid.
21. Judith Thurman, "The Empire's New Clothes," *The New Yorker* (March 21, 2016). www.newyorker.com/magazine/2016/03/21/guo-pei-chinas-homegrown-high-fashion-designer.
22. Yuval Atsmon, "Tapping China's Luxury-Goods Market," McKinsey & Company (April 2011).
23. Michael J. Silverstein, "Don't Underestimate China's Luxury Market," *Harvard Business Review* (December 12, 2012).
24. UNESCO (United Nations Educational, Scientific and Cultural Organization) Institute for Statistics, Adult and Youth Literacy, United Nations, May 2012.
25. "The Power of Parity Advancing Women's Equality in India," McKinsey Global Institute (November 2015). www.mckinsey.com/global-themes/employment-and-growth/the-power-of-parity-advancing-womens-equality-in-india, p. 8.
26. "India's Technology Opportunity: Transforming Work, Empowering People," McKinsey Global Institute (December 2014).
27. "Mobile Internet Users to Reach 371 million by June 2016," *Times of India* (February 4, 2016). timesofindia.indiatimes.com/tech/tech-news/Mobile-internet-users-in-India-to-reach-371-million-by-June-Report/articleshow/50846649.cms.
28. Anita Gurumurthy and Nandini Chami, "The Internet as a Game Changer for India's Marginalised Women—Going Back to the Real Basics," World Wide Web Foundation (October 20, 2015). webfoundation.org/2015/10/india-womens-rights-online/.
29. "Women and the Web: Bridging the Internet Gap and Creating New Global Opportunities in Low and Middle-Income Countries," Intel Corporation and Dalberg Global Development Advisors (January 2013).

30. Danish Siddiqui, "Drought-hit Indian Village Looks to 'Water Wives' to Quench Thirst," Reuters (June 4, 2015). reuters.com/article/india-waterwives-maharashtra-idINKBN0OK1CI20150604.
31. Sandrine Rastello, "India's Plan to Keep Women Working," Bloomberg (March 7, 2016). www.bloomberg.com/news/articles/2016-03-07/mothers-in-law-at-the-office-india-s-plan-to-keep-women-working.
32. The World Bank, Labor force participation rate, female (% of female population ages 15–64) (modeled ILO estimate), 2014-2015. data.worldbank.org/indicator/SL.TLF.CACT.FE.ZS.
33. Sandrine Rastello, "India's Plan to Keep Women Working," Bloomberg (March 7, 2016). www.bloomberg.com/news/articles/2016-03-07/mothers-in-law-at-the-office-india-s-plan-to-keep-women-working.
34. Jonathan Woetzel et al., "The Power of Parity Advancing Women's Equality in India," McKinsey Global Institute (November 2015). http://www.mckinsey.com/global-themes/employment-and-growth/the-power-of-parity-advancing-womens-equality-in-india.
35. Amrita Kohli, "Chanda Kochhar's Heart Warming Letter to Daughter Is Winning Social Media," NDTV (April 15, 2016). www.ndtv.com/offbeat/chanda-kochhars-heartwarming-letter-to-daughter-is-winning-social-media-1395774; and "A Conversation with Indra Nooyi and David Bradley," July 1, 2014, Aspen Institute.
36. Inter-Parliamentary Union, "Women in National Parliaments" (April 1, 2016). www.ipu.org/wmn-e/classif.htm.
37. "Women and the Web: Bridging the Internet Gap and Creating New Global Opportunities in Low and Middle Income Countries," Intel Corporation and Dahlberg Global Development Advisors (2012), p.10. dahlberg.com/document/Women_Web.pdf.
38. Ibid., p. 10.

CHAPTER 4

From Womenomics to Gender Lens Investing

> "Contrary to what many people argue, gender equality is not a zero-sum game in which women win only at the expense of men losing. In fact, gender equality may be the best thing that ever happened to men."[1]
>
> —Michael Kimmel, *Financial Times*, International Women's Day 2015

The evidence is insurmountable. The case has been made. Women are hugely important to the global economy. The obvious next step is to pair economic reality with the significance of women in investment analysis, or to delve deeper into gender lens investing.

The latter lacks a consistent definition and board understanding, and is replete with misconceptions, including the following: that gender lens investing is only about investing in women; will ultimately underperform major benchmarks; is mostly about microfinance; and is just another approach to negatively screen for stocks. Reality is different.

Simply put, gender lens investing is the deliberate incorporation of gender factors into investment analysis and decisions. To expand on this description of the process, it helps to look at each of the three words: *gender, lens,* and *investing.*

First, gender and sex are not the same. Your sex, male or female, refers to biology; gender is sociocultural. A female executive might say, "It's due to my sex that I am able to have a baby but to my gender that my comments are not heard in a meeting. Conversely, a male executive might think, "Due to my sex I'm at greater risk for colon cancer, but it is due to my gender that I shouldn't cry in public."

Gender includes roles, responsibilities, privileges, relations, and expectations of women and men. Of course, all of these elements differ widely by geography, country, ethnicity, class, profession, and more—and are constantly evolving.

Those of us in the profession of financial services who have been immersed in developing the practice of gender lens investing chose the word *gender* because it encompasses biology and culture and it invites analysis that is inclusive of men and women. We wanted to broaden the conversation from "investing in women" (women-owned or -led businesses) to look at all types of investment opportunities and how gender knowledge, including biological and cultural attributes and differences, can inform better decisions.

The dialogue about time off to have children is a good example of how gender distinctions can be used to design more effective policies. Historically, even with national and regional differences in culture and politics, maternity leave policies and data collected by international institutions were all about women—her pregnancy and her job security. Today data and studies of company and country policies reveal much more about the design of programs such as paid leave, day care, and flexible work schedules and how they affect women, men, children, families, companies, countries, and costs.

A gender lens can add perspective on nuanced geographical differences and social expectations. For instance, a multinational consumer goods company operating in India would recognize that an Indian mother-in-law's often-significant role in family purchasing decisions differs by geography and class. A bank may find sharpening their gender analysis of the lifetime value of male and female banking customers, including loan size, loyalty, and referrals, reveals unexpected insights on new profitable segments.

A lens brings out indirect and understated aspects of gender that otherwise would be missed or misunderstood. You might, for instance, be reading this with the benefit of a pair of glasses. Imagine that out of one lens you see particular realities, needs, participation, and perceptions of women and out of the other you see the realities, needs, participation, and perceptions of men. When you look through both lenses, you see the realities (obstacles and benefits) for everyone, with fresh eyes. With gender lenses applied, you see clearly and differentially.

Or think about pointing the lens of a camera, and the way in which you can open and close the aperture to control the depth of field and the light. In this sense, one gender may move into the foreground or become background or blurred, depending on how you manipulate the aperture. Either way, a gender lens helps you frame the context, the issues, and the response more accurately. Elayne Clift, a gender scholar and writer, describes how "One's vision becomes refined..." and "often it is more compassionate and humanistic."[2] That compassion and humanity help to illuminate factors one might not have otherwise considered and ensure a comprehensive understanding of the opportunities and risks therein.

It is through such a lens that Janet McKinley, a co-founder and principal of Advance Global Capital, figured out she could apply the age-old lending practice of factoring to make it easier for entrepreneurs to get financing. With a gender lens she saw an opportunity to design the processes specifically for underserved, underfunded, promising women entrepreneurs, who she knew were also likely to be profitable customers. Based on her experience in microfinance, McKinley knew women often have lower default rates than men. She also knew women who grew businesses beyond microfinance were less successful than men at obtaining commercial bank loans.

How Factoring Works for Women Entrepreneurs

Advance Global is a UK-based trade finance company serving small businesses in developing countries and specializing in women entrepreneurs. When Janet McKinley looked at collateral requirements in multiple countries, she confirmed that women were unlikely to own property, which is often the best source of collateral. She noticed it was equally unlikely a woman would have her name on car loans or any other large asset a woman could use to secure a loan.

Advanced Global saw factoring—a form of debt finance that enables small businesses to sell their invoices to a third party (the factor) at a discount—as the best avenue. The factor pays the invoices and the business increases its working capital so it can grow. In Advance Global's process, factoring also preserves the anonymity of the woman entrepreneur so she can't be slighted or ignored based on her gender. "You don't know anything personal about the person—not gender, not race, not age, not material status, not religion," says McKinley. "You only know a company sells eggs to a supermarket every month, and the supermarket pays the invoice."[3]

A gender lens may also reveal information or patterns that expose investment risk. Investors understand the market risks they are compensated for, such as illiquidity and volatility, but generally know less about the intangible corporate operational, reputational, and litigational risks, or ORL's. A firm with a history of legal complaints around pay equity or sexual harassment could be a ticking ORL time bomb. When a crisis goes public, the reputational risk often directly affects sales and the ability to recruit until the storm has passed. Investors use a gender lens to look at factors such as hiring patterns and lawsuits for this reason. Similarly, a gender lens scanning across a global multinational's supply chain could shine a light on and correct damaging human rights violations before they are publically exposed, and more costly.

The last word in our phrase, *investing*, deserves a moment as well. Today, many philanthropic organizations speak of "investing in women" to describe their work on initiatives designed to address women and girls. This gender lens philanthropy, or gender lens grantmaking, is essential, often underresourced work. But it is not gender-lens investing. These organizations look for social impact, not financial returns. Gender lens investors' return aspirations vary from those willing to accept below market risk-return profiles to those seeking market outperformance, but this is investing, not philanthropy.

We are incorporating gender analysis in investment decision making. As we show throughout the book, there are many different approaches to investing with a gender lens and it can apply across all asset classes, sectors, and geographies.

Investor Attitudes, Ideas, and Returns Are a Changin'

Gender lens investing will require time for broad acceptance but two significant trends in the investment world are converging to accelerate that process. First, investors—even mainstream institutional investors—are taking *sustainable and responsible investing*

(SRI) more seriously. In that regard, the 2015 publication of the BlackRock-Ceres guide to incorporating *environmental, social, and governance* (ESG) considerations into corporate interactions for institutional investors is a notable milestone, pairing the expertise of the largest money management firm in the world and the oldest shareholder engagement advocacy group.

Second, a new type of investor has emerged—the *impact investor*—who considers the social impact of their investment alongside their calculation of financial risk and return.

The convergence (and occasional philosophical clashes) of these two investment trends—the growing acceptance of ESG and return on impact—is driving innovation in investment strategy and capital markets. As the shift accelerates over the next decade, the use of gender factors will grow along with it. (As a sign of the times, former *Wall Street Journal* reporter David Banks started *Impact Alpha,* a new publication for impact investors analyzing alpha and beta in traditional and new capital markets.)

A gender lens adds valuable, and often underrecognized, insights to both SRI (also known today as responsible investing) and impact investment strategies. As the Criterion Institute, a leader in gender lens investing, put it in their report in 2015, "Given the importance of how gender operates in society, culture, and the economy, the ability to analyze it should inform how we assign value and structure investments within systems of finance. This is not standard practice in finance, therefore, the field of gender lens investing is necessary."[4]

For instance, gender is an additional lens through which to evaluate the economic and equality effects of climate change, an area the Wallace Global Fund has been investigating. Susan Gibbs, a senior adviser at the Wallace Global Fund, asks: Could capital divested from fossil fuel sectors and redirected into clean and green energy also help channel new dollars to women and girls? The answer she sees is yes. Innovations in decentralizing energy systems to adapt to climate change can also increase energy access and opportunity for women, Gibbs argues.[5] Indeed, all investments have a gender impact: positive or negative, intended or not.

Responsible and sustainable investing and impact investing have grown 76 percent, to $6.57 trillion, from 2012 to 2014.[6] The 2016 *U.S. Trust Insights on Wealth and Worth*® annual survey of high net worth investors found 51 percent of respondents believe the social, political, or environmental impact of their portfolios is important in decisions on whether to invest. Women are 59 percent more likely to say this than men and a remarkable 93 percent of millennials (men and women) agree.[7] But to fully appreciate the paradigm-changing nature of these numbers—and the practices behind them—it also helps to understand where Sustainable and Responsible Investing comes from and how it has evolved.

Responsible Investing—Then and Now

Thematic screening of investments based on personal ethics or values, often rooted in religious beliefs, began centuries before portfolio diversification. Ethical mandates in Jewish investment laws started in biblical times and remain strong today. In the 1600s, Quakers forbid followers to own slaves. In the 1970s, the success of the Apartheid Divestment movement greatly expanded the profile and number of social investors; a favorite strategy: screening for the "big five" sins: alcohol, tobacco, gaming, pornography, and firearms. These socially responsible investors clashed sharply with the investors who followed economist Milton Friedman's doctrine: "There is one and only one social responsibility of business—to use its resources and engage in activities designed to increase its profits."[8]

Today, that quote from the 1970 *New York Times Magazine* article is more artifact than fact, especially as stakeholder and shareholder maximizers find they agree more than they disagree.[9] Still, Friedman's contention, in the same article, that "discussions of 'socially responsible' business are notable for their analytical looseness and lack of rigor," has continued to reverberate throughout the investment community. Even philanthropists, until recently, shied away from socially responsible investment strategies. The investment committees of major foundations hesitated to consider the foundation's mission in decisions lest they reduce returns. Individual philanthropists were discouraged from questioning the prevailing approach by their advisors. Meanwhile, the few mavericks, mostly faith-based or environmentalists, found themselves constrained by the limited number of socially responsible funds or community investment vehicles.

The introduction of ESG factors enabled the shift from "negative screening" to "positive screening"—in other words, looking for the leading companies achieving a positive social or environmental impact rather than avoiding companies that had poor records. This parallels investors' preferences—70 percent of respondents to the 2016 *U.S. Trust Insights on Wealth and Worth* survey said they "would rather invest in companies that have a positive impact than avoid investments in companies that are harmful."[10] Financial analysts and money managers also started recognizing that ESG factors could add additional rigor to traditional risk–reward analysis. Not to be confused with "buy/sell ratings," ESG data increase an investor's ability to assess important risks and opportunities that sit outside of the balance sheet, but are critical to the financial performance of a company.

Evolving past the world of "looseness and lack of rigor" Friedman described in 1970, ESG-based analysis has become a significant area of interest in academic research, led by top business schools around the world. Harvard Business School's Robert Eccles, with colleagues Ioannis Ioannou and George Serafeim, have been at the forefront of studying ESG factors as leading indicators of management practice and financial returns for over a decade. Their 2011 study concluded that U.S. companies that had adopted formal sustainability policies by 1993 delivered returns 47 percent higher than companies that had no such policies, and exhibited lower volatility as well.[11] Another Harvard Business School paper published about the same time also concluded that firms with good performance on sustainability issues deemed to be material to investors outperformed all firms by 4.05 percent, strongly suggesting the benefits for shareholders.[12] This work has been foundational to the development of the Sustainability Accounting Standards Board's (SASB) Materiality Map, a cross-industry, online tool that compares "material sustainability" issues across industries and sectors.[13] SASB, a nonprofit organization founded in 2011, develops standard social and environmental measures of performance to be used in reporting and benchmarking.

Generation Investment, a private "sustainable capitalism" investment management firm started by Al Gore, offers an impressive ESG investment strategy track record. In 2007, the firm described climate change as an "urgent challenge that affects long-term corporate profitability and therefore must be systematically integrated into investment analysis."[14] Today, Generation invests about $12 billion and its global-equity fund achieved a 12.1 percent return for the period June 2005 to June 2015.[15]

Journalist James Fallows' lengthy 2015 article about Generation Investment in the *Atlantic* shows how the firm "made more money ... than most fund managers who were guided by a straight-ahead pursuit of profit at any social or environmental price."[16] Fallows also interviewed BlackRock CEO Larry Fink, which has about $5 trillion under management. Fink told Fallows that responsible investing strategies are the only way to change economically and socially unsustainable corporate behavior. At BlackRock a centralized investment stewardship team supplies portfolio managers with "specialist insight on environmental, social, and governance (ESG) considerations to all investment strategies, whether indexed or actively managed."[17]

Two global economic mega-trends give the case for ESG analysis and reporting—and gender analysis—a boost: the growth of intangible value and the proliferation of digital data sources. Together, these trends are transforming how investors evaluate business risk and value.

To this point, 80 percent of the value of the S&P 500 was in tangible assets in 1970. A company's property, plant, equipment—things that were found on a balance sheet—drove the valuation. That number today is less than 20 percent. Intangible assets drive over 80 percent of the market value. What is this "intangible value" that we place such faith in? Things like brand and intellectual property and human capital. Surprised? Think of asking a CEO about his or her biggest assets. The answer most often given— "our people." You can't easily find people on the balance sheet, and they can easily walk out the door if they begin to feel they don't believe in the firm, they aren't being compensated fairly, or they don't see opportunity for themselves over the long term.

Or consider how today's consumers (especially younger digital natives) can quickly turn sour on a brand they see failing to provide transparency per its actions. In a 2014 Shelby Study, 60 percent of Millennials said they paid extra for sustainable products and (showing their skepticism) 61 percent said they check for labels on social and environmental impact. With the significant and almost immediate access to information about corporate behavior, these consumers increasingly "vote with their feet" if they hear about companies associated with issues like toxins, child labor, or unfair pay.[18] The upshot: More and more companies are issuing social responsibility reports;

today, more than 7,000 firms issue social responsibility reports, (with over 50 percent of these reports supported by third-party auditors), versus less than 30 companies in 1992. In addition, human capital measures relevant to business performance are starting to appear in regular annual reports and in separate Sustainability reports.

And the reporting doesn't stop there. The *Smarter Annual Report*, the first comprehensive global review of human capital reporting practices, provides snapshots of human capital reports and other metrics published voluntarily by public companies around the world.[19] This study of human capital reporting was inspired by the work of the International Integrated Reporting Council (IIRC), which has led efforts to develop one integrated report that covers all the traditional financial accounting measures required by FASB and ESG and human capital measures in one report. Concurrently, the quality and availability of data on public companies has been enhanced by a growing industry of data providers, with firms like MSCI, Sustainalytics, Bloomberg, and Thomson Reuters leading the way. Morningstar, a leading investment research firm, has begun to provide ESG ratings on mutual and exchange-traded funds (in addition to their traditional risk ratings), adding more legitimacy and more information to investors.

The implications of these trends, and support for them, can be seen in the growth of AUM (assets under management) and signatories to the Principles for Responsible Investment (PRI). The PRI is an international network of investors working together to understand the implications of sustainability and effects on investment decision making and ownership practices. Over 1,300 signatories with AUM of more than $59 trillion (up from $4 trillion at the PRI's launch in 2006) strongly suggests a tipping point in the minds of global investors when it comes to socially responsible investing.[20]

Finally, environmental data has gained legitimacy among mainstream investors as commodity and materials prices became more volatile, as environmental mistakes became more severe and costly (and predictable), and as green consumerism affects corporate revenues and reputations. Global concern for climate change and the development of sophisticated disclosure databases have also accelerated interest in the analysis of environment factors. Social factors, such as human rights and community relations, have lagged in adoption partly because the perception of "doing the right thing" doesn't necessarily drive business results. Inserting new metrics into valuation models and making clear connections to immediate costs requires materiality research. But this hurdle is being overcome as money managers use ESG factors in their valuation models.[21]

Impact Investing Is Another Revolution

While institutional investors awakened to the relevance of ESG factors, *impact investing* has grown up on the shoulders of community investing and microfinance. Impact investing, a term coined in 2007 at a Rockefeller Foundation–sponsored gathering, attempts to marry the social mission of philanthropy with the speed, creativity, and scale of market-based solutions. Impact investors believe entrepreneurial talent and the power of markets to scale businesses can help solve complicated societal problems.

As impact investing gained momentum, the Global Impact Investing Network (GIIN) was launched to increase the scale and effectiveness of impact investing. GIIN defines such strategies as investing in companies, organizations, and funds with the intention of generating social and/or environmental benefits and financial returns. Consider AllLife, a South African company, which provides affordable life insurance to thousands of people living with HIV/AIDS and diabetes. South Africa has the largest HIV epidemic in the world, with over 6 million people, or 19 percent of its population, infected. Women face a higher risk of HIV infection than men due to their greater vulnerability to sexual assault, and lack of access to health care, education, and legal services. Young women and adolescent girls account for a disproportionate number of new HIV infections, and HIV is the leading cause of death among women of reproductive age. Providing life insurance could economically stabilize families and communities.

But what about the financial impact: Can an investor make money? LeapFrog Investments, an AllLife investor that has $535 million in assets under management across two impact funds, believes it can. This optimism is based on AllLife's innovative continuous underwriting process, which is designed to profitably serve a huge population of people who previously could not afford life insurance. Its adherence model makes sure clients go for regular testing and take anti-retroviral medications. LeapFrog focuses on firms providing essential financial services to underserved populations in fastest-growing emerging markets in Asia and Africa, typically investing between $10 million and $50 million and is part of a broader demonstration that impact investment funds can deliver financial and social returns together.[22]

Adding academic rigor to the space, in 2015, the Wharton Social Impact Initiative launched the first-ever academic report on impact investing financial performance and social impact, "Great Expectations: Mission Preservation and Financial Performance." Collecting and examining over 200 variables from 53 impact investing private equity funds, and representing 557 individual investments, early findings suggest that, in certain market segments, investors might not need to expect lower returns as a tradeoff for impact.[23]

The Cordes Foundation is part of the new wave of philanthropic enterprises that illustrate how the best intentions of philanthropy and the result-oriented ambitions of successful businesspeople blend together. Ron Cordes founded and grew AssetMark, a financial firm, while his wife, Marty, developed a passion and expertise for philanthropy, especially for women and girls. After they sold AssetMark, the Cordes' began to move their foundation endowment to impact investments. As Ron puts it, "I went from building what I thought was the best company in the world to building the best companies for the world."

The Cordes' invested in global microfinance funds, as well as diversified funds of funds focused on growing businesses in frontier markets. Capital was also deployed in community development financial institutions as well as social enterprises.

Then came the economic downturn of 2008, and strikingly, they found that the 20 percent of their portfolio in impact investments performed better than their traditional portfolio. Their conviction increased as a result, as did their role in building the impact investing field. Ron supported the development of Impact Assets, an impact investing-focused donor-advised fund. They joined a partnership to build Opportunity Collaboration, an annual conference connecting social entrepreneurs, investors, and philanthropists from around the world.

Stephanie, Cordes' daughter, after attending an Opportunity Collaboration gathering, decided to leave her job in publishing to join the foundation. "When I returned to my role at the magazine, I found myself more interested in the treatment of workers in the supply chain than in the fashion review itself," she recalls. Stephanie spurred her family to make a public commitment in 2014 to moving to a 100 percent impact portfolio.

For Ron and Marty, working with their daughter and other Millennials on global issues brings more joy than they ever expected. The foundation now brings a gender lens to all philanthropy and investing. It was a gradual process of moving from looking at women and girls as beneficiaries to including the role of women as leaders and owners. They started asking questions not just about the intended beneficiaries of the company's efforts but also about the gender diversity in leadership and ownership.

Today, the Cordes Foundation implements a strategy that links the education of girls and women and women-owned businesses to the reduction in poverty. Investing in Women's World Banking Capital Partners, a private equity limited partnership that makes direct equity investments in financial institutions reaching out to women, has been an education in the practices and metrics used by fund managers who see gender as fundamental. Eric Stephenson, portfolio director for The Cordes Foundation (and also a Millennial) said, "We integrate a gender lens everywhere—it's not isolated to one asset class or sector." With Stephanie's leadership, the Cordes' embarked on work to address the capital needs of global artisans, a disproportionately female group. Marty's concentration on the intersection of gender, health, and poverty has informed a variety of other investments. The Cordes' view their approach to impact investing as providing "20×" more capital—100 percent of the portfolio versus only 5 percent of grant making—and they rigorously adhere to seeking market-based returns with 95 percent in the investment portfolio.[24]

Building Bridges Between Philanthropists and Impact Investors

A gender lens might seem an obvious tool for an impact investor, but many of the early social impact finance pioneers didn't see it that way. For some, gender was already mixed into impact. As far as these social impact investors were concerned, their focus on poverty did support women. Others believed it was hard enough to grow businesses in frontier markets without adding a gender analysis or reporting sex-disaggregated data.

In 2008, a team at The Criterion Institute began working to better understand the link between women philanthropists and impact investors. As impact investing grew, Criterion wanted women to be at the table, with their capital and their experience, knowledge, and insights. As more women engaged, they asked which impact investors were using a gender lens or analyzing the benefit for women. Lacking a comprehensive answer, Criterion launched a research study, which concluded that few funds thoughtfully integrated gender into the investment process. Simultaneously, they worked with Shari Berenbach (who later became the head of the U.S. African Development Foundation and sadly passed away in 2015) and Lisa Hall, then at Calvert Foundation. The collaboration led to a new investment offering, WIN-WIN Community Investment Note, that enabled retail investors to provide debt capital to community development and microfinance organizations around the world using a gender lens. This innovation, and the bridge building between philanthropists and impact investors, was a big step forward for gender lens investing.

A WIN-WIN: Women Investing in Women

The Women Investing in Women Initiative (WIN-WIN) was launched on International Women's Day, March 8, 2012, to move the dialogue beyond the "what" and "why" invest in women to the "how." Investors could purchase a WIN-WIN Community Investment Note online or through brokerage accounts starting at $20 or through brokerage accounts for a little as $1,000, with returns up to 3–4 percent based on terms. The full value of the principal is lent to organizations supporting women's economic advancement. As loans are repaid, the capital is lent again, multiplying the social impact an investment has created. At maturity, capital is returned to the investor with interest.

The successes of WIN-WIN were gratifying. In less than two years, nearly 900 investors (over 13 percent of Calvert Foundation's investor base at the time) channeled over $20 million into initiatives and projects that benefited over 20,000 women and their families. But for Calvert Foundation, the most valuable outcomes were the lessons learned.

First, there was a tremendous investor appetite for a gender-lens investment product that enables people from all backgrounds and income levels to align their investments with issues they care about.

"It wasn't until we put the product out into the marketplace—with admittedly limited marketing efforts—that we realized how hungry the industry was for such an investment," recalled Calvert CEO Jennifer Pryce.[25] The staff fielded calls from many organizations and shared their experience and methodology, spawning a set of additional vehicles.

Second, gender analysis is a powerful tool to cut across silos. Instead of narrowing the focus to one sector or issue (e.g., education or health care) the WIN-WIN team sought opportunities across all sectors. The collection of gender metrics in this process yielded a surprising finding: It made a clear case for increasing access to clean energy products and services for women living in the developing world, a solution that had not been seen by other investors. This analysis drove new partnerships and the development of WIN-WIN 2.0 focused on gender inclusive clean energy access in Sub-Saharan Africa.

Through the process of collecting gender metrics on WIN-WIN borrowers, the staff realized the information was applicable to the entire $275 million and growing portfolio of loans. The institution now collects gender-focused data from all borrowers, enabling both deeper assessments on impact as well as potential for new investment areas.

Since WIN-WIN's inception, more responsible and impact investing intermediaries have embraced gender lens analyses, including:

- In 2014, the Aspen Network of Development Entrepreneurs (ANDE) incorporated a gender lens component in their impact manager training. ANDE members also launched a gender lens working group where fund managers share progress and collaborate on challenges.
- Also in 2014, Veris Wealth Partners produced "Women, Wealth and Impact," the first guide from a registered investment adviser suggesting a framework for investors to support gender equality with their portfolios.
- The Forum on Sustainable, Responsible and Impact Investing published "Investing to Advance Women: A Report for Individual and Institutional Advisors."
- Acumen, one of the early impact-focused investors, worked with the International Center for Research on Women to apply a gender lens to its portfolio, releasing a report, "Women and Social Enterprises," in the fall of 2015.

- Demonstrating the intersection of impact and responsible investing, a coalition of Trillium Asset Management, Root Capital, and The Global Fund for Women released "Investing for a Positive Impact on Women," providing a guide for investors looking to apply a gender lens to their entire portfolio.

There will be more and more examples every year.

Different Starting Points for Gender Analysis

Historically, impact investors were portrayed along a spectrum starting with people who have a social objective (and hence, might be willing to accept a lower return or higher risk) and moving to those for whom investment returns come before social and environmental benefits. Investors willing to accept a lower financial return for a larger social impact were called *impact-first* investors. The second group were called *finance-first* investors. Although obviously a simplification, this distinction clarified differing primary motives and increased the legitimacy for investments that might earn less than a market return.

The distinction raises a question for investors incorporating gender factors. Does a gender lens raise an investor's financial acumen, or is it about empowering women and driving global gender equality? Can it be both? We believe it can be both, and as the field matures, more nuanced and creative strategies will provide increasing choice. At the risk of overusing the metaphor of a lens in a pair of glasses, it is useful to remember everyone's prescription strength, function, and style will be different. Some investors use their glasses for particular investment types. Others use them for overarching analysis, or what BlackRock calls the "overlay approach."[26] Some have stronger lenses on very specific data. Others introduce variables and ask questions. It's an evolutionary process that requires experimentation and learning by doing.

Investors who start from a traditional asset class and leverage gender data to drive financial performance are distinct from those whose starting point for investment is solving a social challenge. Often, however, investors try to blend social impact and financial performance, in which case the labels of *impact first* or *financial first* break down. Take, for instance, a fund looking at gender diversity on boards. The fund manager's motivation may be strictly to outperform the benchmark. But some investors may determine that growing this fund, assuming it performs well, would do more to shift gender equality on boards than any other approach, including philanthropically funding a group and advocating for adding more women on boards. Their motivation may be gender equality, but they believe that achieving it though market-rate, business-driven interventions creates the best chance of success. Similarly, gender lens investors with a board seat at a financial services firm might advocate strategies to increase women's access to their services. These changes might also drive long-term profitability.

Gender Equality versus Gender Equity: Is There a Difference?

Gender equality is the concept that both men and women are free to develop their personal abilities and make choices without limitations set by stereotypes, rigid gender roles, or prejudices. Different behaviors, aspirations, and needs of women and men are considered, valued, and favored equally. It does not mean that women and men have to become the same, but that their rights, responsibilities, and opportunities will not depend on whether they are born male or female.

Gender equity means fairness of treatment for women and men according to their respective needs, and what they need to be successful. This may include equal treatment, but often women and men need different treatment to receive the same benefits and to experience their rights. In the development context, gender equity often requires built-in measures to compensate for the historical and social disadvantages of women (such as restrictions on mobility or access to education). Or it may mean projects are targeted to women only.

Source: "Challenging Chains to Chains," Royal Tropical Institute, Agripro-focus and the International Institute for Rural Reconstruction (September 2012), p. 2.

A focus on gender prompts, and even requires, investors to think about power, privilege, and women's historical social disadvantages. Both gender equality and gender equity play roles. For instance, a venture capital firm saying it gives women equal opportunities to pitch their business ideas seems fine until you review the record for the venture industry on implicit bias against women entrepreneurs. Treating men and women equally, and getting the best results, might require adjustments to de-bias the review process. Similarly, providing loan capital to women on equal terms feels fair until you realize they have limited collateral because of legal restrictions to owning property. However, designing for gender equity (addressing what both men and women need to be successful) might surface the opportunity for alternative credit scoring approaches.

Often, treating men and women exactly the same—without recognizing bias against women—may actually reinforce the status quo of a system designed unintentionally to work for the male majority. Raising questions on the design of systems can provoke accusations of "playing the gender card" and a backlash to efforts to raise awareness of gendered needs, realities, and participation. Conversely, clear acknowledgment of realties can catalyze creative and meaningful breakthroughs. Advance Global Capital's use of factoring—where the evaluation is done without knowledge of a client's sex—is the kind of outside the box thinking that raises awareness of gender bias, disrupts business models, and unleashes real economic benefit.[27]

How gender informs and influences investment decisions differs based on goals, sector, geography, and vehicles. But three distinct gender-lens "focuses" have emerged as the field matured (Figure 4.1).[28] While not intended to be limiting to investors, they provide a useful framework, a set of focal points for analysis.

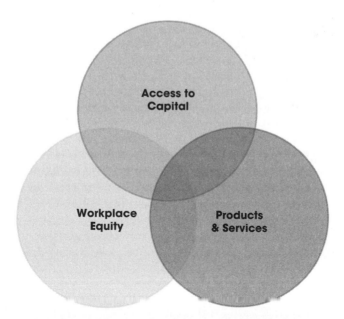

Figure 4.1   Three gender lens focuses.

The first focus reflects on *ownership and access to capital,* an area where investors can break down barriers that constrain the growth of women-owned or women-led enterprises. The second focus highlights gender *equality in the workplace* from the boardroom to the factory floor and across the supply chain. The third examines the tremendous opportunities to direct investors to companies that are conceiving and selling *products and services* that improve the lives of women. They work more like a Venn diagram—investors and companies can focus on just one or they can excel on multiple levels.

Notes

1. "Openings: Why Gender Equality is One for the Boys," *Financial Times* (March 4, 2016). www.ft.com/intl/cms/s/0/947331d8-e062-11e5-8d9b-e88a2a889797.html#ixzz42MtgE8xQ
2. Elayne Clift, "A Gender Lens—Literal and Metaphoric," Women's Media Center (March 18, 2011). www.womensmediacenter.com/feature/entry/a-gendered-lensliteral-and-metaphoric.
3. Personal Interview (Janet McKinley, January 12, 2016).
4. Joy Anderson and Katherine Miles, *The State of the Field of Gender Lens Investing,* The Criterion Institute with The Wallace Global Fund, October 1, 2015, p. 3. https://criterioninstitute.org/wp-content/uploads/2015/10/Latest-State-of-the-Field-of-Gender-Lens-Investing-1-19-2016-V3.pdf.
5. Susan Gibbs, "At the Intersection of Gender and Climate Change: Investment Opportunities," *Impact Alpha* (November 16 2015), impact alpha.com/at-the-intersection-of-gender-and-climate-change-investment-opportunities/.
6. Report on U.S. Sustainable, Responsible and Impact Investing Trends 2014, US SIF Foundation, 2014.
7. *U.S. Trust 2016 Wealth and Worth,* May 2016, http://www.ustrust.com/publish/content/application/pdf/GWMOL/USTp_AR9R6RKS_2016-05.pdf.
8. Milton Friedman, "A Friedman Doctrine: The Social Responsibility of a Business Is to Increase Its Profits," *New York Times Magazine* (September 13, 1970). query.nytimes.com/mem/archive-free/pdf?res=9E05E0DA153CE531A15750C1A96F9C946190D6CF.
9. Judy Samuelson and Miguel Padro, "Reopening the Question of Corporate Purpose," The Aspen Institute Business in Society Program (2014).

10. *U.S. Trust 2016 Wealth and Worth,* May 2016, http://www.ustrust.com/publish/content/application/pdf/GWMOL/USTp_AR9R6RKS_2016-05.pdf.

11. Robert Eccles, Ioannis Ioannou, and George Serafeim, "The Impact of Corporate Sustainability on Organizational Processes and Performance," *Harvard Business School* (2001).

12. Mozaffar Khan, George Serafeim, Aaron Yoon, *Corporate Sustainability: First Evidence on Materiality,* 2015, http://nrs.harvard.edu/urn-3:HUL.InstRepos:14369106.

13. Sustainable Accounting Standards Board Materiality Map. www.sasb.org/materiality/sasb-materiality-map/. (This is updated often.)

14. James Fallows, "The Planet-Saving, Capitalism-Subverting, Surprisingly Lucrative Investment Secrets of Al Gore," *The Atlantic* (November 2015). www.theatlantic.com/magazine/archive/2015/11/the-planet-saving-capitalism-subverting-surprisingly-lucrative-investment-secrets-of-al-gore/407857/.

15. Thematic Research Highlights, Generation Investment, May 2007. www.generationim.com/media/pdf-generation-thematic-research-v14.pdf.

16. James Fallows, "The Planet-Saving, Capitalism-Subverting, Surprisingly Lucrative Investment Secrets of Al Gore," *The Atlantic* (November 2015). www.theatlantic.com/magazine/archive/2015/11/the-planet-saving-capitalism-subverting-surprisingly-lucrative-investment-secrets-of-al-gore/407857/.

17. www.blackrock.com/corporate/en-br/about-us/investment-stewardship.

18. "Sixty Percent of Millennials Willing to Share Personal Info with Brands," The Shelby Report (March 10, 2014).

19. Laurie Bassi, David Creelman, and Andrew Lambert, "The Smarter Annual Report, How Companies Are Integrating Financial," ©2014 Creelman Lambert & McBassi. www.mcbassi.com/wp/resources/pdfs/The_Smarter_Annual_Report.pdf.

20. The Principles for Responsible (PRI) Investment Fact Sheet. www.unpri.org/news/pri-fact-sheet/ Accessed October 18, 2015.

21. Jeroen Bos, "Using ESG Factors for Equity Valuation," *CFA Institute Magazine* (November/December 2014). www.cfapubs.org/doi/pdf/10.2469/cfm.v25.n6.5.

22. "How We Invest and Build," LeapFrog Investments. www.leapfroginvest.com/invest-and-build/.

23. *Great Expectations: Mission Preservation and Financial Performance in Impact Investments* (Philadelphia: The Wharton School of the University of Pennsylvania, October 7, 2015). papers.ssrn.com/sol3/papers.cfm?abstract_id=2694620.

24. Personal communications (Ron, Marty, Stephanie Cordes, May 22, 2016).
25. Personal communications (Jennifer Pryce, April 13, 2016).
26. BlackRock, "overlay approach," https://www.blackrock.com/cor porate/e7-us/about-us/investment-stewardship.
27. Advance Global Capital, *Gender Lens Investing: A Strategy for Uncovering Value and Impact*, September 1, 2015. http://advanceglobalcap.com/gender-lens-investing/.
28. Sarah Kaplan and Jackie VanderBrug, "The Rise of Gender Capitalism" by *Stanford Social Innovation Review* (Fall 2014). ssir.org/articles/entry/the_rise_of_gender_capitalism.

CHAPTER 5

New Paths to Capital

"Even when the world turns against you and ridicules your ideas, 'Press on, regardless.' Try to make things happen, and treat everybody as an equal."[1]
—John C. (Jack) Bogle, Founder, The Vanguard Group

Try this test in a group—whether the group makeup is all men, all women, or a mix: Have everyone close their eyes and quickly picture three entrepreneurs, then ask for them to share whom they chose. Most often the names are men—Bill Gates, Steve Jobs, Richard Branson, and Mark Zuckerberg. Next ask them to picture a woman entrepreneur. Oprah Winfrey or Martha Stewart might come to mind but the group would likely have to think longer to come up with more.

The continuous images and accolades about men in business create our mental models of company founders and successful entrepreneurs. When was the last time you saw a cover story—in digital or print—of a woman entrepreneur who raised the money, built the business, and made the exit? There are examples—for instance, TechCrunch ran an online slideshow on 18 women who "killed it" in 2015, including Robin Chase, who cofounded and sold ZipCar to AvisBudget for $500 million and is back with Veniam, a wifi-on-wheels scheme to build an urban-scale network using cars and public buses as hotspots.[2] A rare example, however, is hardly enough to counter the confirmation bias that men kill it more than women because women don't have what it takes.

Of course, this isn't true. But the reality is that the faces of women entrepreneurs around the world are missing in the media and in action because they are consistently undervalued, and hence struggle to get access to capital. The degree of struggle depends on the context and can be challenging to quantify. But mounting evidence shows women entrepreneurs receive a percentage of investment capital that is not representative of their potential. You can look at the micro entrepreneur in Bogotá, the high-growth entrepreneur in London, the film director in Hollywood, or the fund manager on Wall Street, and see the same pattern. Women lack the capital they need to start businesses and build them. It's been called *capital punishment.*

In Spring 2015, Crunchbase decided to run a series of articles reporting data on female founders. Without much research to go on, they built their own database of 14,341 U.S. startups that received funding and then segmented the recipients by gender. What they found was that only 15.5 percent, or 2,226 companies, had at least one female founder. There was a little good news: The absolute number of companies with a female founder (including the total number of startups) had more than quadrupled from 117 in 2009 to 555 in 2014. Still, the overall percentage of female founders receiving funding was discouraging.[3] In fact, it unfortunately confirmed the ongoing work of the Diana Project at Babson College: Their comprehensive analysis of U.S. venture capitalist investments in women entrepreneurs for a period comparable to the Crunchbase analysis (2011 to 2013) reported that 85 percent of investments went to all male teams. Little wonder that Candida Brush, the Research Director of the Arthur M. Blank Center for Entrepreneurship at Babson and co-author of many Diana Project studies, says, "There is enormous untapped investment opportunity for venture capitalists smart enough to look at the numbers and fund women entrepreneurs."[4]

Widening our aperture to outside the United States and outside the venture world, women entrepreneurs in developing economies are just as vital to growth but just as underutilized in contributing to the formal economy. The International Finance Corporation (IFC) estimates that as of 2011, 31 to 38 percent of small- and medium-sized enterprises (SMEs) in emerging markets are owned fully or partially by women. One in three. All SMEs face challenges, but for women the challenges are "amplified and hard to overcome," says the IRC. Women report more limitations on access to capital to start and grow businesses than men. IFC studies have also shown the terms of women's loans are less favorable than men with the same potential. The 2011 report stated that roughly 70 percent, or 5 to 6 million, of women-owned SMEs in developing economies were unserved or underserved by financial institutions. This amounted to a collective credit gap between men and women of $260 billion to $320 billion.[5]

These numbers, and many others like them, have improved only slightly in the last 5 years or even over the last 10 or 20 years. But it isn't until you apply a gender lens that you can begin to see who gets access to capital and when and why. With that knowledge comes the opportunity to develop gender inclusive financing models for entrepreneurs and better systems of capital allocation for investors.

The Women Entrepreneurs' Gender Dividend

What are the consequences for economies and communities when enterprising women don't get funding to start and build strong businesses? For every narrative of women's lack of access to capital, there is another side of the story—the gender dividend that comes from women receiving investment.

Job Creation

Around the world large corporations employ thousands if not hundreds of thousands of people, but it is the successful SMEs—small and medium enterprises—that serve as the vital engines of new business growth and job creation for countries. This holds regardless of a country's level of economic development.

Despite the obstacles to obtain needed funding, women start businesses all the time. Furthering the point made in the opening of this chapter, the 2014 Global Entrepreneurship Monitor (GEM) reports 200 million women starting or running businesses, and 128 million operating businesses that had survived for more than three and a half years.[6]

The more women participate in the workforce, relative to men, the more likely they are to be, or become, entrepreneurs. The power of this relationship jumps out when you analyze total early-stage entrepreneurial activity in relation to gender-gap indicators measured by the World Economic Forum (WEF). The WEF gap analysis shows ten economies where women are as much, or more, likely to be entrepreneurs than men. They include El Salvador and Brazil in Latin America and the Caribbean; Vietnam, Indonesia, Malaysia, and the Philippines in Southeast Asia; and Zambia, Nigeria, Uganda, and Ghana in Africa.[7] Equally encouraging, in economies with a greater proportion of women starting businesses—in teams of three or more co-founders—there is also a greater likelihood they will have job-creation ambitions. These ambitions speak to a number of cultural factors moving in the right direction. As Harvard Business School's business historian, Nancy Koehn, told *Newsweek* in an interview about the U.S. economy, "Any economist will tell you, the job creation [we] need to fuel any kind of middle class is not going to come from corporations, it's going to come from small businesses … What we need to start thinking about is how we capitalize on this [vast network] of women entrepreneurs. How do we nurture them? How do we fund them?"[8]

Reinvestment

As women increase their incomes and assets, they reinvest in their families and communities. You could say women "pay it forward," even more than men do. In emerging markets, women reinvest an astounding 90 cents of every additional dollar of their income on their families, including education, health, and nutrition. This compares to 30 to 40 cents for men.[9] This outcome creates a virtuous cycle of reinvestment to make families, communities, and countries stronger. Some call it women's "gender dividend."

Another gender dividend comes from women starting or leading companies that practice socially responsible management. This is what Peter Roberts and Li-Wei Chen, professors at Emory University's Goizueta Business School, found when they researched the links between social and environmental performance of B Corps and the composition and career backgrounds of B Corp–founding teams.[10]

What's a B Corp? It is a corporation that has voluntarily completed a rigorous certification process to meet standards of social and environmental performance, accountability, and transparency. B-Corp certification means the company has demonstrated a significant commitment to operating in a manner that creates benefits and protections for employees, shareholders, communities, and the environment. Globally, there are now more than 1,700 certified B Corps.[11] Looking at the gender and career histories of B-Corp founders, Chen and Roberts found that companies with at least one woman on their founding teams reported higher B-Corp ratings. While the research considered size of team, education, and career backgrounds, having one or more women on the startup team was the only factor found to increase performance in a statistically significant manner. The authors note that as all businesses are being called upon to account for the societal impacts of their operations, there is a special opportunity for "socially oriented entrepreneurs to develop and implement creative ideas that generate positive social value in companies that also deliver attractive financial returns. It places similar pressure on the systems and organizations that are required to support these entrepreneurs as they launch and grow." Given the research that women on a startup team is a factor in such outcomes, companies would be wise to consider the gender of their leadership teams. Other research supports women's inclination to embed socially responsible management practices throughout their businesses. Babson professor Candida Brush published research in 2011 that showed women are more likely to start businesses with both social and economic goals.[12]

Innovation

According to the 2014 GEM Women's Report, women entrepreneurs in nearly half of the economies included in the survey are now "equal to, or even outpacing their male counterparts in terms of innovation—demonstrating a growing parity between men and women selling products and services that are new to consumers and not generally offered by competitors."[13]

It may be, given the lack of funding, that only those with remark-able ideas are getting through. However, annual GEM research reports consistently show that when women see a big opportunity they go after it at least as aggressively as men.[14] Unfortunately, we have less research on what an aggressive woman entrepreneur does differently than a man. "In most economies, the prescriptions for success are based on studies of male entrepreneurs," says Babson's Candida Brush. What male gender studies miss is how much women entrepreneurs bring different and diverse experiences than men, and a distinctive understanding of opportunities for the development of new products and markets. (How a gender lens leads to better research, products, markets, and outcomes is explored further in Chapter 7.) Indeed, women apply their personal experiences to identify market opportunities in a way a man might dismiss or would never think of, unless they asked a woman. In healthcare, women are introducing innovations in breast pumps, infant incubators, and applications of big data analytics to find solutions to infertility. And they often lead the funding in these areas as well. As one woman fund manager humorously quipped, "I have an advantage because male VCs are sometimes uncomfortable leading a due diligence conversation about vaginal dryness."

Three working mothers in Los Angeles were not amused by the traffic jams they sat in for hours every week as they ferried their kids to school, sports practices, and friends' houses—and themselves to and from the office. Los Angeles holds the dubious distinction of being one of the most congested cities in America. For Joanna McFarland, Carolyn Yashari Becher, and Janelle McGlothlin, idling away the hours in L.A.'s infamous suburban sprawl's traffic jams had become intolerable. The three professional women and mothers, with a total of 8 children ages 4 and 12 between them, figured there were plenty of other mothers who felt the same. They were right.[15]

Three Mothers and a Fully Funded Car Service

HopSkipDrive is a creative twist on the on-demand taxi business model designed to help moms and dads shuttle tots to teens to and from their games, lessons, play dates, and other activities. Parents request and pay for rides 24 hours in advance using a smartphone app or the company's website. A single ride is $20, or parents can buy a package of 50 trips for $600.[16] Founded in 2014, funding from family and friends underwrote the website and app launch in March 2015. In July 2015, HopSkipDrive raised $3.9 million more in seed funding. As of January 2016, it had received $14 million in two rounds and another $10.2 million in Series A funding, all with well-known Silicon Valley venture firms.[17]

Safety considerations for kids are a centerpiece of the value proposition. Drivers must have at least five years of childcare experience, which has attracted mothers (who often bring their own kids) nannies, nurses, and teachers as drivers. Driver training includes how to handle a sick child and when it is safe to leave once a child is dropped off at the destination. There is a similar competitor in San Francisco called Shuddle, also founded in 2014 by two men with the same business model and emphasis on safety. Shuddle raised close to $21.8 million in two rounds versus HopSkipDrive's $28 million in three rounds. Interestingly, when Shuddle failed to get an additional $10 million to $15 million in a third round, it shut its doors in April 2016.[18]

Outperformance for Investors

Investors focused on financial returns are increasingly interested in understanding the mix of men and women on the leadership team. Why? Because of financial performance and an overlooked market opportunity. A 2013 Dow Jones study of a decade of U.S. venture-backed companies makes the case. It divided the group into two categories: successful (defined as profitable exit or cash flow positive) and unsuccessful. The result? Successful firms were twice as likely to have a woman on the executive team. The seed-stage investor First Round Capital, which pioneered funding in the gap between individual angel investing and a Series A round, publicized a similar conclusion. Reviewing 10 years of their funding performance for over 300 ventures First Round Capital discovered that companies with a female founder performed 63 percent better than firms with all-male founding teams.[19] The outcome of HopSkipDrive and Shuddle adds another case to support their research.

Cindy Padnos, Illuminate Ventures

In the middle of the fast, hyper-connected world of technology investing, Cindy Padnos saw the gender hurdles in funding before many others did. She also saw the promise. Padnos wrote several seminal whitepapers on the success of women entrepreneurs in the technology sector shortly after she launched her fund, Illuminate Ventures, in 2009. Illuminate focuses on early and seed-stage investing in enterprises in cloud computing and mobile technologies with an exclusive focus in the enterprise software sector.

Without making gender an investment criterion, Illuminate actively sought ways to avoid it being a barrier. Padnos chose to be much more aggressive than her peers in pursuing a large and diverse deal flow. Strategically, she stacked an advisory council with over

40 of the top names in enterprise technology—and made sure that more than half of those spots were filled by world-class tech women who could grow Illuminate's referral network of more diverse talent. By deliberately seeking to expand access, Illuminate expanded its pipeline. The result? With two successful funds under management, nearly 40 percent of Illuminate's portfolio companies include at least one women founder in a field where less than 5 percent is the average. Interestingly, the diversity didn't stop with just women. Illuminate's founders include much higher than average ratios of Latino and Asian entrepreneurs as well. Equally importantly, Illuminate's performance now stands as an important validation point that diversity may improve performance for companies and investment outcomes. In just 5 years Illuminate's portfolio companies have gained over $1.65 billion in follow-on financing from larger VC firms and completed six successful exits via M&A and one IPO. The firm's initial fund ranks in the top quartile of performance within the Cambridge Associates U.S. Venture Capital Index.[20]

The Battle of the Biases

The collective experiences of women entrepreneurs are driving an essential, and increasingly public, conversation about gender bias. The research demonstrating that women entrepreneurs, and startup teams with more women on them, are good investments has moved out of the PhD classroom: Academic articles and news on the topic regularly trend on Twitter and Facebook as well as in popular news outlets such as Fast Company and Huffington Post. This is not to say that women-led ventures are always better investments than those run by men, but the growing research certainly removes any shadows of doubt about competency that hangs over women. So why, still, do women-founder teams continue to find themselves overlooked? How can it possibly be that only 24 out of the 10,238 venture deals minted from 2012 to 2014 were raised by African-American women founders?[21]

Although investors like to believe they invest solely based on the business concept and the entrepreneurs' track record, they may be underestimating their biases. Consider the recent research by a team from Harvard Business School, MIT Sloan School of Management, and Wharton Business School. They asked an investor group to listen to a man and a woman present identical pitch decks. One group heard the female voice, the other the male voice. Investors, both men and women, were 60 percent more likely to invest in the pitches presented by a man's voice. The researchers also found when the groups could see the person giving the pitch, an attractive man had a significant advantage over both attractive and unattractive women.[22]

These studies show *implicit bias,* or what social scientists call implicit social cognition. All human beings have these biases shaped by our brains being hard-wired to favor people who look, act, and sound like us. So it is no surprise that in the real world of male-dominated venture capital in the United States, only 6 percent of venture capital funding goes to women-led businesses: The United States doesn't lack ambitious women but does have an investment culture riddled with men and their implicit biases.

When the team at Village Capital, a global incubator and accelerator for social entrepreneurs, devised a process to reduce the complexity and cost of seed-stage due diligence, little did they know what they would learn about implicit bias. To give a sense of scope, since founding Village Capital in 2009, Ross Baird has executed over 40 programs in ten countries, with more than 600 graduates raising over $142 million in follow-on capital, and creating 8,800 jobs through their enterprises.

Entrepreneurs who make the extremely competitive cut to get into Village Capital's incubator spend an intensive three months working together. Through the process they become embedded in the due diligence process, including—and this where they really innovated on the funding process—voting as a group to choose which firm will get funded by Village Capital. Typically, this investor evaluation and investment decision would be made by out-side experts, not through a peer review. During those three months, Village Capital's startups openly rank each other three different times against the same criterion: team, product, customer, financials, scale, and return on capital. The collaborative feedback process is no less rigorous, but it does tame the competitive beast. "In the typical winner-take-all startup competition, two people get funding, 15 people get skewered and ripped apart by people trying to make themselves look good, and the non-winners just don't get anything," says Baird. In this process, "when people give feedback to each other, they are more thoughtful about what they say. They care a lot about each other and if they are unfair to each other, it comes back to them," says Baird. "In the peer-reviewed process everyone gets something out of it."[23]

Village Capital did not set out to correct for human bias or behavior driven by implicit biases, but the new process did show the limitations of traditional quantitative and impersonal investment due diligence. It also gave women a chance to shine. In this more democratic, transparent, and collaborative model, women entrepreneurs impressively outperformed their male peers. Although only 15 percent of the participants were women, 40 percent of the investment winners were women. Baird surmises this happens because the process favors entrepreneurs who are more substantive and less flashy. "We find that women tend to under-promise, over-deliver and hit milestones, but are maybe not as free to brag about themselves up on stage." Village Capital has found that women co-founders were 2.7 times more likely than men to get funded through peer-to-peer due diligence, and the differential continues to increase as the structure of the program has improved.

Microfinance Through a Gender Lens

Finding opportunities to invest in women entrepreneurs requires a critical review of sizes and structures of firms providing capital to different markets. You might find yourself drawn to a certain part of the world, a particular industry sector, a type of business, or a funding structure (including traditional structures of debt or equity or innovative models like pay for success or revenue rights). Of course, your choices depend on your capacity, interests, experience, passion, risk tolerance, and return and social impact objectives. We start with a look at microfinance, a gender-lens lending practice inspired by womenomics.

In the mid-1970s, Dr. Muhammad Yunus, a Bangladeshi economics professor, frustrated by theories and lending practices that failed the rural poor in Bangladesh, began making small loans to village women with his own money. In 1983, he founded the Grameen Bank, the first full-service bank to the "unbanked," a finance term used to describe people who don't have a bank account or a credit history. Grameen pioneered a peer-to-peer lending process where groups of five villagers (same family members not allowed) are given five days of training and each person invests two dollars per day. Then the group loans the pooled capital to two members. They meet weekly to ensure the loans are paid back. Each loan repaid increases the number and size of the loans the group may access. The strong social incentive to fulfill one's obligation in a small group reduces the need for outside oversight and increases the incentives to share knowledge and support.[24]

Today there are over 10,000 microfinance institutions (MFIs) worldwide, with different legal statuses and of varying size, that invest in innovative entrepreneurs.[25] Commercial microfinance funds, such as MicroVest, Blue Orchid Microfinance Fund, and Developing World Markets MicroFinance, LLC, offer market rate returns and the opportunity for portfolio diversification. They note the MFI sector's historically low correlation with other sectors, which is not surprising given the nature of its underlying assets (loans to extremely poor individuals). In fact, the Symbiotics Microfinance Index (SMX–MIV Debt) showed no correlation to any of thirteen leading indices spanning diverse asset classes, geographies, and strategies.[26] While not all funds focus on women, as it turns out, women are often a better credit risk than men. Indeed, researchers using a global dataset covering 350 MFIs in 70 countries found that "more women clients are associated with lower portfolio-at-risk, lower write-offs, and lower credit-loss provisions."[27]

The growth and impact of microfinance lies not only in access to capital, but behavioral changes in lenders and loan recipients. For instance, Grameen peer groups commit to "Sixteen Decisions" covering areas such as water access and sanitation, dowries and family planning, and planning for current and future investments. Embedded in these interactions and commitments are sociological factors that enable investors to adjust calculations of risk and return. Better sanitation practices reduce the risk of loan defaults due to family illnesses. Family planning increases women's control of childbirth, and so on. It is not simply that women are better risks than men, but the design of the system itself takes into account living conditions, culture, and other factors that help reduce the risks for the lending institutions.

But how might an investor understand which MFIs are truly implementing practices that will reduce financial risk and increase social returns? Just as the power of microfinance comes from more than the loan itself, a gender lens in microfinance elucidates material factors beyond the sex of the borrower. Women's World Banking (WWB), a global nonprofit with a global network of 40 financial partners from 29 countries, is devoted to giving low-income women access to the financial tools and resources they need to build security and prosperity. To fully deploy the potential of a gender lens in its work, WWB has developed Gender Performance Indicators for use in benchmarking and research. Based on three decades of work understanding and serving the financial needs of low-income women in developing countries, the indicators cover all aspects of MFIs' social and business missions.[28] These gender performance indicators provide quantifiable insights on how customers are served, enabling investors to monitor progress and make decisions to achieve long-term performance. The data collected and analyzed looks at performance from three main perspectives: the women receiving the capital (the client), the financial institutions investing (the institution), and the outcomes for both.

Women's World Banking: Gender and Private Equity Investment

Women's World Banking (WWB) Capital Partners invests equity in companies with specific financial inclusion strategies and a strategic focus on women. They see increasing women on boards, in management, and throughout employee ranks as the "sharp edge of the wedge" for change. Fund investors include both institutions and individuals. C. J. Juhasz, a WWB fund manager, finds herself in board meetings with portfolio companies that are expanding healthcare, savings, or pension strategies. Juhasz regularly raises questions about gender and its relationship to achieving established goals. Reflecting on these experiences, she notes, "There's often a sense of more important focus areas than the percentage of women in the client base or on the board. Despite all the supporting data, gender as a factor in success is a concept that must be nurtured and protected, especially around the connection to financial results."[29] WWB are rallying other investors to the gender leadership approach. Among other initiatives, they are looking to insert covenants, including gender indicators, in term sheets and shareholder agreements. These non-binding covenants provide a baseline of understanding of gender and performance relevant for all investors.

Client Focus

These indicators move beyond the number of women served to reveal the market penetration, the usage of various products, retention, and churn, satisfaction, and engagement of women clients (also as compared to men). For instance, Fundacion delamujer, a Columbian MFI, learned that 75 percent of the clients who had been with the firm for four years or longer were women. Given that acquiring a new customer costs up to five times more than retaining an existing one, and clients with longer tenure have higher average assets, this information is valuable. But sometimes it is hard to get. Ujjivan, an Indian MFI with 423 branches, noticed less than 1 percent of clients were submitting customer feedback or complaints. Women may not feel comfortable complaining to their lender, but they aren't shy about telling their friends. (By some estimates, Ujjivan determined women are four times as likely as men to complain about a bad experience.) To ensure they were hearing from all clients proactively, Ujjivan provided customers with cards which outlined complaint resolution procedures. Within six months it increased by 88 percent.[30] These indicators provide a comprehensive look at best-in-class retail banking practices that are not always standard in service to low-income consumers.

Institutional View

This perspective recognizes that to serve women clients well, the organization needs women employees and leaders on its teams. WWB's Gender Performance Indicators include board diversity and employee promotion and retention. One might think a financial industry service created for women would include women on the board and in the ranks. This has not been the case. As Mary Ellen Iskenderian, WWB's President and CEO, wrote in the *Harvard Business Review*, "In the industry as a whole there has been little focus on gender *within* lending institutions. In fact, our data indicate that the percentage of women in senior management and boards has been decreasing over the past eight years."[31] Unfortunately, this means microfinance organizations will continue to miss the benefits to decision making provided by the sharing of diverse perspectives.

Measures of Outcomes

Elements like well-being, self-determination, and economic improvement turn the focus from customer service to the impact of loans on clients lives. This may take the form of evaluating repayment performance or percent change in household income by gender. Some MFIs collect data on the percentage of clients with children not in school or housing conditions, to track progress in breaking the cycle of intergenerational poverty. The most forward thinking also look for unintended consequences. For instance, Ujjivan's analysis of loan purpose found of the 25.6 percent of loans for non-business purposes the majority were passed on to family members. With that knowledge, they now train loan officers to be aware of trends where women take out loans on behalf of others, creating a contractual obligation to repay a loan they do not actually control.

The overall impact of microfinance is beyond the scope of this chapter, but some lessons are clear. Microfinance is not a silver bullet for poverty alleviation. Not all microfinance lending is supportive of women. Although women are the face of microfinance, without an active gender lens it is more rhetoric than reality. Investors who want social and financial returns must demand that execution matches expectations, and must measure that execution intelligently.

The Missing Middle: Larger than Micro

Definitions of SMEs vary by geography and sectors, but for the purposes of this discussion our definition is businesses with between 5 and 500 employees. In developing economies, as we noted earlier, SMEs are the largest job creators in the formal economy, yet they are the least likely to get financing. Larger, established companies have access to traditional corporate finance while micro-entrepreneurs increasingly find options through microfinance. SMEs sit in the middle, with capital requirements exceeding microfinance but without access to institutional finance. Hence, SMEs are called sometimes the *missing middle.* The IFC estimates that in emerging market countries the finance gap for SMEs is between $900 billion and $1.1 trillion.[32]

To our knowledge, no bank hangs out a sign saying "no women served here," but the barriers to women's participation and enterprise growth are apparent. These challenges fall into three overlapping and reinforcing categories—individual, structural, and cultural. Individually, women may have less experience, education, and confidence. Structurally, they have fewer assets, often because of the laws we described in Chapter 3 that prevent women from owning property and restrict inheritance by gender. Even assistance programs can be gender-biased and structurally undermine women: Some of Latin America's state-sponsored redistribution programs, for example, have resulted in male farmers owning 70 to 90 percent of the land that supports formal sector commerce.[33,34] And finally, culturally, women are expected to put their household duties first while they also face unconscious gender discrimination in lending practices if they aspire to work outside the home.

Fully understanding these barriers and how to address them provides great opportunities for business growth and for social impact. Mara Bolis, a Senior Advisor at Oxfam, saw the opportunities early. Bolis had worked with women who started small businesses and supported their families through the Oxfam Savings for Change groups. She saw the constraints for those who wanted to create businesses that go beyond the subsistence level. "That these ambitious women cannot get the capital they need is criminal," Bolis said. She also observed how Oxfam's Women Economic Leadership (WEL) training methodology (which includes banks, technical assistance providers, and entrepreneurs) helped "peel away mental models that prevent women from accessing opportunity... WEL is not directive or prescriptive, per se. It is an interactive approach empowering women in conjunction with the principles of business."[35] The program's gender lens introduces relevant business tools with a sophisticated look at the household roles and responsibilities of men and women.

In 2014, Bolis and a team launched Oxfam's Women in Small Enterprise (WISE) program for women graduating from microfinance lending programs. It addresses access to capital, technical assistance needs, and policy. The WISE program brings together experts in small-enterprise finance, gender justice, community development, market access, and advocacy. The collaboration extended to over 40 different organizations that share the goal of empowering women business owners. The first lending partner selected was Banco GyT Continental, Guatemala's third largest bank. The review process applied a gender lens to all the usual parameters (strategy, markets and products, sales and services, credit, and technology) and listed required actions to improve services for women in the program as a requirement of the financing.

Learning from the initial WISE experiences, future recruiting will be more selective and the loan amounts slightly smaller and a new highly motivated partner is on board—a smaller regional cooperative bank. The team now also looks at how existing private-sector value chains can be reconfigured to bring economic opportunity to women cultivating small-scale farms. While realistic about the challenges, Jim Daniell, chief operating officer of Oxfam USA, is compelled by the opportunity, saying simply, "We want to prove that investing in women-led small businesses is good business."[36]

BLC Bank in Lebanon is a banking on women success story in a region where there is little good news. BLC's success provides an encouraging example of a regional bank in a developing country that has deliberately and successfully advanced its capacity to lend to women. In 2002, the Lebanese Central Bank acquired 95 percent of the shares of BLC Bank and installed a new management team. In a country where 70 banks serve a population of 4 million, BLC had to find a way to quickly differentiate its brand and strategy.

Using a gender lens, the bank found that while Lebanese women own 33 percent of businesses they receive only 3 percent of bank loans. BLC joined the Global Banking Alliance for Women (GBA), a research and network hub for banks building sustainable profitable women's market programs. Together, BLC and GBA launched the We Initiative Women's Market program in 2012. It created a collateral-free loan to increase access for women and to open accounts on behalf of their children. In only two years, the We Initiative generated significant business returns and currently represents more than 18 percent of the bank's profits, with double-digit growth projected for the next three years. The We Initiative has positioned BLC Bank as the Bank of Choice for women in Lebanon and as a global example for Women's Market best practices.[37]

The IFC's Banking on Women Is Good Business

The International Finance Corporation (IFC) was founded in 1956 with the same pioneering fervor for investing in the future as today's social impact financiers. A member of the World Bank Group, IFC opened its doors with a staff of twelve and $100 million in authorized capital. Today it boasts a balance sheet of over US$87 billion, presence in more than 100 countries, and an emerging markets portfolio invested in most every major industry in the world.

IFC increased its commitment to economic opportunity for women through the 2010 launch of its "Banking on Women" business. The team, led by Patience Marime-Ball, camped out in data rooms of leading banking clients on multiple continents to collect and disaggregate customer data on profitability, cross selling, loyalty, deposit stability, asset quality, and more. Working side by side with commercial banks, they developed metrics and proposals compelling to bank CEOs. In 2014, after a strong track record of success in investing in and providing advisory services to banks, IFC announced the Women Entrepreneurs Opportunity Facility (WEOF) jointly with the Goldman Sachs *10,000 Women* initiative. With a target size of $600 million, this partnership leverages the lessons and network from Goldman's *10,000 Women* initiative and IFC's experience with financial institution clients in emerging markets looking to increase bottom line bank value by providing more and better financial services to women customers. IFC invests in banks in emerging markets, which in turn lend and provide other financial services to women customers and women-owned small and medium businesses. IFC also helps local banks build a value proposition to address the non-financial business hurdles for women customers.

Two WEOF features stand out. The first is the size of the aspiration—moving capital to up to 100,000 women through IFC's banking clients. Of course, in the context of the market opportunity in what IFC has estimated to be a US$300 billion annual credit gap, there is little question about the absorptive capacity for more lending. The second feature is the permanent impact WEOF can have on the banking system because it has introduced a fundamental change in the capabilities of emerging market financial institutions to serve women.

As of June 2016, IFC's Banking on Women business has built a cumulative committed investment portfolio of US$1.2 billion, dedicated to financing women-owned SMEs through banks in over 30 countries.[38] Jessica Schnabel, IFC's current Global Head for Banking on Women, is not surprised: "Women entrepreneurs and women customers comprise the most significant emerging market in the world. Providing valuable banking services to women is key to building long-term bank value in emerging markets today."[39]

Governments and impact investors are excited by the job creation and growth possibilities of SME businesses looking for loans in the $2,000 to $2 million range. Consider the ambitions and accomplishments of Bukky George, the ninth of thirty-five children born into a polygamous family from rural Nigeria. George moved, with her mother and her two siblings, to Lagos where her mother was the head of nursing at one of the local teaching hospitals in their neighborhood. George attended pharmacy school and did her national youth service work at Glaxo SmithKline Beecham (GSK), with rotations through sales, quality control, and production. After a stint in the United Kingdom working for a small owner-run pharmacy, she returned to Nigeria to become a medical rep for GSK and an assistant manager for another drug company.

After four years, like every natural entrepreneur, she was restless. Her personal and professional experiences enabled her to see a market gap in Nigeria for a retail pharmacy chain just as urban populations around the country were exploding. In 1999, George founded HealthPlus, Limited, in Lagos. She established a vision for a pharmacy brand known for excellence in customer service, training, and information management. She sweated the details, a skill she had honed during her days as a medical rep. A loan from Access Bank, a multinational Nigerian commercial bank, enabled George to expand her franchise into one of the fastest-growing pharmacy chains in Nigeria. In 2008, she incorporated another company, CasaBella International Limited, a one-stop store for grooming and beauty solutions for men and women. CasaBella opened in July 2010 at The Palms Mall in Lagos, and now has ten branches. George's move was shrewd as she leveraged the existing retail back-end systems of HealthPlus.[40]

By 2015 HealthPlus had twenty branches and employed over 500 people; more than half are women.[41] As the first integrative pharmacy in Nigeria, HealthPlus is attracting women employees who may follow in George's footsteps. Bukky George's story inspires entrepreneurs everywhere to believe they can grow beyond the missing middle.

HealthPlus has grown to the point where it qualifies as part of a subset of SMEs known as Small and Growing Businesses, or SGBs. Members of the Aspen Network of Development Entrepreneurs (ANDE), a global collaborative promoting entrepreneurship in emerging market countries, targets ambitious SGB entrepreneurs with businesses that have significant potential for growth, and are typically seeking $20,000 to $2 million in capital. ANDE has teamed up with Value for Women, a UK-based social enterprise to bring together a global multidisciplinary team of business and gender specialists to better understand the issues of women-led SGBs. The SGBs led by women, which have been described as "the most missing of the missing middle," have enormous potential as drivers of economic growth in many countries, but not without better access to capital.[42]

Women Gender Capitalists Who Fund and Mentor Women

Whitney Johns Martin has devoted her life to supporting women entrepreneurs. A practicing attorney who founded a mergers and acquisitions consulting business, she was the chairman of the Federal Reserve Bank of Atlanta and served on a number of corporate boards. A former president of the National Association of Women Business Owners, in 1998 Martin created the U.S. Small Business Administration's first Small Business Investment Company (SBIC) for women-led companies. The fund successfully deployed over $50 million and earned the distinction of the SBIC "Portfolio Company of the Year." But Johns Martin was just getting started.

She founded Texas Women Ventures (TWV) to help women-owned businesses in the Southwest reach their full potential. The fund includes companies with an established track record who are achieving $10 million to $100 million in annual revenue. The debt capital allows the business owner(s) to maintain majority ownership and control over running the company.

Over the years, investees in earlier funds have become investors in later funds, demonstrating the interest of women entrepreneurs in paying it forward. Gail Warrior epitomizes this desire. Her firm, The Warrior Group, a commercial general contracting firm with national expertise in permanent modular construction, was an early TWV investment. As CEO, Gail experienced the power of capital and connections to grow her business. Now a limited partner in the most recent TWV fund, Gail has also created the Warrior Women's Mentoring group.[43]

Canada's Vickie Saunders, named one of the 100 most influential leaders of 2015 by "Empowering a Billion Women," alongside Marissa Mayer, Melinda Gates, Sheryl Sandberg, and Michelle Obama, is a champion of missing-middle women entrepreneurs who have eschewed traditional growth funding because they find the process unattractive and the terms biased. Saunders finds that these women prioritize building their companies on their own terms, and specifically maintaining control.

Saunders should know. As a serial entrepreneur, World Economic Forum Global Leader for tomorrow, and CEO of SheEO, a consultancy and incubator, Saunders has worked with hundreds of women entrepreneurs. She's observed their passion, talent, and grit. And she's seen the walls keeping them from funding. But Saunders doesn't just want to see women climb over walls that exist in the current field; she has a bigger plan. She believes the "chasing unicorns" angel model—angel investing with the hopes you find and fund the next Facebook—is an inefficient use of capital. "In economies built on SMEs starved for capital the winner-take-all model hasn't worked," Saunders asserts. "We need a new one."

That was her motivation for launching "Radical Generosity," a model where 500 women each make $1000 donations to a fund. And in doing so they get no return, not even a tax deduction. The women vote on five enterprises to receive low interest five-year loans from the aggregate $500,000. Then it gets more interesting. The five chosen entrepreneurs get together and negotiate who gets how much. These negotiations have two rules: It can't be an equal split and all the money can't go to one venture. In addition to the investments, the entrepreneurs are part of a guided development program with two calls per month with program leads, including access to the 500 women funders on a monthly basis. Saunders set these rules realizing women might not advocate for themselves or make it fair for everyone. But everyone understands the power of collaboration. One group was clear, she says: "Everybody in here is incredible and is going to do something amazing with their life. And if it's not this venture, it's going to be another one and we all want to be working together."[44]

Many Radical Generosity applicants have strong businesses that could or should qualify for traditional loans. And while the 500 investors did not take an investment risk, Saunders believes this step may move more women to say, "We grew these businesses, what can we do next?" She also sees crowdfunding being rolled into the model. Saunders's goal? By 2020, a million women will be working through a franchise model.

The New Girl Networks

Despite academic studies and media coverage highlighting the lack of funding for high-growth women entrepreneurs, change remains elusive. While people debate what the "right" percentage of deal flow ventures with at least one women founder should be, it's tough to argue it should be the current 15 percent. Recall from the Diana Project's most recent picture of the venture capital funding world that businesses with all-men teams are still more than four times as likely to receive VC funding than companies with even one woman on the team.[45]

But reframe the conversation to talk about the importance of venture capital to every economy's innovation and job growth and it is no longer about gender inequity or leaving women out of the financial process. It is about making sure capable capitalist women are present, valued, and funded so that more capital drives innovation and makes economies stronger.

Enter New Girl Networks such as Plum Alley Investments and Astia Ventures, a response to what woman VCs called "the built-in male network in the venture community, that takes people a long time to break into."[46] These and other examples show the power of combining funding and community building with women entrepreneurs and investors. These women-founded funds welcome men and women as investors, but research shows that venture-capital firms with women partners are twice as likely to invest in companies with a woman on the management team and three times more likely to invest in companies with women CEOs.[47] Unfortunately, only 6 percent of U.S. venture firms had women partners in 2014, a decline from 10 percent fifteen years earlier, according to the Diana Project. Similarly, a *Fortune* review of U.S. venture capital firms that had raised at least one fund of $200 million or more between 2009 and 2014 indicated that only 4.2 percent of the senior partners at these firms are women.[48]

From Wall Street to Plum Alley Investments

Andrea Turner Moffitt and Deborah Jackson both started their careers on Wall Street. Jackson worked at Goldman Sachs and then Shattuck Hammond Partners, where she discovered her love for technology. She leveraged this into a series of women-focused companies and initiatives—from a website connecting entrepreneurs to customers, to a subscription-based newsletter, to an accelerator and a crowd funding site. Turner Moffitt was an investment banker and hedge fund analyst at Citibank, but she was looking to make a broader impact on the world and found few role models in the bank with the same passion.

Turner Moffitt teamed up with Sylvia Ann Hewlett, a professor at Columbia University and founder of the Center for Talent Innovation, to conduct groundbreaking global research on the capabilities, needs, and attitudes of women investors across six countries. The international study based on a survey of men and women with at least $100,000 of annual income and $500,000 of investable assets found that women, despite their growing incomes and assets, do not feel their unique perspective as investors is fully valued by the financial services industry. Sixty-seven percent of women said they "feel misunderstood" by their financial advisor. Seventy-one percent of women versus 56 percent of men say they want an adviser who helps them align their investments and life goals.[49]

Turner Moffitt and Jackson teamed up in 2015 to launch Plum Alley Investments, a membership-based private investment company providing access to curated investment experiences and deal flow in private companies led by women and gender diverse teams. The investments are made through syndicates, allowing individuals more choice than a fund mechanism.

The first syndicate provides a window into the opportunity. Laura Mather, PhD, CS, founded Unitive, a Silicon Valley-based software company, to tackle unconscious bias in hiring across major corporations. Plum Alley members invested $430,000 in the company's $7.5 million plus in a series A round.

Plum Alley is open to men and women. Members have the opportunity to connect with a high-caliber peer group, continue learning in a community, select from a curated set of opportunities, and use financial resources and expertise to help build smart businesses.

Some people blame the lack of pipeline of women-led startups for the minimal VC funding of women. That is, women are not starting ventures at the same rate as men in high growth industries. Sharon Vosmek, CEO of Astia, the angel group investing in inclusive teams, completely disagrees: "Invest now. Enough with the conversation. Enough with the pipeline filling."[50] Founded in 1999,

Astia was one of the earliest new girl networks in Silicon Valley to identify and promote high growth women entrepreneurs. From there, Astia expanded from training and networks to drive access to capital through an angel network and a fund. Investors include men and women and all investments are in gender inclusive teams. In addition to changing the look and experiences of people who are considered players in the venture world, Astia is deliberately seeking to increase recognition of women as innovators, and the flow of investment into businesses started by women.

With respect to performance, the results have been outstanding. Since 2003, 60 percent of firms that qualified for Astia training secured funding or an exit within one year. In its first three years, Astia Angels made 28 investments in some of the most cutting-edge U.S. women-led startups, including a company that has created a wearable biosensor to monitor body chemistry and a company that uses electricity to transform water and salt into disinfectants for food production and processing industries.[51,52]

Vosmek is indignant about the passive responses of the venture capital establishment to the current debate. "It is easier to make it about the women but much harder to say my firm doesn't speak to women," says Vosmek. Indeed, research confirms that much of the venture funding happens through male-dominated networks, which relish their separateness and entrenched *maleism*. Investors understandably ask gating questions, including, "Who introduced us?" "Whom did you study with?" "Whom have you worked with?"

The trouble is, when the circle is never opened, affirmation and implicit bias ensures that not only do the people in the club look alike, their deals do, too. But there are encouraging hints of change to come, precipitated by recent investments in younger entrepreneurs. As one entrepreneur commented, "I can't prove it, but my perception is that I get a fuller hearing from firms with a positive experience with a woman-led portfolio company." Research confirms that male VCs who have had successful exits with women entrepreneurs are more open to investing in women-led teams.

Women across the planet already own and are continuing to start businesses. They differ greatly in size and aspiration. Some women are simply supporting basic life needs while others are creating great wealth. Underestimating and underfunding the potential of women, now and in the future, makes no sense. As Andrea Turner Moffitt of Plum Alley told *Fast Company*, "Funding is like oxygen for companies."[53] Why would anyone want to cut off any source of oxygen for companies or countries? The answer is that they really don't want to. But the problem is that they don't realize the folly of their ways.

Notes

1. Art Carey, "Vanguard Founder's Enduring Wisdom," *Philadelphia Enquirer* (September 16, 2013). articles.philly.com/2013-09-16/business/42083490_1_jack-bogle-john-bogle-part-jeremiad.

2. Connie Loizos, "18 Female Founders Who Killed It in 2015," *TechCrunch* (December 22, 2015). techcrunch.com/gallery/21-female-founders-who-killed-it-in-2015/.

3. Gené Teare and Ned Desmond, "Female Founders on an Upward Trend, according to Crunchbase," *TechCrunch* (March 26, 2015). techcrunch.com/2015/05/26/female-founders-on-an-upward-trend-according-to-crunchbase/.

4. Candida B. Brush, Patricia G. Greene, Lakshmi Balachandra, and Amy E. Davis, "Diana Report Women Entrepreneurs in 2014: Bridging the Gender Capital Gap," Arthur Blank Center for Entrepreneurship, Babson College, September 2014. www.babson.edu/academics/centers/blank-center/global-research/diana/documents/diana-project-executive-summary-2014.pdf.

5. Peer Stein, Oya Pinar Ardic, and Martin Hommes, *Closing the Credit Gap for Formal and Informal Micro, Small and Medium Size Enterprises* (International Finance Corporation, August 2013), p. 19. www.ifc.org/wps/wcm/connect/4d6e6400416896c09494b79e78015671/Closing+the+Credit+Gap+Report-FinalLatest.pdf?MOD=AJPERES.

6. Donna Kelley, Candida Brush, Patricia Greene, Mike Herrington, Abdul Ali, and Penny Kew, "GEM 2014 Women's Report, GEM: Special Report Women's Entrepreneurship" (November 17, 2015). http://www.babson.edu/Academics/centers/blank-center/global-research/gem/Documents/GEM%202012%20Womens%20Report.pdf.

7. "The World Economic Forum Gender Gap Report 2014." reports.weforum.org/global-gender-gap-report-2014/.

8. Jessica Bennett and Jesse Ellison, "Women Will Rule the World," *Newsweek* (July 5, 2010). http://www.newsweek.com/women-will-rule-world-74603.

9. Jackie VanderBrug, "The Global Rise of Female Entrepreneurs," *Harvard Business Review* (September 4, 2013). hbr.org/2013/09/global-rise-of-female-entrepreneurs.

10. Li-Wei Chen and Peter W. Roberts, "Founders and the Social Performance of B Corps," Goizueta Business School Emory University, 2010.
goizueta.emory.edu/faculty/socialenterprise/documents/founders_
social_perforormance.pdf.
11. www.bcorporation.net/.
12. Candida Brush, "How Women Entrepreneurs Are Transforming
Economies and Communities," *Forbes* (February 16, 2013). www.forbes
.com/sites/babson/2013/02/16/how-women-entrepreneurs-are-
transforming-economies-and-communities/#719904d25466.
13. Brianna DiPietro, "Women Entrepreneurs Thriving Worldwide," Babson College blog. www.babson.edu/news-events/babson-news/Pages/
2015-global-entrepreneurship-monitor-womens-report.aspx.
14. Donna Kelley, Candida Brush, Patricia Greene, Mike Herrington,
Abdul Ali, and Penny Kew, "GEM 2014 Women's Report, GEM: Special
Report Women's Entrepreneurship" (November 17, 2015).
15. "L.A. Has the Worst Traffic in America" *CBS News* (March 16, 2015).
losangeles.cbslocal.com/2016/03/15/study-l-a-has-worst-traffic-in-
america/.
16. Claire Martin, "HopSkipDrive, a Ride Start-up for the After-School
Set," *New York Times* (June 27, 2015). www.nytimes.com/2015/06/28/
business/hopskipdrive-a-ride-start-up-for-the-after-school-set.html.
17. "HopSkipDrive." www.crunchbase.com/organization/hopskipdrive#/
entity.
18. Caroline Said, "Shuddle for 'Uber Kids' Hits the End of the Road," *San
Francisco Chronicle* (April 14, 2016). www.sfchronicle.com/business/
article/Shuddle-Uber-for-kids-service-reaches-end-7249450.php?
cmpid=gsa-sfgate-result.
19. 10years.firstround.com/#method.
20. Personal communications (Cindy Padnos, June 18, 2016).
21. Davey Alba, "It's Embarrassing How Few Black Female Founders Get
Funded," *Wired* (February 2, 2016).
22. Alison W. Brooks, Laura Huang, Sarah W. Kearny, and Fiona Murray,
Investors Prefer Entrepreneurial Ventures Pitched by Attractive Men (Boston:
Massachusetts Institute of Technology, February 2014). www.pnas.org/
content/111/12/4427.full?sid=45375246-9dd9-45f2-9c51-fec71b2299ab
http://www.pnas.org/content/111/12/4427.full?sid=45375246-9dd9-
45f2-9c51-fec71b2299ab.
23. Personal communications (Ross Baird, June 16, 2016).
24. Without oversight, these same social pressures can create unintended
consequences, such as suicides.
25. Microfinance Market Outlook 2015, November 2014. ResponsAbility.
26. Symbiotics Microfinance Index and Microvest Short Duration Fund LP.

27. Bert D'Espallier, Isabelle Guérin, Roy Mersland, *Women and Repayment in Microfinance* (Institute of Research for Development, November 18, 2010.).

28. "Gender Performance Indicators: How Well Are We Serving Women?" Women's World Banking, 2013. www.womensworldbanking.org/wp-content/uploads/2013/09/Womens-World-Banking-Gender-Performance-Indicators.pdf.

29. Personal interview, (C.J. Juhasz, July 24, 2015).

30. "Gender Performance Indicators: How Well Are We Serving Women?" Women's World Banking, p. 15, 2013. www.womensworldbanking.orrg/wp-content/uploads/2013/09/Womens-World-Banking-Gender-Performance-Indicators.pdf.

31. Mary Ellen Iskenderian, "Women as Microfinance Leaders, Not Just Clients," *Harvard Business Review* (March 16, 2011). hbr.org/2011/03/women-as-microfinance-leaders/.

32. IFC Financing to Micro, Small and Medium Enterprises Globally (FY 2013) accessed Sept. 11, 2015.

33. C. Deere, and M. Leon, "The Gender Asset Gap: Land in Latin America," *World Development,* 31(6) (2003), 925–947.

34. World Bank, *World Development Report, 2012: Gender Equality and Development.* Washington, DC, 2011. siteresources.worldbank.org/INTWDR2012/Resources/7778105-1299699968583/7786210-1315936222006/Complete-Report.pdf.

35. Lynda M. Applegate and Aldo Sesia, "Oxfam America's Women in Small Enterprise," Harvard Business School Case 814-011, (February 2014). www.hbs.edu/faculty/Pages/item.aspx?num=46398.

36. Ibid.

37. "BLC Bank Profiting Through Strategic Differentiation," Women's World Global Banking Alliance Case Study, 2014. www.gbaforwomen.org/news-events/blc-case-study-highlights-womens-market-success-story-in-lebanon/.

38. "The Women Entrepreneurs Opportunity Facility," GoldmanSachs.com (May 25, 2016). www.goldmansachs.com/citizenship/10000women/partnership-infographic/.

39. Personal Interview (Jessica Schabel, February 25, 2016).

40. Bukky George, CEO HealthPlus Limited and CasaBella International, Career Development Network, CDNet, Nigeria. cdnetng.org/?q=node/5918.

41. LinkedIn profile, HealthPlus Limited. Accessed May 25, 2016. www.linkedin.com/company/health-plus-limited.

42. Tim Chambers, Rebecca Fries, and Hannah Schiff, "The Problem of Under Investment in Women-Led Small Businesses: An Ecosystem Perspective from Latin America," Value for Women Policy Brief, The

Aspen Institute, 2013. Adapted from M.E. Bianco et al., *The Most Missing of the Missing Middle* (United Kingdom: Oxfam, 2013).

43. Personal communications (Whitney Johns Martin, April 20, 2016).
44. Personal communication (Vickie Saunders, September 11, 2015).
45. Candida Brush, Patricia Greene, Lakshmi Balachandra, Amy Davis, *Diana Report Women Entrepreneurs 2014: Bridging the Gender Gap in Venture Capital*, September 2014.
46. Ibid., p. 3.
47. Ibid., p. 11.
48. Dan Primack, "Venture Capital's Stunning Lack of Female Decision Makers," *Fortune* (February 6, 2014). fortune.com/2014/02/06/venture-capitals-stunning-lack-of-female-decision-makers.
49. Andrea Turner Moffitt, and Sylvia Hewlett. "Harnessing the Power of the Purse: Female Investors and Global Opportunities for Growth," Executive Summary Center for Talent Innovation, 2015, p. 3. www.talentinnovation.org/_private/assets/HarnessingThePowerOfThe Purse_ExecSumm-CTI-CONFIDENTIAL.pdf.
50. Personal communications (Sharon Vosmek, August 3, 2015).
51. Joe Whitworth, "Ozone Purification Secures Funding to Accelerate Market Launch," FoodQualitynews.com (November 23, 2015). www.foodqualitynews.com/R-D/Astia-Angels-and-Wheatsheaf-Group-invest-in-OZO-technology.
52. Jennifer Hicks, "Beyond Fitness Trackers at CES: Tiny Wearable Biosensor Continuously Monitors Your Body Chemistry," *Forbes* (January 7, 2016). www.forbes.com/sites/jenniferhicks/2016/01/07/beyond-fitness-trackers-at-ces-tiny-wearable-biosensor-continuously-monitors-your-body-chemistry/#47bad5ae6019.
53. Gwen Moran, "How Women Entrepreneurs Can Get More Funding," *Fast Company* (April 19, 2016). www.fastcompany.com/3058997/how-women-entrepreneurs-can-get-more-funding.

CHAPTER 6

Inside and Outside the Workplace

"When women are at the table, the discussion is richer, the decision-making process is better, management is more innovative and collaborative, and the organization is stronger."[1]

—Joseph Keefe, President and CEO of Pax World Investments, LLC

Companies enjoy the publicity from announcing pay equity reviews and new parental benefits. These are steps in the right direction, but the real and hard effort to create fully inclusive workplaces—where women are present everywhere and men and women are working more productively together—requires a lot more from leaders than policies, programs, and good press.

Saleforce.com decided to do a corporate pay equity analysis of its 17,000-person workforce in 2014. When Cindy Robbins, Salesforce's head of human resources, and Senior Vice President Leyla Seka first proposed the assessment to CEO Marc Benioff, they weren't sure there was a problem. It turns out there was. In November 2015, the company announced it would spend $3 million to eliminate pay inequities that applied to female and male employees.

Benioff later admitted he was initially skeptical about the value of doing it, and told *SiliconBeat*, "I think I got called out this year, and it was a difficult moment for me as a leader, for sure."[2] But he also changed his mindset when he realized the concept of "equal pay" was a powerful aspirational goal for the company. Indeed, Cindy Robbins reported on her blog in March 2016 that the pay equity study triggered changes in recruiting and high-potential mentoring programs that resulted in a 33 percent increase in women's promotions in 2015.[3]

It takes a deeper dive inside the intricacies of a firm, and a long view of change, for a company to collectively understand how gender affects all parts of its businesses and begin to implement approaches that will make an enduring difference. It also takes a smart gender lens researcher to separate public relations from actions with substantive impact.

Think about Gender in a Value Chain

When Harvard Business School's Michael Porter coined the term *value chain* in 1985 in the classic business strategy book *Competitive Advantage: Creating and Sustaining Superior Performance*, he opened the door to a new way of evaluating a company's competitiveness from the inside. Companies are not just a random assemblage of people, money, buildings, and equipment. How these assets are deployed determines a company's competitiveness, and the value created for customers and investors is determined by how well particular activities are performed and how the linkages between them are managed.

The notion of a value chain elegantly breaks down each activity of an enterprise into strategically relevant pieces and enables someone to look at them individually to show how they connect. Take this idea a step further and imagine using your gender lens to look closely at an enterprise or even a business unit or a team to see how gender influences business process design and performance in all parts of a company's value chain.

Consider late and over-budget projects in an IT department. A Mercer study tells the story of a male chief information officer who did a gender lens analysis of his teams to see if this could shed light on project management performance. What he found out is the teams with at least one woman completed projects on time, and within budget, significantly more frequently than did the all-male teams. After doing the analysis, he required teams to be gender diverse before approving a project launch. Soon the department's managers realized they would need to hire more women if their projects were going to move forward.

Another Harvard professor, Iris Bohnet, has written a new book called *What Works, Gender Equity by Design* that is as ground-breaking as Porter's. In her book, Bohnet explores how studying gender- and sex-based differences and biases in human behavior leads to opportunities to achieve incremental or exponential innovations throughout a firm. Bohnet, a behavioral economist, calls herself a behavioral designer. "Much like interior designers or landscape architects, behavioral designers create environments that make it easier for our biased minds to get things right."[4]

RobecoSAM's Five Areas for Gender Equity Analysis

RobecoSAM, the Swiss fund manager responsible for the research underlying the Dow Jones Sustainability Indexes, conducts an annual Corporate Sustainability Assessment (CSA) of over 3,000 companies. In collaboration with EDGE, they added gender equity questions that address five major areas: board nomination, talent management, pay equity, employee satisfaction, and occupational health and safety.[5]

In subsequent conversations with other clients, the idea surfaced to create a gender score using the questions in the CSA, and adding more. Research began with some encouraging results. For instance, the team divided the reporting companies into two portfolios by gender score (controlling for the effects of industry, region, and market capitalization).

The high gender-equality portfolio outperformed the lower by 11 percent from 2004 to 2014, and it also outperformed the market universe of 4,000 stocks.

The strength of the findings differed by sector and geography, but provided a strong enough investment signal to build a fund. In 2015, the RobecoSAM Global Gender Equality Impact Equities Strategy launched. The global strategy invests in companies in the top half of gender scores versus their peers. The team considers valuation and momentum factors, as well as a fundamental analysis to deliver a concentrated portfolio of high-conviction stocks that seek to outperform the MSCI World Index. RobecoSAM also publicly claims, "Through this strategy, we aim to drive change at companies, ultimately creating a positive societal impact."

Source: "Equal opportunity: Moving beyond board diversity," http://www .robecosam.com/images/RobecoSAM_Global_Gender_Equality_Impact_ 3-pager_en.pdf.

Tracking Four Gender in Business Themes

For investors and companies, we believe there are four essential themes to any gender-lens analysis. They may serve as part of a broad effort to understand and expose opportunities for change, or be part of a deeper examination of a single issue.

Collective Intelligence

In 2006, MIT's Sloan's Thomas Malone, a scholar who studies organizational design, information technology, and leadership behavior, established Center for Collective Intelligence (CCI) to study what it means for people to problem solve more intelligently as a group.[6] In one study Malone conducted with Anita Woolley, a Carnegie Mellon economist, they found collective intelligence was strongly correlated with two emotional intelligence factors (the average social sensitivity of its members and their ability to take turns contributing) and one gender factor (the proportion of women). Groups with at least one woman as a team member outperformed the all-male teams. Woolley and Malone pull no punches: They say "teams with more women make better decisions and boost problem-solving and creativity."[7]

A London Business School collective intelligence study across companies, industries, and levels in 17 countries examined the effect of women on knowledge transfer, experimentation, and task performance on R&D teams.[8] Researchers found that the team's self-confidence, experimentation, and efficiency (all critical to innovation) were optimized when there were 50 percent more women on the team. Imagine a board member, upon hearing about a groundbreaking R&D initiative in the firm, asking about the gender composition of the selected team before the budget and timeline.

Investors who understand the significance of gender in team dynamics will ask different questions about the gender composition of teams at all levels.

Attracting and Retaining Talent

Company leaders talk a lot about talent management but few companies report specific metrics, in part because they have not done it before, and in part because investors don't ask enough questions. Investors should inquire about the state of hiring and retention for strategic senior positions, and roles throughout the company critical to strategic and operations execution.

And they should be mindful that Millennials, much more than previous generations, scrutinize any potential employer's record on hiring and retaining women. Among Millennials, 74 percent of men and 82 percent of women who responded to a global PwC study in 2014 said an employer's policy on diversity, equality, and workforce inclusion was a deciding factor on whether they should work for a company. Fifty-five percent of respondents of both genders agreed with a statement in the survey that, in essence, said they are not seeing the women and minorities in companies that claim diversity is a priority.[9] Collecting data on the percentage of women and minorities to show diversity in different roles, and reporting changes, is not difficult for an HR department to do, and should be a routine part of analyses of key roles and workforce planning.

Built-in Bias in Business Systems

Most of us want to think we are fair, unbiased, and work in meritocracies but researchers like Iris Bohnet show us otherwise. Bias in hiring processes is especially common.[10] For example, Bohnet looked at employers' hiring decisions for a position that required both math and verbal skills. To inform their decisions, employers were given the results of the applicant's performance on a set of relevant activities (either math or verbal problems). Fifty-one percent of the employers given separate information for male and female candidates chose an employee who underperformed relative to other candidates. Think of it—half the time they chose weaker candidates due to perceptions or biases as to male or female math or verbal abilities. Poor hiring decisions plummeted (down to only 8 percent choosing underperformers) when employers considered all candidates side-by-side, regardless of gender. In other words, direct comparisons of men and women (versus an interview where implicit bias is not corrected) increase the likelihood of selecting qualified candidates.[11]

A McKinsey/LeanIn.org study describes four kinds of bias that surface in many business processes and situations. The first is likeability bias: Competent women are seen as less likeable and likeable women are seen as less competent. Next is performance evaluation bias. Women are often evaluated only on what they have accomplished while men are evaluated more on their potential. The third bias is performance attribution: Women are given less credit for success and blamed more often for failures. The final bias is the motherhood bias we talked about in Chapter 4: Women and men are seen as less committed to careers when they step away for family reasons. In fact, more than 90 percent of people think their career will be negatively impacted if they have a child (women) or take parental leave (men). They are probably right.[12]

Relating to Customers and Business Partners

There are plenty of jokes about all-male teams designing the next women's bra. Jokes aside, though, it is not a new idea that teams working on product usage and features for women should include women. Women make the majority of purchasing decisions for their families, so it makes sense for consumer product companies to have women well represented in strategy, R&D, marketing, and customer service teams. Too many companies don't.

The U.S. government requires companies awarded federal contracts to disclose gender and racial diversity by seniority level of any contractors they hire to work on the project. Corporations that have made public diversity commitments have begun to ask their contractors and suppliers to report their status on diversity as a requirement for doing business with them. For example, Wal-Mart, as part of its Women's Empowerment program launched in 2012, asked its largest professional service and merchandise suppliers (with more than $1 billion in sales) to increase women and minority representation on their sales teams that handle Wal-Mart accounts. Inside Wal-Mart, the focus on compliance started with global accounts and cascades down to smaller relationships.[13] Any supplier strongly dependent on Wal-Mart as a customer is going to have a hard time doing business with them if they don't meet its demands. That is a risk an investor in that supplier would want to know.

Analyze Inside, Outside, and Look Forward

A thorough value chain analysis starts with the board room and moves through conference rooms, cubicles, customer service operations into factories, and throughout the supply chain. It shines a light on business units and departments and teams, support functions, and line roles. The best analyses demand rigorous data collection. For example, anyone researching Google's new parental leave policy will discover the company used human capital analytics to figure out why women were twice as likely to quit as the average Google employee. To their surprise, the team at Google discovered that Google had a "parent gap," not a gender gap. And it was specifically a problem with young mothers, who were twice as likely to quit. The data influenced Google's design of a new policy giving new mothers five months off (replacing the 12-week industry standard of maternity leave) and new parents seven weeks of leave.[14]

The analysis requires scrutiny of all the targets the company sets and where accountability for delivering them lies. It raises the tougher questions about how women and men are engaged in core business operations and broader value chains, and challenges measures that are not getting the results that matter. This is a flexible framework for analysis but it resists easy answers (i.e., what might be said to the press). Using it is as much a learning experience as it is detective work.

Companies committed to reaping the benefits of this level of analysis stand out based on their actions. Some of the most transparent are working with EDGE Gender Certification (EDGE is the Economic Dividends for Gender Equality, formerly the Gender Equality Project). EDGE's three-part consultative and certification process covers policies and practices (infrastructure), results over time (statistics), and employee perceptions (experience). The approach makes intuitive sense since policies are only relevant if they deliver results and perceptions often highlight well-meaning but ineffective practices. This isn't a simple or superficial exercise. Cosmetic giant L'Oreal USA's certification process took six months and included a review of policies, an extensive employee survey, and a deep dive of gender data for a workforce of over 10,000 people.[15] Key assessment areas included pay equity, recruitment and promotion, leadership development, work flexibility, and culture.

Aniela Unguresan, CEO and co-founder of EDGE certification, sees two significant shifts in organizational approaches to gender issues among the companies EDGE has observed or certified. First, the responsibility for diversity and gender equality has moved from global human resources to diversity councils, chaired by business leaders with profit and loss responsibilities. Second, the bar for diversity and gender equality progress has been raised.

Just having a program description and participant numbers used to be an adequate response to gender questions. No longer. These organizational trends reinforce recognition of gender equality as a business performance issue and validate its consideration by business executives and the financial analysts who follow them.[16]

The Board of Directors

In 2015, the GAO issued a report highlighting the growing body of literature that shows the advantages of increased diversity, and specifically gender diversity, on corporate boards. They explicitly highlighted a broader perspective leading to better decision making, as well as emphasizing the importance of a board that reflects a company's employee and customer base, and the need for a broader talent pool from which to select candidates.[17]

Large institutional investors, especially pension funds, have generally understood the relationship of governance to financial returns.[18] Teacher's Insurance and Annuity Association (TIAA) is well-known for the demanding reviews and comparisons of board accountability and for considering carefully how actions pan out over time. Rosemary Kenney, Senior Director of Corporate Governance and Compliance for TIAA, recently opened a panel discussion at an MSCI event by saying, "We have a longstanding interest in the quality of boards."[19] And for good reason. TIAA serves more than 4 million active and retired educators working for more than 15,000 institutions and, as of 2015, had $866 billion in combined assets under management.

Stephanie Sonnabend is another successful businesswoman who knows the importance of effective boards. She presented regularly at Sonesta International Hotels Corporation—her family's hotel business—board meetings, and pushed aggressively and successfully for the first female board member. Recognizing one woman at the table was not enough, Stephanie formally joined the board in 1996, and in 2001 when she became president of the firm, she recruited a third woman.

Sonnabend has been a consistently vocal activist for gender diversity on corporate boards. Researching the issue with the Boston Club, a women's leadership organization, they realized, "Most people don't know what a board is, what it does or who is on it. The strongest opposition to diversity is apathy and inertia," Sonnabend says. "And it wasn't just in Massachusetts; it was true across the country."[20]

Four elements for change were missing: a definition of diversity, a goal, transparency, and visibility. In 2011, she founded 20/20 Women on Boards, a research and advocacy group pushing for 20 percent female board representation in the United States by the year 2020.[21] The 20/20 organization, along with others like the 30% Coalition and ION, have championed the issue with companies, government, and the media.

One sign we are moving in the right direction is that board diversity research has gone mainstream. The CFA Institute, one of the largest investor associations in the world, now asks separate questions in its annual opinion survey about board accountability and board diversity. (Though, in its Environmental, Social and Governance 2015 survey, 78 percent of respondents ranked board accountability as important or very important in investment analysis and decisions versus only 41 percent for board diversity. There is progress to be made.)[22]

It's no longer hard to find multiple studies linking women on boards and corporate financial performance. Catalyst Research's study of Fortune 500 financial performance (2004–2008) showed that companies with three or more women on the board of directors outperformed those with none by a 46 percent return on equity.[23] A 2014 Credit Suisse analysis across 40 countries from 2005 to 2014 showed companies with more than one woman on the board had a compound annual return 3.7 percent higher than sector peers with no women on the boards.

Of course, linking diversity to financial performance is not simple. Not all researchers find conclusive evidence of a positive impact on a company's financial performance, based on different definitions and methodologies—and in some cases, other relationships are discovered. Thomson Reuters global and multi-sector analysis of 1,843 international companies from 2009 to 2013 showed the share price of firms with "mixed" (men and women) boards tended to have slightly lower volatility than companies with no women on boards.[24] The Peterson Institute 2016 global survey of 21,980 firms from 90 countries in 2015 found no definative financial benefit to gender diverse boards.[25]

Overall, the collective research suggests there is value in gender diversity on boards, but it requires more than counting the number of women. The recruiting process, the committee assignments, and the broader corporate commitment to gender lens analysis all matter. MSCI, which has published a global "State of the Union on Boards" report since 2010, found that companies in the index "with strong female leadership"—three or more women on the board, or its percentage of women on the board above the country average—generated 36 percent higher returns on equity per year versus companies that did not have the same level of women on their boards.[26] A company is also categorized as having "strong female leadership" if its CEO is a woman and there is at least one woman on the board. (MSCI disqualifies companies that otherwise would meet its criteria if they have been implicated in discrimination allegations in the past three years, as captured by its controversies database. Controversies disqualified 53 companies in 2015.) This research, like others, stops short of claiming causation. Yet the correlation of gender diverse boards and corporate performance is striking.

Barclay's Women in U.S. Corporate Leadership Index and ETN

In 2013, Sue Meirs' (chief operating officer of Funds Structured Market Sale at Barclays), review of the research on gender and performance left her puzzled. The research showed strong correlations between gender diversity and investment performance, but there were few products for investors who wanted to put their capital behind women in leadership while targeting market rate returns.

The following year, Barclay's launched its Women in Leadership Exchange Traded Note (ETN), linked to the performance of Barclays Women in Leadership North America Total Return USD Index. (ETNs are contracts between investors and banks that are backed only by their issuer's credit as opposed to exchange-traded funds and mutual funds that hold the actual assets.)

The Barclay's index, which uses data from Institutional Shareholder Services, Inc. and is a highly regarded source of data on governance and responsible investment, is designed to provide investors with exposure to eighty-three U.S.-based companies listed on the NASDAQ and New York Stock Exchanges that have strong female representation on their executive leadership teams. To be included, a company must have either a female CEO or at least 25 percent of female members on the board of directors, or both.[27]

In Meirs' view, the ETN and other products launched under the Women's Leadership Index, are "an arbitrage opportunity. Here is an investment product that takes advantage of the fact that the women in management indicators we have chosen correlate with higher financial performance and yet are not being included in investor's analysis or valued highly enough by the market. We think investors have an opportunity to take advantage of that."

Barclays ETN combines basic U.S. equity exposure with an opportunity for the investor to express their support for gender diversity through their investment choice. While those benefits matched some investor's interests, Meir also thought the product might draw attention to the cumulative research around diversity and performance. On launch day, her phone began to ring with firms asking if they were being included in the index, demonstrating the power of public benchmarks and capital. Speaking on Canadian Public Television, she noted: "Over time, this creates incentive for companies to say 'What are we doing that is causing us to be below the standard? Should we be doing something different for our own benefit?'"[28]

Even those convinced by the research may assume there aren't enough women with "executive experience" (often a nominating committee requirement). They assume, too, that boards nominating women need to lower their standards. But step outside this argument for a moment and consider the qualities of a great board as a team, and then apply a gender lens. What might you see?

Tony Lingham, a professor of organizational behavior at Case Western Reserve University, developed a thirty-item team dynamic assessment tool, called TOOL, to assess how a board functions. Dysfunctional boards suffer from groupthink, less dialog, and cronyism. One study using TOOL found boards that function well as a team (i.e., high collective intelligence) have 800 percent greater impact on firm profitability than any one, lone, well-qualified director.[29] The researchers also found gender issues: Women tended to pursue ideas in the best interest of the shareholders even if there was conflict with the board's consensus opinion. Men, by contrast, tend to be more concerned with being collegial with teammates. These findings suggest self-interested shareholders should look more at the composition of the board than at the individual credentials of the next candidate.

If group intelligence is not enough, risk may be a motivator for looking more closely at companies with women on boards. For instance, a global MSCI analysis of companies in the bottom quartile of gender diversity (versus country peers) suffered 24 percent more governance-related controversies than the average.[30] Kellie McElhaney of the Haas School of Business at the University of California–Berkeley analyzed a company's ESG performance against the governance of 1500 companies. Her research was to establish a relationship: "Firms with higher numbers of women on their boards are more proactively managing their ESG performance, and hence, improving the firm's social, environmental and governance impact(s)." Indeed, she found these firms were more likely to invest in renewable power generation, and measure and reduce carbon emissions in their products. But they were also more likely to address the environmental risks embedded in their financing decisions and avoid corrupt business dealings.[31]

Again, these analyses of board diversity only show correlation, but strong research shows that diverse groups are collectively more intelligent. They will ask more questions and probe broadly to expose and reduce risks. And when women join boards, studies show that overall attendance at board meetings improves. This is not because the women show up, but because the male attendance increases. Interestingly, a few public companies, mostly outside the United States, now publish statistics on board attendance in their annual reports.

Despite the research, the advocates, the publicity, and efforts to recruit more women on boards, their numbers have climbed only five percentage points over the last ten years.[32] EY found in its analysis of board performance in 2014 annual meetings there were more men named William, John, Robert, and James on boards of the S&P 1500 than the total number of women.[33] "The pace of change is absolutely glacial," says Karyn Twaronite, EY's firm global diversity and inclusion officer. "The idea that we can essentially pick out four common men's names, at random, and find this shows there's a long way to go." One has to ask the question why. It may be, in the words of Joe Keefe, CEO of Pax World and chair of the 30% Coalition, "The status quo dies a hard death; you have to drive a stake through it."[34]

Senior Management

A 2015 Peterson Institute global study of 22,000 public companies found that an increase in the percentage of women in top management positions from 0 to 30 percent would be associated with a 15 percent rise in profitability. That is an impressive correlation.

And they further clarified the pattern, saying, "The largest gains would be for the proportion of female executives, followed by the proportion of female board members; the presence of female CEOs has no noticeable effect on performance. This pattern underscores the importance of creating a pipeline of female managers and not simply getting lone women to the top."[35]

How do investors find useful and accurate information on corporate progress with respect to women in management at the senior levels? Which companies are retaining and promoting women? How are those women impacting business decisions, strategy, and execution?

The answer cannot be forced without a lot of digging.

As with most research on gender and corporate performance, it is relatively easy to find CEO lists. At the next level, a few companies report on senior management in human capital metrics (mandatory or voluntary), notably those among the companies that have adopted the IIRC's integrated reporting framework.

Global surveys of corporate practices and opinions by region, size, and industry—like the annual Mercer Report, "When Women Thrive Businesses Thrive," launched in 2014—provide benchmark data.[36] For example, in the 2016 survey (respondents in 583 companies based in 42 countries) women made up 35 percent of the average company's professional workforce. At higher levels, women made up 31 percent of managers, 26 percent of senior managers, and 20 percent of executives.

These and emerging new human capital metrics are a good place to start to single out companies that take gender diversity seriously. They are also good places to track progress.[37] But they are clearly only a beginning. Gender as a factor in operational and managerial efficiency and effectiveness can show up in employee engagement surveys, human rights safety records, and many other aspects of running a company. How do we get beyond just counting women or reporting percentage increases to get a better sense of the gender factors that affect people's effectiveness from day-to-day and year-to-year?

Until recently, too many companies and analysts only paid lip service to concerns about the lack of women in senior management roles and provided little data at all. This is changing. Credit Suisse's CS3000 database includes gender diversity for key senior management roles (CEO, CFO, Operations, and shared services). The Credit Suisse study suggests that women in management are more of an influence on corporate performance than simply women in the boardroom." (This research stops short of claims for causality as does a lot of research.) Cristian Dezsö and David Ross examined the relationship between a firm's financial performance and women in senior management in the top 1500 U.S. firms from 1992 to 2006. They concluded that firms that promote women to senior management positions enjoy superior economic performance, especially companies that are focused on innovation.[38] Why? They cite a complementary set of interpersonal management skills that encourage inclusiveness and listening to other employee voices.

McKinsey did its first study of gender and corporate executive pipelines of American Fortune 500 companies in 2012, and teamed up with LeanIn.org in 2015 to update their findings. The 2015 *Women in the Workplace* study of 25 North American companies showed women underrepresented at every level of corporate pipelines, a finding similar to the 2012 report and the Mercer study (see Figure 6.1).

Even though people often assume more women leave corporate jobs than men, their study found the reason for the "leaky pipeline" is that women face a "steeper path to corporate leadership" than men. Bias by culture and organizational designs play a big role.

EDGE and Mercer research of 167 companies found that having a pay equity policy was the strongest correlation to outcomes in making progress or achieving gender balance in management. Perhaps a solution to plugging the "leaky pipeline" is through pay equity? Yes, says EDGE's Aniela Unguresan. "It is the most clear expression of a company equally valuing men and women. It goes to the heart of the way an organization operates."[39]

Salesforce.com is certainly another bit of evidence she's right. And Cisco CEO Chuck Robbins said at Davos in 2016 that pay equity is part of a $2 million plus investment Cisco is making in putting the data into the review process. "If we review the sales numbers, let's also review the people numbers, and let's invest in the capabilities to ensure all employees are compensated fairly and equitably."[40]

The growing pressures for disclosure of pay equity data make it possible for management to share and shareholders to see for themselves where a company really stands on this issue. Activist fund managers are pushing their agendas for more transparency and better information to serve their clients. Meanwhile, in a number of countries, disclosure regulations aren't just coming, they're here.

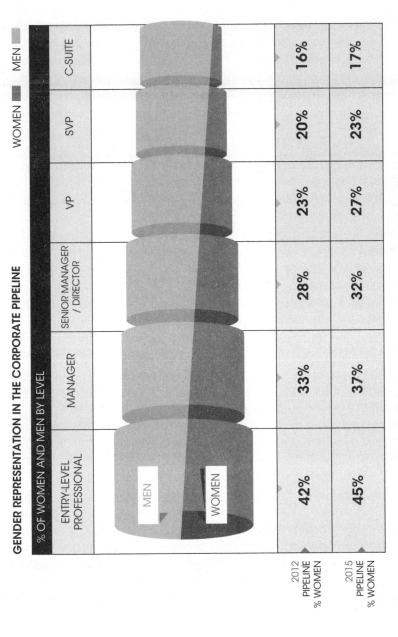

Figure 6.1 Women are underrepresented at every level of the corporate pipeline.

Source: Women in the WorkPlace Corporate Pipeline, McKinsey & Co. and LeanIn.org, 2015

From 2012 to 2015, disclosure on gender equality and management and pay equity to the U.S. Securities and Exchange Commission increased over 33 percent and 50 percent, respectively. And the pace may quicken. For instance, in the United Kingdom—spurred by his country's significant pay gap of 19.1 percent and ranking sixth in the European Union—then–Prime Minister David Cameron announced requirements for companies with over 250 employees to publish average earnings of women and men. This follows Austria, which requires yearly publication, and Sweden, where every three years firms must publish a progress report and plan for pay equity. The U.S. Equal Opportunity Commission (EEOC) announced a proposal in January of 2016 to require employers of over 100 employees to report annual compensation data broken down by race, ethnicity, and sex; if approved, the requirements would go into effect in September 2017.

Despite this incredible momentum, pay equity reviews are not a silver bullet to the broader issue of women being underrepresented in leadership positions; this requires making connections between pay gaps and the corporate pipeline, as EDGE's Aniela Unguresan argues. Where there are patterns that can be detected in multiple data, there are sure to be deep insights to find.

People at Every Level

Good data about people in any enterprise is an extremely valuable source of information: They are the ones who really know if a company is working well and is a place where great employees and leaders will do great work. The annual 100 Best Companies to Work For list compiled by *Fortune* and Great Place to Work® has long been one of the most widely read and promoted employee opinion surveys. In 2016 they launched the 100 Best Place Workplaces for Women.[41] Although the rankings rely strongly on absolute numbers of women and percentages, two-thirds of the ranking is based on qualitative responses to questions posed to female employees on issues such as the support they get for their lives outside of work, what they think about their managers and the senior management, their access to information and leaders, and how connected they feel to their co-workers and other people around the company.[42]

Companies on the *Fortune* list may in time benefit from trends in gendered employee engagement that Gallup has documented for years. Over four decades, 195 countries, and 27 million employees, Gallup employee engagement data has found that employees working for female managers outscored those working for male managers on multiple metrics. They conclude that female managers excel at setting basic expectations for their employees, building relationships and a positive team environment, and providing employees with opportunities to develop within their careers.[43]

Processes like hiring, firing, and promoting can be hotbeds of gender bias and—because of that—are areas where companies have the chance to collect essential data. To isolate the greatest opportunities for change, McKinsey/LeanIn.org recommends tracking the number of women and men at all stages in the hiring process (sourcing, screening, interviews and hires, promotion rates for men and women and promotion rates for line and staff positions, number and reasons for men and women leaving at all levels).[44] The resulting data can provide motivation for programs like Google's online platform for employees called "re: Work"—a strong indicator of the company's commitment to raising awareness of unconscious bias and providing a range of tools to address it.[45] The program's website includes a video of the workshop called "Unconscious Bias @ Work." Over 30,000 Googlers (over half the company) have participated. In fact, it is the largest voluntary learning program at Google.

Corporations have begun to learn from each other in exciting ways. SheWorks is a partnership of ten companies—a mix of well-known global multinationals (Coca-Cola, E&Y, and Intel) and domestic leaders (Kuwait Energy, Brazil's Odebrecht Group, the Ooredoo Group in Oman, and Zulekha Hospitals in Dubai)—with the World Bank's private sector partnership group and a number of other partners including EDGE. The commitment of this geographically, industrially, and culturally diverse group is to put "gender smart" business ideas into practice. Specifically they seek to improve employment opportunities and working conditions for women while driving business benefits. Members have pledged to implement measures such as mentorship programs, flexible working arrangements, and leadership training to increase diversity in management.[46] Through the partnership, companies share resources, experience, and learn from each other.

Often of their work starts with somewhat broad areas, like safe workplaces: including effective anti–sexual harassment programs, and data analytics on stress, productivity, and turnover. Absenteeism, an easy to understand metric, presents an obvious risk factor. Few organizations report it, and if they do, it is a line item with no explanation. If organizations recorded the causes for employee absenteeism, additional data to help identify gender issues or shape gender-friendly policies could emerge. For example, if women were missing more work than men due to school closures, the company could consider designs such as work from home on days where school systems were closed, emergency daycare, etc.

Gender differences may also show up in workplace safety data around workplace violence. According to the Institute of Finance and Management, one in four organizations believes that domestic violence is a significant contributor to the risk of workplace violence. As such, identifying threats or instances of domestic violence is not only beneficial for the employee at risk, but prudent for a company in their efforts to minimize workplace violence. Furthermore, research indicates that about 50 percent of battered women who are employed are harassed at work by their abusive partners.[47]

When domestic violence is perpetrated by an employee, or an employee is the victim of such violence, there is a chance that warning signs are observable by a manager or coworker of the employee. So, beyond the positive social impact of an employer being aware of and taking action against domestic violence for the employees' sake, it is prudent for the stability, productivity, and safety of the organization as a whole to do so.

Employers should beware that data may illuminate some complex issues: In one example, Oxfam International research in developing economies revealed that as women's income increases domestic violence may decrease—but it also may increase.[48] For an employer in such an environment, the cultural norm creates both a financial and moral challenge. Imagine a growing SME agricultural processing business with fifty percent female employees. The business cannot sustain its growth with significant absenteeism or turnover in female employees—and, likewise, they do not want to knowingly increase their employees' risk of violence at home. The solution in such a scenario may be complicated, but the first step is knowing the problem exists—and it takes asking the right questions and tracking the right data to do so.

Investors using a gender lens can request details—such as HR policies, presence of domestic violence training, and more granular data on absenteeism—and review it for cultural and gender sensitivity that will not only help to make socially impactful investment decisions, but ones with decreased risk and increased stability.

Leading employers also move beyond the easy answer. Have you ever heard someone managing an organization say, "We just can't seem to keep women in that role"? This is often a challenge relating to retaining women in sales roles. Consider the recent research looking at the design of a sales training program for cookstoves conducted by the Johns Hopkins Bloomberg School of Public Health, ESVAK Kenya, and Envirofit International in Kenya.[49] Although this story is about a salesforce in rural Africa, the principles of training with gender in mind translate to sales teams in any type of enterprise.

Envirofit sells clean cookstoves designed to reduce the cost, time, and health hazards of preparing meals in rural communities. Globally, men sell 90 percent of cookstoves, but 90 percent of three billion people who use cookstoves are women who live in these remote, hard-to-reach areas. The distribution model relies on what Envirofit called "last-mile entrepreneurs"—individuals in the community who are employed as sales agents.

In 2012, Envirofit piloted a women's empowerment training program for clean cookstove entrepreneurs in Kenya. Multiple factors contributed to the low representation of women in salesforces, but the one that intrigued Envirofit was Kenyan women's lower confidence than men in their entrepreneurial capabilities and their higher fear of failure. The existing training programs ignored this gender difference.

The firm tested an empowerment training model to equip salespeople (women and men) with business skills and utilize their personal motivations. The motivational component was the real innovation—including an introspective self-examination of key areas of people's lives: emotions, relationships, health, body, money, and work.

Sound's great for women, right? To find out, salespeople were randomly assigned to two groups: One received four days of traditional "entrepreneurial" training; the other had four days of "agency-based" training. The agency-based design benefited the psychological state of the women, as hypothesized. For instance, the measure of "grit," which in women is related to perseverance, increased from 69 percent to 90 percent of all women sampled.

In both groups, women entrepreneurs outsold their male counterparts by three to one. Women who purchased from other women were more likely to report consistent and correct usage and benefits than those who purchased from men. An intentional focus on gender inclusion in their salesforce drove increased revenue, stronger referrals, and lowered returns. And reviewing the training process to see what motivated women made the results of the whole team better. Using gender knowledge in the design of the training, Envirofit unlocked hidden sources of competitive advantage that could apply to any type of salesforce.

Supplier Relationships

In an era of rampant consumption and increasing transparency, the risks and rewards of managing a global supply chain require a gender lens. Every manufacturing company is watched critically by its customers. Nike felt this pressure early in the 1990s when it received criticism for sweatshop labor. The 2013 collapse of the Rana Plaza in Bangladesh again prompted customers to question, Who made my shirt? And are the workers who make them—who are primarily women—safe?

A gender-lens on multinational companies' supply chains is another powerful tool for management and investors. In 2014, The Harvard Kennedy School and the U.S. Chamber of Commerce Foundation launched a series of roundtables with corporate leaders looking for business advantages through empowering women in the supply chain.[50] They found encouraging examples from boardroom commitments to training programs in mines, farms, and factories. Particular initiatives, however, deliver only limited value unless there is a strategy to engage with women in core business operations and value chains.

For example, in 2010 Coca-Cola launched its "5 × 20" global commitment to economically engage five million women entrepreneurs across the company's value chain by 2020. The implementation, through locally tailored programs, targets specific women in six elements of Coca-Cola's value chain: producers, suppliers, distributors, retailers, recyclers, and artisans. Despite varied backgrounds, the women find similar benefits in the access to business skills, financial services, mentors, and peer networks. In northwest South Africa, for instance, women reported a 44 percent growth in sales and a 25 percent average jump in income. As of 2016, 5 × 20 has reached over 1.2 million women entrepreneurs in sixty countries.[51]

Still, supplier diversity and inclusion programs historically have struggled to meet goals. "We don't know where to find qualified women business owners to source from in international markets" is the painful refrain Elizabeth Vazquez hears repeatedly. In 2009 she founded WeConnect International with several leading corporations. Today WeConnect International educates and connects women-owned businesses based in over 100 countries with corporations representing over $1 trillion in annual purchasing power. Working with Vital Voices and other partners in two years they trained over 40,000 women business owners and track over $3 billion in new spending through connections to regional and global corporations looking to increase supply chain diversity.[52]

Multinational corporate supply chains sourcing from women-owned ventures can be significant and strategic. Part of Wal-Mart's Women's Empowerment Program includes the goal of sourcing over $20 billion in goods and services from women-owned businesses and doubling their sourcing from international women entrepreneurs by 2016. Ninety percent of Wal-Mart shoppers surveyed said they would be more likely to buy a product if they knew it was produced by a woman-owned business.[53] To tap this market, in 2014 Wal-Mart helped WeConnect International and WBENC launch the WomenOwned logo for in-store sales and an "Empowering Women Together" destination for online purchases from women-owned businesses.

Companies can strengthen the resiliency of their supply chains with a gender lens in other ways, too. For instance, 80 percent of garment workers globally are women: often young, under-educated, and living away from home. They lack formal training as well and the ability to advocate on their own behalf. In 2007, Gap, CARE, the International Center for Research on Women (ICRW), and Swasti Health Resource Center launched a workplace educational program called PACE (Personal Advancement and Career Enhancement) to provide training in time management, job skills, health, and financial literacy. As important, the program provides communication tools; training in legal literacy, gender norms, and influences; goal setting; and decision making.

In a 2013 evaluation PACE participants "reported that their self-esteem had increased by 50 percent, that they enjoyed a heightened sense of self-worth, and that they were able to communicate more effectively with their supervisors and managers." This is certainly a positive outcome, but how does it enhance the bottom line? Factory owners experienced increased productivity, efficiency, and retention, in some countries at remarkable rates. In Cambodia, PACE participants were 66 percent more likely to stay employed with their factory. Local communities also became engaged as women shared their knowledge and practices with friends and families.[54]

This shift to partnering throughout a supply chain to see women workers as an investment has also been taken on by a set of companies partnering with Business for Social Responsibility. The benefits are impressive. HERHealth companies, which invest in women's health and wellness, have achieved a 3 to 1 return on their investment from reduced absenteeism and turnover as well as enhanced productivity.[55]

Intel's Capital Investment in Women and Diversity

A different look at the supply chain begins with an organization's investment funds, which are the bets it makes to grow new markets or on potential acquisitions. Intel's Capital Diversity Fund, launched in 2015, is a $125 million fund strategically focused on businesses led by women and underrepresented minorities. This fund supports the firm's Diversity in Technology Initiative, which aims for the company to reach full representation of women and underrepresented minorities in its U.S. workforce by 2020. CEO Brian Krzanich's comments reflect a "shared value" approach to gender-lens investments: "We believe that a diverse and inclusive workplace is fundamental to delivering business results. Our goal with this new fund is to meaningfully support a technology startup workforce more reflective of society, and ultimately to benefit Intel and the broader economy through its success. The fund had made six investments by September 2015, using the same rigor and process of any other Intel investment.[56]

Salesforce's Marc Benioff told CNN in an interview that he regrets not creating gender inclusive practices sixteen years ago. "When I started Salesforce I wanted to start a new technology company. I wish I could rewind time and put women's equality issues in the culture from the beginning."[57]

We suspect that a lot of the executives, leaders, entrepreneurs, and researchers we profiled in this chapter feel the same way. Whether they follow the leader, react to peer pressure, or truly believe, there is no reason not to consider how relevant gender analysis could impact all aspects of business—from startups to global giants.

Successful entrepreneurs, who are now startup investors like Mitch Kapor of Lotus Notes fame and his wife, Freada Klein Kapor, are also encouraging new companies not to have those regrets. The "Founder's Commitment" of Kapor Capital provides a four-part roadmap for startups to foster diverse and inclusive cultures early. Thirty-eight of Kapor's 74 investments (51 percent) have a founder who is a woman or a "person of color from an underrepresented background." Fifty-two of its portfolio companies—almost two thirds—have signed the Commitment, and it has become a standard term in all of Kapor Capital's new investment agreements.[58]

It is very early days in the development of methods and measures to evaluate gender performance in business. It takes time and patience to piece together the information that is relevant for a specific investment decision. And "there is no one-size-fits-all approach to gender inclusive leadership," says Colleen Ammerman, Director of the Harvard Business School Gender Initiative. "To deliver performance benefits companies must be willing to make investments and learn over time, not simply grab an off-the-shelf solution."[59]

The good news is there is less need for overly simplified packaged solutions when diverse solutions are emerging that are better for women and bottom lines.

Notes

1. Joseph Keefe, "Gender Equality as an Investment Concept," Pax World Investment, 2016.
2. Michelle Quinn, "Salesforce Adds $3 Million to Female Workers' Pay," SiliconBeat (November 5, 2015). www.siliconbeat.com/2015/11/05/will-tech-follow-salesforce-and-adjust-womens-pay/.
3. Cindy Robbins, "Equality at Salesforce: An Equal Pay Update," SalesforceBlog (March 8, 2016). www.salesforce.com/blog/2016/03/equality-at-salesforce-equal-pay.html.
4. Iris Bohnet, *What Works: Gender Equality by Design* (Cambridge MA: The Belknap Press of Harvard University Press, 2016), p. 4.

5. RobecoSAM Corporate Sustainability Assessment Methodology, 2016. www.sustainability-indices.com/images/corporate-sustainability-assessment-methodology-guidebook.pdf.

6. http://cci.mit.edu/.

7. Anita Williams Woolley, Christopher F. Chabris, Alex Pentland, Nada Hashmi, and Thomas W. Malone, "Evidence for a Collective Intelligence Factor in the Performance of Human Groups," *Science* (October 29, 2010). www.sciencemag.org/cgi/content/abstract/science.1193147.

8. London Business School, *Innovative Potential: Men and Women in Teams*, 2007. The Lehman Brothers Centre for Women in Business.

9. PWC, *Next Generation Diversity: Developing Tomorrow's Female Leaders* (PriceWaterhouseCoopers, 2014), p. 18. www.pwc.com/gx/en/women-at-pwc/internationalwomensday/assets/next-generation-diversity-publication.pdf.

10. Iris Bohnet, Harvard Business Review, *How to Take the Bias Out of Interviews*, April 18, 2016, HTTPS://HBR.ORG/2016/04/HOW-TO-TAKE-THE-BIAS-OUT-OF-INTERVIEWS.

11. Iris Bohnet Alexandra van Geen Max H. Bazerman, Harvard Business Review, *When Performance Trumps Gender Bias: Joint Versus Separate Evaluation*, March 16, 2012. http://hbswk.hbs.edu/item/when-performance-trumps-gender-bias-joint-versus-separate-evaluation.

12. "Women in the Workplace", McKinsey & Co. and LeanIn.org, 2015, p. 20, womenintheworkplace.com/ui/pdfs/Women_in_the_Workplace_2014.pdf?v=5.

13. "Women's Economic Empowerment Initiative Goals," corporate.walmart.com/global-responsibility/womens-economic-empowerment/our-goals.

14. Bohnet, p. 105.

15. Elizabeth Segran, "EDGE Is Like the LEED of Gender Equality Certification—Can It Help Fix the Gender Gap?" *Fast Company* (August 26, 2014). www.fastcompany.com/3034742/edge-is-like-the-leed-of-gender-equality-certification-can-it-help-fix-the-gender-gap.

16. Personal Interview (Aniela Unguresan, September 16, 2015).

17. *Corporate Boards: Strategies to Address the Representation of Women Include Federal Disclosure Requirements* (Washington, DC: United States Government Accounting Office, December 2015), p. 1.

18. In fact, in a 2015 CFA Institute Study respondents were 28 percent more likely to say they incorporated Governance factors than Environmental or Social factors in their decision making. CFA Institute, 2015 Environmental, Social and Governance (ESG) Survey, "ESG Issues in Investing: Investors Debunk the Myths."

19. Personal communication (Rosemary Kenney, March 9, 2016).

20. www.2020wob.com/about/idea.

21. www.2020wob.com/take-action/form-2020-team.

22. "Environmental, Social and Governance (ESG) Survey", June 2015, page 9, https://www.cfainstitute.org/Survey/esg_survey_report.pdf

23. "The Bottom Line: Corporate Performance and Women's Representation on Boards 2004–2008", Catalyst, March 1, 2011, http://www.catalyst.org/system/files/the_bottom_line_corporate_performance_and_women%27s_representation_on_boards_%282004-2008%29.pdf.

24. Climb to the Top—Tracking Gender Diversity on Corporate Boards by André Chanavat and Katharine Ramsden, October 2014, page 9, http://thomsonreuters.com/content/dam/openweb/documents/pdf/corporate/corporate-responsibility/tracking-gender-diversity-on-corporate-boards.pdf.

25. Marcus Noland, Tyler Moran, Barbara Kotschwar "Is Gender Diversity Profitable? Evidence from a Global Survey", Peterson Institute for International Economics, February 2015, page 7, https://piie.com/publications/wp/wp16-3.pdf.

26. "Women on Boards: Global Trends in Gender Diversity on Corporate Boards," MSCI (November 2015), p. 2. Time period was between 12/2009 and 8/2015. Strong female leadership is defined as three or more women on the board, a female CEO and one woman on the board, or a percentage of women on the board over country average—without having been implicated in discrimination allegations in the past three years. The latter criteria disqualified 53 companies.

27. "WIL: Barclays Women in Leadership ETN." etn.barclays.com/US/7/en/etnsnapshot.app?instrumentId=269035.

28. Gender Capitalism: The Agenda with Steve Paikin, Air date: February 11, 2015, http://tvo.org/video/programs/the-agenda-with-steve-paikin/gender-capitalism.

29. Solange Charas, International Journal of Disclosure and Governance, May 2015, Volume 12, http://link.springer.com/journal/41310/12/2/page/1"Issue 2, pp 107–131.

30. Ibid., p. 6. Time frame 2012–2015, normalized for market capitalization.

31. Kellie McElhaney, "More Female Board Directors Add Up to Improved Sustainability Performance," Berkeley Haas (October 14, 2012). newsroom.haas.berkeley.edu/research-news/more-female-board-directors-add-improved-sustainability-performance.

32. Sixteen percent of S&P 1500 board seats are held by women, 15 percent of S&P Midcap 400 and 12 percent of S&P SmallCap 600 directorships are held by women. For more detailed information on the trends and current composition see the E&Y report and website, http://www.ey

.com/GL/en/Issues/Governance-and-reporting/Women-on-US-boards—what-are-we-seeing#gender-diversity-is-rising.

33. Jena McGregor, "There Are More Men on Corporate Boards Named John, Robert, William, or James than There Are Women on Boards Altogether," *Washington Post* (January 25, 2015). www.washingtonpost .com/news/on-leadership/wp/2015/02/25/there-are-more-men-on-corporate-boards-named-john-robert-william-or-james-than-there-are-women-altogether/.

34. Personal Interview (Joseph Keefe, November 2, 2015).

35. Marcus Noland, Tyler Moran, and Barbara Kotschwar, *Is Gender Diversity Profitable? Evidence from a Global Survey* (February 2016). www.iie .com/publications/wp/wp16-3.pdf.

36. "When Women Thrive, Businesses Thrive," 2016 Executive Summary Mercer McLennan Companies. www.mercer.com/content/dam/mercer/attachments/private/nurture-cycle/WWT-Executive-Summary-2016.pdf.

37. Laurie Bassi, David Creelman, and Andrew Lambert, "The Smarter Annual Report How Companies Are Integrating Financial and Human Capital Reporting" (2015).

38. Cristian L. Dezsö and David G. Ross, *Girl Power: Female Participation in Top Management and Firm Performance*, Columbia Business School, August 2008.

39. Personal Interview (Aniela Unguresan, September 16, 2015).

40. www.mercer.com/newsroom/top-ceos-in-davos-say-men-matter-in-driving-gender-diversity.html.

41. *Fortune*'s Best Companies to Work For, 2016. fortune.com/best-companies/.

42. "100 Best Workplaces for Women," *Fortune*. fortune.com/best-workplaces-for-women/.

43. "The State of the American Manager: Analytics and Advice for Leaders," *Gallup International*, p. 27.

44. "Women in the Workplace," McKinsey & Co. and LeanIn.org, (2015). p. 20. womenintheworkplace.com/ui/pdfs/Women_in_the_Workplace_2015.pdf?v=5.

45. rework.withgoogle.com/guides/unbiasing-raise-awareness/steps/introduction/.

46. *Putting Gender Smart Commitments into Practice: SheWork's One-Year Progress Report* (Washington, DC: International Finance Corporation, 2015). www.ifc.org/wps/wcm/connect/ebeb1f8049f25315b48fb7e54d141794/PuttingGender-Smart+Commitments+Into+Practice.pdf?MOD=AJPERES.

47. *Domestic Violence: Prevalence and Implications for Employment Among Welfare Recipients* (Washington, DC: U.S. General Accounting Office, 1998).

48. Christine Hughes, Mara Bolis, Rebecca Fries, and Stephanie Finigan, "Women's Economic Inequality and Domestic Violence: Exploring the Links and Empowering Women," Oxfam (July 31, 2015). policy-practice.oxfam.org.uk/publications/womens-economic-inequality-and-domestic-violence-exploring-the-links-and-empowe-560892.

49. www.envirofit.org/images/news/Lessons_learned.pdf.

50. Nelson, Jane, Marli Porth, Kara Valikai, and Honor McGee, *A Path to Empowerment: The Role of Corporations in Supporting Women's Economic Progress* (Cambridge, MA: The CSR Initiative at the Harvard Kennedy School and the U.S. Chamber of Commerce Foundation Corporate Citizenship Center, 2015).

51. *The Coca-Cola Company's 5by20 Initiative Reaches More Than 1.2 Million Women Entrepreneurs*, Apr 12, 2016, http://www.coca-colacompany.com/press-center/press-releases/the-coca-cola-company-s-5by20-initiative-reaches-more-than-1-2-million-women-entrepreneurs.

52. "Clinton Global Initiative Commitment." weconnectinternational.org/en/clinton-global-initiative-commitment.

53. Patrick Clark, Bloomberg News, Coming Soon to Walmart: A New Way to Find Products from Women Entrepreneurs, June 26, 2014, http://www.bloomberg.com/news/articles/2014-06-26/coming-soon-to-walmart-a-new-way-to-find-products-from-women-entrepreneurs.

54. Weiss, Ellen. P.A.C.E graduates make important gains in their personal and work lives, October 2, 2013, www.icrw.org/media/news/icrw-finds-gap-inc-pace-program-yields-high-returns-women-and-businesses.

55. Racheal Meiers, "Women and Sustainability: Investing in Women's Health," *BSR* (March 2011).

56. Intel Capital Press Release, Intel Capital launches $125M Diversity Fund to invest in startups run by women underrepresented minorities, June 9, 2015, http://www.intelcapital.com/news/news.html?id=333.

57. Poppy Harlow, Marc Benioff: Now I Understand Women's Equality, CNN, June 15, 2015, http://www.cnn.com/videos/business/2015/06/15/salesforce-ceo-benioff-workplace-equality.cnn.

58. Megan Rose Dickey, "Kapor Capital Will Start Requiring New Portfolio Startups to Invest In Diversity and Inclusion," *TechCrunch* (January 21, 2016). (@meganrosedickey) techcrunch.com/2016/01/21/kapor-capital-founders-commitment/.

59. Personal Interview (Colleen Ammerman, March 8, 2016).

CHAPTER 7

Getting Beyond Pink

"Remember when you were 9 or 10 and you were this independent little girl climbing trees and saying, 'I know what I want, I know what I think'? she says. That was before gender descended for most of us."[1]

—Gloria Steinem

In the musical adaptation of J. M. Barrie's children's classic *Peter Pan*, the lost boy of Neverland sings soulfully, "If growing up means it would be beneath my dignity to climb a tree, I'll never grow up, never grow up, not me." Peter, a brilliantly rendered and comforting character, is widely accepted by all kids and adults. But adult consciousness of gender has descended upon young girls—especially tweens. For them, engaging in the cultural framing and conversations about gender has become part of growing up. Eight-year-old Annie Rose was outraged when she opened her *Star Wars* version of the famous board game, Monopoly, only to discover that Rey of *Star Wars, Episode VII: The Force Awakens* was not in the game. Rey is the most fierce and independent female lead in the almost 40-year history of George Lucas's epic movie franchise.

Annie became an instant heroine in the battle against sexism in product design and marketing when her mother, Carrie Goldman, tweeted this letter:

Dear Hasbro,

How could you leave out Rey? She belongs in Star Wars Monopoly and all the other Star Wars games! Without her, THERE IS NO FORCE AWAKENS ... and without her, the bad guys would have won! Besides, boys and girls need to see women can be strong as men ... Sincerely—Annie Rose (age 8).[2]

Annie Rose is not the only young girl to shout out on gender. Twelve-year-old sixth-grader Madeline Messer was so frustrated by the absence of female avatars in her action figure iPhone video games she decided to analyze 50 popular video games to get proof. Her findings were published in an OpEd in the *Washington Post*. In her sample, programmers "built in" boy characters in 98 percent of the games. And "what shocked me," she opined, "was that only 46 percent offered girl characters," adding that 18 percent of the characters were genderless potatoes, cats, or monkeys.[3]

Man or woman, child or adult, no one is neutral about gender. In the words of Stanford sociologist Cecilia Ridgeway, we are "framed by gender."[4] But where Ridgeway's book delves into the question of why gender inequality between men and women is so persistent – and is certainly worth reading—we frame a discussion of the role gender research and analysis can play in developing products and services and growing markets. From toys and banking services, to computer operating systems and treatments for heart disease, basic awareness of gender differences and deeper gender research is improving the quality of men's and women's lives while revealing how cultural gender biases limit innovation.

A Gendered Quest for Better Innovation

News reports regularly cover the lack of women working in industrial and software design, and all types of basic and applied scientific and medical research. Far less attention is paid to gaps in gender knowledge which compromise human health and safety, regardless of who is in the lab or at the drawing board.

Consider crash test dummies used in automotive safety testing. In 1949, the U.S. Airforce commissioned Samuel W. Alderson of

Alderson Research Labs and the Sierra Engineering Co. to create the first crash test dummy, "Sierra Sam". Named after his inventor, Sierra Sam was used to test aircraft ejection seats, aviation helmets, and pilot restraint harnesses. When the first mandatory federal seatbelt law for automobiles passed in 1968, Alderson built another version of the first test dummy for General Motors and Ford. But the first adult-size female dummy wasn't built until 1987 when the Centers for Disease Control awarded a grant to Ohio State University to create one to test the effectiveness of seatbelts and shoulder harnesses.

You would think that after the addition of a female prototype, separate safety tests on dummies designed for male and female auto drivers would have immediately become standard. Not so. The National Highway Transit and Safety Administration has only used a female dummy in federal compliance crash tests since 2003, mostly to ensure an air bag's safety.[5]

Len Vinsel, Assistant Professor of Science and Technology Studies at the Stevens Institute of Technology, makes a compelling argument that women's safety was compromised for decades by the way in which automotive companies fought safety regulation and conducted safety tests. "Although marketers had begun to account for the tastes of women as potential consumers well before the 1960s, many automakers claimed that considering women's health in engineering was too radical," Vinsel writes. Auto executives throughout the industry believed there was no female dummy because it was unnecessary, and they thought it would cost too much and take too long to develop, Vinsel says.[6]

Gender knowledge gaps in automotive engineering and safety testing, and in the information available for car buyers, is still a problem today. The need for female and male dummies in different tests is clear. Lynda Tran, a NHTSA spokesperson told a *Washington Post* reporter in 2012, "Studies show that women, having smaller bones and lower bone density, are at greater risk than men of suffering injury or death in crashes. Their less muscular necks make them more vulnerable to whiplash. In general, smaller people cannot tolerate crash forces as well as can full-sized men."[7]

Similarly, airbags designed for the average-size male will hit men in the upper chest, which creates a cushion for their bodies and heads. A small woman, however, might hit the inflated airbag with her chin first. This would cause her head to snap back abruptly, potentially causing serious neck and spinal injuries. Len Vinsel cites tests with female mannequins where small women were almost three times as likely as their average male counterparts to be seriously injured or killed.

From her office in Palo Alto, Londa Schiebinger, a History of Science professor at Stanford University, advocates for this type of deep gender analysis in R&D to drive product and service innovations ranging from slight shifts to complete disruptions.[8] Schiebinger, one of the world's leading experts in "gendered innovation," asks how we can harness the creative power of inclusive sex and gender analysis for innovation and discovery. She argues that organizations and initiatives must make gender a variable when establishing research priorities, methods of analysis, and data gathering. Explaining her passion, Schiebinger says, "Once you start looking, you find that taking gender into account can improve almost anything with a human endpoint–stem cell research, assistive technologies for the elderly, automobile design, transportation systems, osteoporosis research in men, and natural language processing."

Thinking broadly, Schiebinger likes to say there are three "fixes" for achieving gender equity for women in STEM professions. The first fix is to increase the number of women studying and working in these fields. She believes common fixes in this category, including coaching women to be more competitive, instruction in self-promotion, and mentoring, are essential but not sufficient. The second is to fix the institutions. This focuses on changes in processes and structures (e.g., institutionalizing flexibility in work assignments or equity in performance reviews and promotions). The third is "fixing the knowledge" through gendered innovation processes "that integrate sex and gender analysis into all phases of basic and applied research to assure excellence and quality in outcomes."[9]

And in her role as director of the EU/US Gendered Innovations in Science, Health & Medicine, Engineering and Environment, Schiebinger also chairs a group of more than sixty experts from Europe and North America who reported on twenty one practical case studies of gender analysis methods used in research to stimulate new knowledge and technologies and create products and services that are more responsive to societal needs. The cases cover a large variety of products and services, including heart disease diagnostics, animal research, scientific text-books, video game design, seat-belt design for pregnant women, and the design of public transportation systems, among others.

Most basic research with animal models in studies focuses on males and excludes females, according to the report which looked specifically at early phase clinical trials for health and biomedical research. Animal research for trials repeatedly focused on male animals, under-represented females, and failed to report sex disaggregated dated in the published results. Researchers may have hoped by only including male animals to reduce the cost of research or to avoid the impact of fluctuating female hormone levels on experimental outcomes. This practice, however, results in less knowledge about disease in females, the inability to use sex as a variable in studies, and missed opportunities to understand how uniquely female characteristics, such as pregnancy, affect and are affected by diseases. Currently, U.S. legislation requires "sufficient representation of women to allow for sex analysis" only for Phase III clinical trials.

In one example of possibilities that could otherwise be missed, studying sex differences in animal models could lead to new post-traumatic brain injury treatments, as data from both male and female animals informs observations of gender differences in a disease. Traumatic brain injury is more common in men than in women, but by studying the impact of treatments on male and female rats, and specifically on female rats through the estrous cycle and during pregnancy, researchers identified a potential role of progesterone in protecting against brain damage.

Young Madeline Messer will be glad to know that Londa Schiebinger and her colleagues are as concerned about the state of play in video games as she is. "The stereotype of gaming as masculine persists, even though women have become active gamers," their report asserts. Innovation researchers applied gendered disaggregation data gathering techniques to improve the overall quality of the game experience. Researchers are then able to analyze how gender intersects with, and is influenced by, factors beyond gender, such as age, experience, and geographic location. Taking the examples off the screen and to the streets, another case shows how disaggregating gender data and combining it with factors such as income, marital, and family status can lead to design of public transport systems which address the needs of diverse populations (e.g., a single woman head of household who needs to make stops on her commute for kids' schools).

Problems to Avoid When Analyzing Gender

Dr Schiebinger's team documented state-of-the-art methods of sex and gender analysis as well as general methodology. They summarize a set of common challenges found across their case studies.

- *Being blind to potential differences of sex and gender*—may result in missed business opportunities, with certain groups of people being left out, poorly accommodated, etc.
- *Treating "women" and "men" as homogeneous groups*—ignores differences among women and among men.
- *Over-emphasizing differences between women and men*—can cause engineers to overlook significant commonalities between women and men.
- *Designing to stereotypes*—may result in unpopular products.

Source: "Gendered Innovations: How Gender Analysis Contributes to Research", European Commission, 2013, p. 117.

Or consider computer software and hardware, now a ubiquitous part of our lives, and one that is gender neutral, right? Not according to the new field of Gender Humane Computer Interface (Gender HCI), which poses a provocative question: "What if females and males would be better supported at problem-solving if the problem-solving software they used were changed to take into account individual differences that often cluster by gender?" HCI researchers looking at gender issues rarely considered in software development, and drawing on psychology, computer science, marketing, neuroscience, education, and economics, found that males and females do in fact solve problems, communicate, and process information differently. The differences cluster in five areas: motivations, information processing style, risk approach, computer self-efficacy, and willingness to explore and tinker. Furthermore, HCI researchers have found that male software designers often inadvertently design software or hardware the way they would interact with it, and thus don't consider that there might be gender differences. In spreadsheet problem-solving tasks, for example, an HCI study found that women end users were significantly slower than men to try out unfamiliar features. This is gender knowledge that software developers could use to greatly improve software utility for women and make improvements for all users.

Margaret Burnett, a professor of computer science at Oregon State University and an HCI innovator, created the GenderMag Kit (Mag being shorthand for *magnify*) to identify gender-related differences and usability issues for men and women. The GenderMag magnifies the five gender differences by bringing to life carefully construed personas or archetypes of software users named Abby, Patricia, Patrick, and Tim.[10] Each persona conducts a "cognitive walkthrough" with a software system to test user interactions (ease and difficulty to accomplish explicit tasks). For software developers, the GenderMag process (which can be done in three hours) brings out the implications of their design decisions. For instance, a field study on four software development teams who used GenderMag to evaluate their products showed 25 percent of the software features they evaluated had gender-inclusiveness issues to resolve.[11]

Burnett and other advocates of gender-led innovation in software development attended the first-ever "Hack for Her" summit sponsored by Microsoft in 2016. Christina Chen, Microsoft's General Manager, Emerging Devices Experience, told the assembled crowd the company is aiming "to increase awareness of gender-inclusive product development" and opportunities to better serve diverse user groups. Chen called Hack for Her a "Microsoft-led movement that brings together people of diverse backgrounds, skills and professions to create experiences that work well for women—and spawn new market opportunities."[12]

Klaus Schroeder, a Danish industrial designer and speaker at the inaugural Hack for Her, added to the fomenting feeling of a movement: "Why develop for and with women? Because it's a game-changer for business and innovation … Applying a female lens to the experiences we deliver is a big opportunity for improvement in many industries and organizations, not just at Microsoft."[13]

Perils of Thinking Pink or Blue

To be *punked* by a friend, according to the Urban Dictionary, is "a way to describe someone ripping you off, tricking you or teasing you." When you are "pinked" by a company, it means the exact same product is marketed to men and women, and packaged differently. A favorite men's razor is simply repackaged to be pretty in pink for girls and women. A high-performance ski in green in the men's section of a store is identical to the pink ski in the women's section.

There is no change in the materials, weight, design engineering that could enhance performance for one sex or the other. (Thinking back to our seatbelt stories, you can imagine this is also dangerous if the women consumers assume the pink product has been specially designed, engineered, or tested for women.) Some companies charge a premium—often called a "pink tax"–on the female version of the product.[14] Young Madeline Messer discovered how video game makers use this gendered pricing strategy. In the fifty game apps she studied, 90 percent of the downloads of boy characters were free while only 15 percent of the girl characters were. The 60 percent of girls who downloaded the app for a game called Temple Run had to pay more for a girl character. That system, Messer wrote, "seems ridiculous."

A group of women in France calling themselves the "Collectif Georgette Sand," named after the woman novelist Amantine-Lucile-Aurore Dupin, who wrote under the pseudonym George Sand, collected 40,000 signatures to challenge the Monoprix supermarket chain for marking up their prices with a pink tax. The five-pack of pink disposable razors, for instance, was priced at €1.80, while the packet of 10 blue disposable razors was priced at €1.72.[15]

Furthering the complexity, just because *changes* in product design happen, doesn't mean those changes were supported by solid gender research or best for women. Simply shrinking a men's product to make it smaller for women is also common—"shrink it and pink it," as the saying goes. This often happens with athletic market products, gear, and clothing. As Christine Day, ex-CEO of Lululemon, put it, "They are making women mini men, not celebrating the diversity of who women are."[16] Alternatively, brands like LuluLemon, Patagonia, and Title Nine, have become leaders in the "athleisure" category by designing products for women that are fashionable, comfortable, and celebrate their diversity.

Looking at younger generations specifically, the $22 billion U.S. toy industry, including manufacturers and retailers, are waking up to the fact that some girls love running around in a Captain America suit and playing video games as much as they love playing with Barbie dolls and pink princesses. The Twitter site @LetToysBeToys, sponsored by a UK-based nonprofit advocacy group started by parents, asks the toy and publishing industries to "stop limiting children's interests by promoting some toys and books as only suitable for girls, and others only for boys." They argue that gender-based marketing of typecast toys for boys or for girls interferes with a child's imagination. Alternatively, the group wants retailers and manufacturers to "categorize and label toys by theme or function, rather than by gender, and let the children decide which toys they enjoy best." After a parent protested on Twitter about an in-store display at Target of "Girls' Building Sets" the big-box family retailer stopped labeling toys for girls or boys in their stores. The Disney Store eliminated girl and boy designations from its children's Halloween costumes in 2015 and has embraced generic labels on backpacks and other accessories.[17]

But rather than going from the simple assumption that "boys will be boys and girls will be girls" to being completely neutral, a stronger approach embraces gender differences in product design and marketing. Take bicycles, for example. Sure, many little girls will want a pink bike with colored tassels on the handlebars. And for years, women's bikes were either men's bikes painted a different color, or only slightly modified. Today, women who love biking have more options. In 2010, in recognition of the growth of women in cycling and their differing needs, Giant Manufacturing Co., Ltd., the world's largest bicycle manufacturer launched Liv/giant, a global brand "committed to the female cyclist."[18] Liv/giant Cycling invites women into the cycling lifestyle, providing not only products but also cycling education and networks for women bikers with different skills and interests. "The biggest thing about Liv/giant [is that] we really truly are a community," says Jackie Baker, the brand's global marketing manager. "We want to be that go-to resource for all women who are into cycling, whether you are Marianne Vos [the Olympic champion] or whether you are on your third day out on the bike." The Liv/giant team, including the designers, engineers, and managers, are primarily women, which stands out in an industry that is primarily run by men. (The Liv example illustrates the value chain approach; every decision about this bike, from concept to sale, was touched by women.)

Liv/giant bike designers begin with "white paper" and design what they believe best addresses the women's market, including and featuring a 27.5 wheel size, with lighter weight. This "gives you that flickability, that playfulness," says Abigail Santurbane, the Liv/giant category manager.[19] Liv/giant also changed store layouts to be less intimidating to newcomers—both to the brand and to the sport. And they recognized that the brand promise went far beyond the metals in the bike, to the vision for girls and women as part of a racing movement.

Historically, there has been hesitation—even outright refusal—on the part of men and women in businesses to address gender differences in product design and marketing because a "woman's" product might be seen as inferior to a "man's." Making things different—even with good reason—opens one up to criticism of those differences, so all too often it's avoided. Leaders say "We don't think women need different products" or "We don't believe in offering a women's product." In the financial services industry, we hear this all the time.

However, the people who make these arguments are not listening to women who, in survey after survey, say the customer service in financial firms, especially in the investment advisory segment, fails women.[20] More than half of women with investible assets of $1 million think that their financial advisor doesn't understand them, according to the Center for Talent Innovation, a New York–based business management research thinktank.[21] Their international survey of women and men from the United States, United Kingdom, India, China, Singapore, and Hong Kong strongly suggests women care less about whether a man or a woman is their advisor, and much more about whether their financial advisor is "gender smart." As study authors Andrea Turner Moffitt and Sylvia Hewlett wrote, "What women want everywhere" is a service environment "where they feel welcome to ask questions and are assured they feel heard and understood. Advisors who understand and honor a woman's financial, personal, and social priorities are likely to win her trust, satisfaction and loyalty."[22] In other words, it's not just the products themselves: the way the service is offered is an important part of the overall service experience. The study defined a satisfying experience as one where the advisor takes the time to educate them, where they feel safe to learn, and where they have confidence that the strategy the advisor delivers aligns with their life goals.

Australia's oldest bank, Westpac, plc, provides an example of the value created when the distinct needs of women are understood. In the 1990s, Westpac executives took note of women's rising educational attainment levels, labor force participation, and assets under their control. These trends inspired an internal research project to determine the distinct needs and preferences of women, to inform the design of new service offerings for women. Westpac's market research revealed women did not necessarily need different financial products than men but they did have different priorities for service. Specifically, women tend to expect more information before making a commitment to apply for a loan. They tend to be less financially educated. They are less likely than men to be part of a business network. And poignantly, their surveys showed Australian women felt a lack of respect from the financial community.

In 1999, Westpac became the only Australian bank with a women's unit dedicated to women's needs as customers, including providing networking support for women entrepreneurs seeking capital and building their businesses and careers. This was accomplished through the unit's *customer value proposition* (CVP). The subbrand, Ruby, takes a holistic approach to finance, including education and a network of peers and mentors. Internally, the brand created momentum as staff were excited about the tools and opportunity to target customers. Its online portal, "Ruby Connection," reaffirmed the commitment to education and community (as the portal was not used to sell product) while still attracting women clients. In person networking events for women owners of small and medium-sized businesses and high net worth women clients round out the offering.

The CVP was connected and fundamental to Westpac's long-term vision. "I saw becoming the Bank of Choice for Women as a long-term strategy integral to our core business, not just an add-on," says Larke Riemer, Westpac's director of Women's Markets, who spent three decades with the bank and led the Women's Markets unit before retiring in February 2015.

In March 2014, Westpac Women's Markets unit boasted 2.1 million women who are primary account holders and contributed AUD $1.55 billion in annualized revenue to Westpac's bottom line. Furthermore, Westpac's women customers have higher Net Promoter Scores (meaning they'll recommend the brand to others) than men, which drives business across the bank's divisions and supports the growth of the firm's footprint beyond Australia and New Zealand.

As of November 2015, Westpac had 13.1 million customers served by five divisions covering consumer, commercial, and wealth management services.[23] It is also a member of the Global Women's Banking Alliance, supporting women's initiatives in the Pacific Rim region. Westpac is also recognized by the World Economic Forum as one of its Global 100 "Most Sustainable Corporations in the World."[24]

Westpac had started back in the 1990s to become an employer of choice for women at the same time it was introducing Ruby and developing its women's marketing strategies. In the mid-2000s, the bank lost some of its internal focus on women in management. The appointment of a woman CEO in 2010 revived their focus and the momentum. In 2010 Westpac, it announced a target of 40 percent women in leadership roles, which it achieved three years later. The firm is tracking for 50 percent women in its leadership by 2017.[25]

Westpac and Liv/giant provide examples that underscore that women are not a niche market and do have desires and needs that warrant a deeper understanding. Surprisingly, many firms have not fully evaluated their customer segments using a gender lens. Investors can benefit from asking the question, "Does this leadership team fully understand the opportunities the women's market presents for our product?"

Raising Gender IQ in Marketing and Branding

Opportunities to improve a brand's gender image can be right in front of a company's eyes, but it takes gender diverse product development and marketing teams to see them. Take the July 2015 overhaul to Facebook's "friends" icon. The need for a change was seen by a new designer, Caitlin Winner, who discovered a "chip" in the shoulder of the iconic woman in the company glyph kit. The chip was placed exactly where the male icon would be placed in front of her for the "friends" icon. Her observation motivated her to update both the male and female icons, noting, "As a woman, educated at a women's college, it was hard *not* to read into the symbolism of the current icon; the woman was quite literally in the shadow of the man, she was not in a position to lean in."[26] After giving the woman a hip bob and smoothing the shoulders of the man, she placed the woman in front of the man, and adjusted their sizing to appear more equal. Facebook's Global Director of Diversity Maxine Williams promoted the shift and praised Caitlin's "fearless approach to changing our design." "The more diversity there is in our population, the more we will be able to check ourselves on bias in product decisions and elsewhere," she said.[27] The icon change, while subtle, was magnified through social media. And Facebook amplified the value of the icon update by linking it to its cultural embrace of diversity, which appeals to the talented, highly sought after employees it wants to attract.

The portrayal of girls and women in advertising campaigns is becoming less sexist and more respectful in many industries, but not fast enough. Women leaders in the advertising industry—executives, agency founders, and creative directors—interviewed by the *New York Times Magazine* in 2016 say they still feel they work in "a white man's world." This perception persists despite women making up almost 50 percent of those working in the advertising industry—though only including a relatively small number in top executive positions.

Only 11 percent of the creative directors of U.S. advertising agencies are women, according to the 3% Conference, an organization advocating for retaining more women in creative roles at agencies.[28] It is not surprising that with so few women in creative roles, the majority of ads still portray either stereotyped women—mothers mopping floors, girls' nights out—or macho stereotypes—men boxing and riding bulls—or worst, the blatant use of sexually suggestive ads to sell products.[29] Unfortunately, consumer critics fed up with these ads find it hard to be heard. This is why organizations like the Representation Project exist: Its mission is to ensure the voices of individuals and communities challenging stereotypes, and gender disrespect, are heard and addressed by ad agencies and advertisers. Since the 2013 Super Bowl and the ads that aired during it, the #notbuyingit campaign from the Representation Project has called out sexism in the media. The project's success spawned a list of "all-time worst offenders" as well as an app to monitor future ads. Impressions to date total more than 60 million and have pressured major brands like GoDaddy, Amazon, and Bud Light to make substantial changes in their portrayal of women.[30]

With the distribution channels at everyone's fingertips these days, brands that inadvertently exclude or exploit sexist or negative images of women may find themselves on the wrong side of a viral media explosion. And enough of the alternatives, which celebrate women's diversity, have gone viral that they are now in their own ad category known as *femvertising*. The category kicked off in 2004 with Unilever's Dove Campaign for "Real Beauty," a rebuttal to the traditional media beauty norms. The multi-year and multi-media effort celebrates women's physiques of all types and inspires the typical girl and woman to be comfortable in their own skin.

The first stage of the campaign centered on a series of billboard advertisements, initially in Germany and the United Kingdom, and later worldwide, which showcased photographs of ordinary women (not professional models).

SheKnows Media, a digital marketing company, put out a survey in 2014 to find out precisely how women felt about femvertising ads. In the survey of 628 American women, 52 percent said they had purchased a product because they liked the way the company portrayed women in the ads. Fifty-six percent of those respondents were in the Millennial demographic. Forty-three percent said female empowerment ads made them feel good about supporting the brand. Additionally, 45 percent said they had shared an ad they considered "pro-female" with friends and 46 percent started following a company on social media after seeing an advertisement. Over 90 percent recalled at least one particular femvertising campaign, with many citing the "Dove's Real Beauty" as their example.[31] In an oversaturated world where capturing your viewer is becoming harder and harder, the statistics above are nontrivial to brands.

With that compelling survey data in hand, SheKnows launched the first #Femvertising Awards in 2015.[32] While social media agencies like SheKnows are first movers, the major global advertising houses have taken notice and are following. "It's the beginning of a change—a change that will stick because what we are starting to see is it works," Andrew Robertson, CEO of global marketing powerhouse BBDO Worldwide, said in an interview at a New York Advertising Week event in 2014. "It creates stronger relationships with women, which in turn results in selling more stuff … and I think, as people see and get confidence from that, we will see more and more."[33]

Should investors take advertising into consideration? They do, and for a variety of reasons. If you want your capital to speak in support of campaigns like the Representation Project, you probably question firms that still advertise like it was 1970. Of course it's all too easy for a firm to create a commercial without actually doing anything else—especially some of the harder and lasting work like women on boards, in management, pay equity, and so on. Making superficial changes or *pinkwashing* has been compared to *greenwashing* (when companies falsely claim environmental benefits). On the other hand, decades of overwhelming research confirms how much media influences consumers, so those *pinkwashed* commercials—though not all a company can or should do—do make a difference. Advertising is ubiquitous and unavoidable. So it is not only possible, but also likely, that images that empower women can contribute to changing attitudes in society and to sales, and that the two should work together. Investors also need to consider patterns of marketing and advertising that typecast and undervalue women for the market risk they represent. A number of ESG funds use a gender lens to consider the portrayal of women in advertising and media as an indicator of the executive team's sensitivity to gender bias and awareness of women's markets.

Getty Images, one of the world's leading vendors of high-quality stock photography, saw a market opportunity after observing these trends. In partnership with Sheryl Sandberg's LeanIn.org, they launched a carefully curated collection of photography for companies inclined to refresh their images of women. Before the partnership, the three most searched words in Getty Images were "women," "business," and "family," but all they had to offer were photos of stereotyped bankers in pantsuits, multi-tasking moms, and girls going wild on a night out. Missing were women as surgeons, soldiers, scientists, sculptors, and athletes, women on business trips or working at an office while pregnant, and more—as well as photos of men taking care of children, cooking, or doing projects in the home. These images will help companies of all sizes shift out of some of the stereotypes of gender norms. Sales of photos from the collection grew 65 percent in the first year, demonstrating the resonance of women depicted in many roles and strong demand for updated images by corporate and other types of users of stock photos.

Products for the Base of the Pyramid

Every eight seconds someone on the planet dies from inhaling smoke from traditional stoves and open fires; it is the fourth-leading health risk in the world.[34] Forty percent of the global population relies on traditional use of biomass for cooking and heating, which causes this exposure to smoke. In addition to dangerous, this is inefficient: Women spend hours collecting wood, up to four hours a day or 60 days a year. These methods of cooking and heating are not only a burden on women and create hazardous conditions in homes, they also produce significant amounts of CO_2, a major contributor to climate change.

Clean cookstoves have been shown to reduce fuel use by 30 to 60 percent while providing health benefits and time for women. The UN reports universal adoption of cookstoves would be the equivalent of reducing global CO_2 emissions by 25 to 50 percent.[35] Achieving these goals, however, depends on the women using the cookstoves. A world away from the corporate offices of large consumer product companies, the principle of co-creation from product development through marketing, distribution, and maintenance remains essential. Experience shows that without women as part of the design team, cookstoves end up underutilized or in storerooms.

Many products and programs in the energy sector are designed without a clear gender lens, and employment in the sector remains male dominated.[36] In contrast, Potential Energy, a cookstove manufacturer and distributor, gained valuable insights from customers, such as Wudeh, who lives in Meki, a small village in Ethiopia. Wudeh, her husband, two children, and another relative live in a thatched-roof house made of mud and straw. There is no ventilation. She spends hours each day collecting fuel and cooking over a simple, wood-burning cookstove, which results in eye infections and chronic coughing for her young daughter. At a community cookstove demonstration, Wudeh used a new model (developed in California's Lawrence Berkeley National Laboratory) to cook Shiro Wat, the Ethiopian lentil and Berber spice specialty. Along with her excitement about the potential reduction in smoke, she shared her concerns about hyena attacks because of the needed ventilation holes, her desire to use different pot sizes, and the challenges she has with fragile clay pots constantly needing repair. All of these considerations guided Potential Energy's approach, and caused them to innovate on their proposed design—deciding, for example, against clay, even though it would have lowered the manufacturing cost.

To move forward, Potential Energy and other cookstove suppliers need investments to scale production and distribution, finance working capital, and enhance management capacity. Unfortunately, the cookstove market is still perceived as immature. And it is true that current transaction sizes are small, which means significant investor risk. Enter the Global Alliance for Clean Cookstoves (GACC), a public-private partnership with the audacious goal of transitioning 100 million households to clean cooking solutions by 2020. Through work on technology standards, policy frameworks, and robust evidence of the market potential base gathered in eight countries, the GACC wants to change perceptions and create the environment to attract capital. GACC's conviction around the importance of women's empowerment and gender inclusion in cookstove enterprises led it to create a full guide to support firms in making enhancements across the value chain.[37] The case studies included provide investors and entrepreneurs clear roadmaps to ensuring their products will be well designed and utilized.

Investing in young girls—their current needs and their futures—is another strategy with big potential. The "Girl Effect," launched by the Nike Foundation, proposes that 250 million adolescent (12 to 18) girls living in poverty represent 250 million solutions to the world's social challenges.[38] Development agencies across the globe tout the unique position of girls to elevate themselves, help each other as their lives are transformed, and end the cycle of intergenerational poverty. The evidence is clear: When girls can learn, earn, and save without harm, families benefit and agricultural productivity goes up, while rates of child marriage, teen pregnancy, and HIV/AIDS go down. Films like *Girl Rising* and *A Path Appears* spread the girls' message, attract supporters, and support others.

Given that powerful impact, imagine if there were many more companies that understood the opportunity to design products or services to give an adolescent girl the time and light she needs to study, the teaching resources she needs to finish school with an education she can use to launch a business of her own. With this vision, in 2014 The Nike Foundation and The UK Department for AID (DFID) and USAID launched SPRING, a business incubator and accelerator focused on products and services specifically for girls at the bottom of the pyramid (living on less than $2.50/day).[39] SPRING is thinking big: The aspirational goal is to create products that affect the lives of 200,000 girls in eight countries by 2019 and 50 million girls by 2030. The incubated business must impact girls in at least one of four ways: generate income, save time or labor, save and invest their earnings and assets, or make them feel safe and secure. The program integrates these goals into venture design from product conception through distribution and maintenance.

The Power of Unreasonable Capital

Like SPRING, Nike and the Unreasonable Institute saw the opportunity to accelerate the growth of entrepreneurs positioned to transform the lives of girls. Its Girl Effect Accelerator finds and supports, in their own words, "wildly innovative" and successful, growing startups with proven track records of impacting poverty.[40] "This is a brilliant way to invest in carefully curated businesses that can truly transform girls' lives," says Holly Gordon, the co-founder and chair of Girl Rising global campaign advocating for girls' education.[41]

During due diligence they asked the key question: "How might aligning around key issues affecting women and girls enhance results?" The first program in November 2014 considered 150 companies and narrowed the winners down to ten. Twenty mentors, including marketing expert Seth Godin, the product designer and social venture innovator Paul Polack, and designer Hanna Jones, joined the two-week intensive program. TED-style videos marked the concluding event. A $500,000 revolving debt vehicle provided access to a line of credit.

What kind of companies do they fund? School operators educating over 100,000 children. Solar franchises bringing lighting to thousands of households a day. Mobile platforms enabling talented artisans to make and sell their jewelry to customers all over the world, and sustainable fuel producers reclaiming waste from coffee and rice husks.

The original intent was to move from the accelerator to launch a fund. But the founder's perspective shifted from a smaller fund focused on girls to integrating gender into the measurement of all companies. As they put it: "Unreasonable believes that our best lever for ending global poverty is investing into solutions that benefit women and girls without excluding boys and men… Though the core product or service of our portfolio companies may be gender agnostic, we believe that what you measure is an indicator of what you value and that what you measure often changes behavior overtime. To this end 100% of our investments will track their impact on women and girls in poverty."[42]

Some ventures, such as the Sub-Saharan Africa's BanaPads, which makes eco-friendly feminine hygiene pads, and Totohealth, a provider of SMS and voice technology to assist parents with maternal and child health, benefit from deep anthropological research and human-centered design—the design technique made famous by firms like IDEO. Other companies in energy, water, and sanitation access explore the role of girls in sales, distribution, and maintenance. Suzanne Biegel, Investment Director on the SPRING program, points out, "We are developing an evidence base of what works for girls, how girls help businesses to be successful, and we are sharing that knowledge with investors and other ecosystem actors. We see an unprecedented opportunity to build a pipeline of investable ventures with a positive 'girl effect.'"

Solar lamps that enable young boys and girls to study after dark and not with candlelight are a potential boon to advancing children through secondary and tertiary school. But they are especially important for girls, who—among other things—may be tasked with household chores while the sun is still up while their brothers are able to read at that time. Many models provide only enough light for a single person, the equivalent of a reading lamp, and in a family with many boys and girls, most often it is the boy, not the girl, who gets the light first or second. In fact, she may be last in line after her father and her brothers. A design that lights the entire home changes that dynamic. Beyond this, however, one also needs to consider the role of family members in the purchasing decision, and how this varies by region. Katherine Lucey, CEO of Solar Sister, has confronted these questions as her company has expanded around the world.[43] She sees clearly, for instance, the role of the mother-in-law in purchasing and how it differs by region. Anyone who fails to address this in their sales and distribution model misses an opportunity.

Investor Questions Uncovering Innovation

Many investors leverage gender insights in their analysis around products. They will see new markets, shifting interests, and opportunities for transformative product categories. Especially in due diligence, probing for a leadership team's understanding of and commitment to gender-based analysis can prove invaluable. Consider the dialogue possible when starting with these questions:

- What do you know about the differences or similarities of customers by gender? Does this differ by age, income, or geography? Where and why do you track sex-disaggregated data?
- How does sex or gender impact your design process? Do you use human-centered design approaches? How are women

engaged in your design process? Who are the design decision makers?

- Does your company have a reputation for designing for women? What innovations can you identify?
- Are there differences in how men and women learn about your product, decide to purchase, use, or continue to relate to your firm (e.g., return products, require service, promote your product)? What will the gender differences be in distribution and maintenance?
- How will your brand portray women and girls? Boys and men?
- If your offering is wildly successful, what affect will it have on women and girls?

Consider Rivet Ventures, the venture firm which targets early-stage companies whose products and services cater to a predominantly female demographic. They seek out contrarian entrepreneurs, those who are thinking about unsolved female customer pain points and who have the skill to create and leverage a customer community. Rivet sees women-centric markets as a key opportunity often missed by traditional firms. But they look for entrepreneurs who have gone beyond identifying a growth market driven by women or girls. They want leaders who can answer questions such as those above. "If the female voice is substantial to your ability to grow as a company, you should have an approach to it," says founder Shadi Mehraein.[44]

Rivet looks at multiple sectors from personalized beauty to wearable technology to mobile platforms for teen girls and aging parents. For example, Mayvenn is a startup targeting the haircare market with an initial focus on stylists and salons selling hair extensions to African Americans. It is a $9 billion market driven by consumers spending three times more than other demographics on these products, and which are mostly purchased at local beauty stores. Another Rivet portfolio company, GoldieBlox, has created construction and engineering games for girls.

Rivet's three founders—Mehraein, formerly of Focus and Bessemer Ventures, Rebeca Hwang, co-founder of YouNoodle, and Christina Brodbeck, who was part of the founding team at YouTube—are still an unusual trio of women in the male-dominated world of venture capital. Brodbeck notes, "The costs of starting a company have come down, and the technology barriers have come down. In consumer products we are seeing more gender diversity in founders—but venture hasn't changed to reflect the breadth [of] entrepreneurs starting businesses."[45]

Fortunately, a gender lens is equally available to all investors. And while imperative for those focused especially on women-led markets, it can improve any product, from bikes to banking. Opportunities to invest in gender research innovation methods and resulting products and services abound—from startups, to established consumer industry leaders, tech companies, and many more. And if social impact is your aim, there are a wide variety of inspired entrepreneurs and investors who are focusing on gender in economic development and social change. As you will see in the next chapter, innovation in creating products and services with a gender lens are moving in lockstep with the expansion of gender lens investment vehicles.

The Perfect Storm in Women's Health

Anula Jayasuriya, managing director of EXXclaim Capital and an experienced life sciences venture capitalist, hopes to significantly broaden the way in which investors think about opportunities in women's health. "The term *women's health* is not a great term because it is ambiguous and to most people it means OB/GYN health," says Jayasuriya, who argues it includes much more, including disease, geriatrics, mental health, etc. her other "big frustration" is that when wealthy women think of women's health, "they want to save women and children in economically disadvantaged regions. I admire them greatly for their selflessness, but I would like them to spend a bit more time thinking about the women in developed economies whose health is also not well served, and how their investments could improve it."

Jayasuriya has an MD, a PhD, and an MBA from Harvard University and a Masters in Pharmacology from Cambridge in addition to a vast and impressive professional experience working in biotech and life sciences. Since 2001, she has invested in life sciences and health care. Jayasuriya formed EXXClaim capital to capture the value in a "compelling yet underinvested business opportunity in women's health."

She sees trends in demographics, gender research, digital technology, and women's role as the "chief medical officers" of their families converging to create a "perfect storm for transforming women's health into an attractive investment area." First, women outlive men by five to eight years; empowered, engaged, and affluent, yet they are suffering from higher levels of chronic disease. Second—and encouragingly—scientific advances in understanding fundamental sex differences in human biology results in different disease mechanisms, symptoms, treatment responses. Third, new digital platforms spur radical shifts in the delivery of health care in the United States.

Her portfolio focuses on areas beyond those that are "only in women" (reproductive, gynecological, hormonal) to areas that are "different in women" (including Alzheimer's, cardiac, and depression) and areas where women are the primary decision makers (pediatric, elder care). This definition of women's health includes medical devices, diagnostics, digital health, wellness, and more. EXXClaim's seed portfolio of eight investments is performing well, a rejoinder she can use when male VC colleagues make comments like "women's health is just a sliver of the pie" or "I avoid Bikini medicine." Among the products developed by the companies in EXXClaim's seed portfolio are an early detection device for ovarian cancer; a pregnancy tracking app provided by the insurer for free and with no ads; a male reproductive health product; a smart, portable, and nearly silent breast pump; a device to prevent nightmares in children, and a solution to the problem of mild female urinary incontinence. We trust these didn't strike you as "bikini medicine" opportunities or insignificant market sizes.[46,47]

Notes

1. "At 81, Feminist Gloria Steinem Finds Herself Free of the Demands of Gender," Fresh Air, National Public Radio, October 26, 2015. http://www.npr.org/2015/10/26/451862822/at-81-feminist-gloria-steinem-finds-herself-free-of-the-demands-of-gender.
2. Katie Baillie, "'Where's Rey in the Star Wars Monopoly Set?' Asks 8-Year-Old Girl," Metro (January 5, 2016). metro.co.uk/2016/01/05/wheres-rey-in-the-star-wars-monopoly-set-asks-8-year-old-girl-5601710/.
3. Madeline Messer, "I'm a 12-Year-Old Girl. Why Don't the Characters in My Apps Look Like Me?" The Washington Post (March 4, 2015). www.washingtonpost.com/posteverything/wp/2015/03/04/im-a-12-year-old-girl-why-dont-the-characters-in-my-apps-look-like-me/.
4. Cecilia L. Ridgeway, Framed by Gender: How Gender Inequality Persists in the Modern World (New York: Oxford University Press, 2011). sociology.stanford.edu/people/cecilia-ridgeway.

5. "Female Dummy Makes Her Mark on Male Dominated Crash Tests," *The Washington Post* (March 25, 2012). www.washingtonpost.com/local/ trafficandcommuting/female-dummy-makes-her-mark-on-male-dominated-crash-tests/2012/03/07/gIQANBLjaS_story.html.

6. "Why Carmakers Always Insist on Male Crash-Test Dummies," Lee Vinsel blog (December 30, 2013). leevinsel.com/blog/2013/12/30/ why-carmakers-always-insisted-on-male-crash-test-dummies.

7. Katherine Shaver, "Female Dummy Makes Her Mark on Male Dominated Crash Tests," *The Washington Post*, March 25, 2012.

8. Londa Schiebinger, The John L. Hinds Professor of History of Science, Stanford University. web.stanford.edu/dept/HPS/schiebinger.html.

9. *Gendered Innovations: How Gender Analysis Contributes to Research* (European Commission, 2013). ec.europa.eu/research/science-society/ document_library/pdf_06/gendered_innovations.pdf.

10. GenderMag Personas Foundation Document. http://eusesconsortium .org/gender/GenderMagPersona-FoundationDocuments/Foundations .html.

11. "A Method for Evaluating Software's Gender Inclusiveness Interacting with Computer," GenderMag (January 27, 2016). iwc.oxfordjournals .org/content/early/2016/01/27/iwc.iwv046.full.pdf+html.

12. Christina Chen, "First-ever Hack for Her Summit Champions Gender Inclusiveness for the Benefit of Everyone," Microsoft (January 26, 2016). blogs.microsoft.com/blog/2016/01/26/first-ever-hack-for-her-summit-champions-gender-inclusiveness-for-the-benefit-of-everyone/ #sm.001p7idap6p6d7v10ce21mryr04o9.

13. Klaus Schroeder, *Gender Dimensions of Product Design* (New York: United Nations, October 2010). www.un.org/womenwatch/daw/egm/gst_ 2010/Schroeder-EP.13-EGM-ST.pdf.

14. Catey Hill, "6 Times It's More Expensive to Be a Woman," *MarketWatch* (April 12, 2016). www.marketwatch.com/story/5-things-women-pay-more-for-than-men-2014-01-17.

15. Georgette Sand, "Monoprix: Stop aux produits plus chers pour les femmes! #Womantax," Change.org (2016). Monoprix? www.change .org/p/monoprix-stop-aux-produits-plus-chers-pour-les-femmes-womantax.

16. John Kell, "Ex-lululemon CEO Advising Adidas on How to Target Women," *Fortune* (February 17, 2016). fortune.com/2016/02/17/ lululemon-day-advising-adidas/.

17. Hiroko Tabuchi, "Sweeping Away Gender-Specific Toys and Labels," *The New York Times* (October 27, 2015). www.nytimes.com/2015/10/28/ business/sweeping-away-gender-specific-toys-and-labels.html.

18. Jen See, "Liv/Giant Ditches 'Pink and Shrink' Approach to Building Women's Bikes," *Velonews* (August 1, 2013). velonews.competitor.com/ 2013/08/news/livgiant-no-more-pink-and-shrink_297617.

19. Ibid.
20. Reshma Kapadia, "Women's Retirement Planning: What Wall Street Misses," *Barrons* (February 13, 2016). www.barrons.com/articles/ womens-retirement-planning-what-wall-street-misses-1455343712.
21. Sylvia Ann Hewlett, Andrea Turner Moffitt, and Melinda Marshall, "Harnessing the Power of the Purse: Female Investors and Global Opportunities for Growth," Center for Talent Innovation (May 2015). www.talentinnovation.org/_private/assets/HarnessingThePowerOf ThePurse_ExecSumm-CTI-CONFIDENTIAL.pdf.
22. Ibid.
23. Westpac Group, Company website overview, date accessed 2016. www .westpac.com.au/about-westpac/westpac-group/company-overview/ our-businesses/.
24. World Economic Forum. www.weforum.org/organizations/westpac-banking-corporation.
25. Chief Executive Women, *CEW Case Studies: Westpac*, 2015. www.cew.org .au/wp-content/uploads/2015/03/•-CEW_CaseStudy_Westpac_ WebFinal.pdf.
26. Karissa Giuliano, "This is why Facebook just changed its friend icon," CNBC, www.cnbc.com/2015/07/09/facebook-just-changed-the-friends-icon.html. medium.com/facebook-design/how-we-changed-the-facebook-friends-icon-dc8526ea9ea8.
27. Caitlin Winner, "How We Changed the Facebook Friends Icon," NPR (July 7, 2015). www.npr.org/sections/thetwo-way/2015/07/08/ 421240583/facebooks-new-logo-is-a-visual-nod-to-gender-equality.
28. The 3% Conference: Campaigning Creative Female Talent+Leadership, *Introducing 3% Certified* 2016. www.3percentconf.com/certified.
29. Sydney Ember, "For Women in Advertising, It's Still a 'Mad Men' World," *New York Times* (May 1, 2016). www.nytimes.com/2016/05/ 02/business/media/for-women-in-advertising-its-still-a-mad-men-world .html?action=click&pgtype=Homepage&version=Moth-Visible& moduleDetail=inside-nyt-region-4&module=inside-nyt-region&region =inside-nyt-region&WT.nav=inside-nyt-region.
30. The Presentation Project.org, *Tell Super Bowl Advertisers You're Watching* (January 27, 2016). therepresentationproject.org/tell-super-bowl-advertisers-youre-watching/.
31. Michelle Castillo, AdWeek, *"Why would I buy from a company that doesn't respect me?" one survey respondent asks*, October 10, 2014, http://www .adweek.com/news/technology/these-stats-prove-femvertising-works-160704.

32. *Which Ads Best Inspire and Empower Women? Vote in the First #Femvertising Awards,* Adweek.com (June 2, 2015). www.adweek.com/news/advertising-branding/which-ads-best-inspire-and-empower-women-vote-first-femvertising-awards-165115.

33. Catherine Clifford, "Market to Empowered Women: It's Ethical and It's Good for Business," *Entrepreneur Magazine* (October 2, 2014). www.entrepreneur.com/article/238039.

34. Global Alliance for Clean Cookstoves. http://cleancookstoves.org/impact-areas/health/.

35. United Nations Foundation, *What We Do: Global Alliance for Clean Cookstoves.* www.unfoundation.org/what-we-do/campaigns-and-initiatives/cookstoves/.

36. Energy, Environment and Development, *Re-thinking Gender and Energy: Old and New Directions.* Energia/EASE Discussion Paper, May 2004. www.energia.org/fileadmin/files/media/pubs/cecelski2004_rethinking-ge.pdf.

37. Global Alliance for Clean Cookstoves, *Scaling Adoption of Clean Cooking Solutions through Women's Empowerment.* cleancookstoves.org/binary-data/RESOURCE/file/000/000/223-1.pdf.

38. Girl Effect, *Social Change for Girls.* www.girleffect.org.

39. Melody McDaniel, "Spring Accelerator," USAID (May 19, 2016). www.usaid.gov/what-we-do/gender-equality-and-womens-empowerment/spring-initiative.

40. girleffectaccelerator.com.

41. Girl rising, About us webpage. girlrising.com/about-us/index.html#what-is-girl-rising.

42. Unreasonable Capital. unreasonablecapital.com.

43. Solar Sisters. www.solarsister.org/about.

44. Personal Interview (Shadi Mehraein, July 23, 2015).

45. Personal Interview (Christina Brodbeck, July 23, 2015).

46. Madeleine Johnson, *Why Investing in Women's-Health Technology matters: Some men call it "bikini medicine," but it saves lives,* July 20, 2016, www.lennyletter.com/health/interviews/a478/why-investing-in-womens-health-technology-matters/.

47. Personal Correspondence (Anula Jayasuriya, February 9, 2015).

CHAPTER 8

A New Field in Motion

"Another world is not only possible, she is on her way. On a quiet day I can hear her breathing."[1]

—Arundhati Roy

You can feel the change in the air. It's there. Just about everywhere in the world, every day, there is someone talking, writing, or arguing about changes in gender equality and equity.

For decades, the gap in educational and occupational opportunities between men and women has been narrowing. The pace is erratic, geography matters, and the inequities still range from frustrating to unthinkable, but "she" is on her way to a more inclusive world. And "he" is going with her. Harvard economist Claudia Goldin called the "converging roles of men and women" among "the grandest advances" in society and the economy in the last century.[2] At the same time, while more and more women succeed in all types of paid professional endeavors—and maintain their demanding roles as wives, mothers, daughters, volunteers, ministers, athletes, and so forth—the gaps between men and women in earnings, opportunities, and responsibilities persist.

Gender lens investing is a product of and a force in this grand arc of converging economic roles. It reaches from the dreams of a million adolescent girls in Sub-Saharan Africa to become small business owners and transform the prospects of their continent to the idea that investors can fund a software company making mobile apps for these young women to manage their businesses, and everything in between.

The rapid broadening and deepening of the field builds from the quality of the data, research, and investor experiences. For years, Joy Anderson of Criterion Institute hosted a gender lens investing "Convergence," with leaders who were developing models to incorporate gender analysis into financial analysis. It is now paying off. "Gender lens investing is a field on the rise. It is growing in attention, in money moved, the number of investment products and in the expectation of what it will deliver," she says. Anderson sees both gender analysis and financial analysis as methods of assigning value to something. As she puts it, "Gender analysis can shape what matters in finance. And shifting what matters in finance can help to create a more gender equitable world."[3]

In 2012, when gender lens investing first emerged from backroom conversations and onto the main stages of galvanizing events like TEDx Women and SOCAP (a leading social capital market event for impact investors and social entrepreneurs), most of the gender-investment vehicles were new and lacked track records. Only one Wall Street firm offered a product. Microfinance and community development funds, which had more history, lacked detailed reporting around their impact to women and girls.

Only four years later, however, there are over 50 vehicles, some attached to established firms like Barclays, State Street Global Advisors, RobeccoSAM, and Morgan Stanley. Social investors, like Root Capital and the Calvert Foundation, have quantified the benefits of gender inclusion and uncovered investor appetite. The relevant data are growing at the company and country level. Bloomberg has launched a Financial Services Gender-Equality Index and Melinda Gates announced she will invest $80 million over three years to plug data gaps on women and girls. Though we have a long way to go, these early actors will spur the field as they create examples, build track records, and demonstrate the opportunities that exist.

With gender investment opportunities on all continents and across asset classes, choices abound. Further, as we discussed in Chapter 4, where you direct your lens depends on your motivations and investment philosophy. Some investors see investing in women entrepreneurs in emerging markets and are willing take on outsized risks. Others want to maintain a more traditional risk/return profile while investing in companies that support their values. But broadly speaking, investors increasingly consider gender due diligence essential to smart decision making. This chapter provides a snapshot in time; the practice is growing and evolving too quickly to do more than that. We lack a complete picture but we make do with what we have now. The following examples showcase the emerging art and discipline of investment analysis using a gender lens and the resulting range of opportunities for all types of investors.

The Public Equity and Debt Markets

Public equities, the earliest focus of social impact investors, has also attracted gender lens investors. The opportunity was perhaps first seen by one of the pioneers in this field, Linda Pei, who founded the Women's Equity Fund in 1993. Pei was born in the 1940s in China, the third daughter of a family from a rural village. At the end of World War II, her father had a chance to take a job in Japan. Her mother, not knowing if she could take all four siblings along, almost left Linda with relatives just because she was the "third daughter." China's long history of devaluing girls drove Linda's passion for ensuring that women were not left behind and spurred her creation of the Women's Equity Fund. "My conviction," she said, "is that when companies treat women equitably, those companies are likely to exhibit superior long term profitability. Why is this the case? Because companies that embrace diversity have a much wider range of talent to choose from." Joe Keefe, the CEO of Pax World Management, and an architect of the Women's Equality Principles at Calvert, shared that passion and purchased Pei's fund. In a remembrance of Pei, who died of cancer in 2007, Keefe wrote, "Linda was also one of the first people to understand and articulate the financial case for gender equality."[4] Now called Pax Ellevate Global Women's Index, the fund's strategy has shifted slightly as data sources expand and the criteria become more specific: representation by women on the board of directors, representation of women in executive management, women CFOs, women CEOs, and whether the company is a signatory to the UN Women's Empowerment Principles.

Other equity investors have built their investment strategies around women in management. For instance, Makeda Capital only invests in U.S. companies with women CEOs and excludes tobacco, firearms, and gambling industries from its portfolio. In 2013, the wealth management group at Morgan Stanley created The Parity Portfolio to invest in companies that have a gender-diverse board.

Only companies with at least three women board members are included in the portfolio. The intent is to encourage companies in these industries to think more deeply about the gender benefits of having women on their boards.

New gender-based indexes, such as the Barclays Women in Leadership North America Index, have begun to spur investment houses to introduce products. For example, in April 2016, BMO Investments Inc. launched the first Canadian gender lens fund—the BMO Women in Leadership, using Barclay's Women Leadership in North America as the reference index. Joanna Rotenberg, head of personal wealth management for BMO Financial Group, said in a release that the new mutual fund enables investors to promote change by rewarding gender-diverse companies.[5]

CalSTRS and State Street's Journey from Panels to Products

It's easy to take potshots at high-profile conferences for too much talk and too little change. Davos, Milken, Skoll, and others create remarkable forums raising global issues and reviewing them from all angles. Often it can feel like a year later the same conversation occurs, albeit with different panelists. But sometimes more happens. Sometimes an exchange begets an idea and connection leads to a new reality. This is what happened when State Street Global Advisor (SSGA) Executive Vice President Kristi Mitchem and CalSTRS CIO Chris Ailman shared the stage at the 2015 Milken Institute's annual conference.

CalSTRS had for years supported gender diversity in corporate America. In pursuit of this goal, they had advocated for the business case, and even supported a database of women candidates for boards. But the numbers didn't move. The picture was the same for women in senior leadership. CIO Ailman had a hypothesis that investment capital was the lever for change. He was ready to test it. Mitchem agreed.

Focusing on institutional investors, SSGA saw an opportunity to create a new gender lens product that was transparent, liquid, and sector neutral. But they needed reliable historical data. They found this in the nonprofit governance organization BoardEX's database on women in senior management. CalSTRS provided seed capital and SSGA was able to design and register a product in just a few months. The SPDR® SSGA Gender Diversity Index ETF (Ticker: SHE) launched in March 2016. The ETF tracks the performance of the SSGA Gender Diversity Index, comprised of US large cap companies excelling in board and management gender diversity. Mitchem's goal is to shine a beacon on the strong performance of companies with diverse teams and their best practices, to make the Index an aspirational club other companies would want to join.

Many firms have significant opportunity to improve, and might find real-world solutions from their peers. Mitchem notes that SHE isn't a Women's Index—it is an index that celebrates the power of diversity. That's something that both sexes can get behind. Or put another way—there is HE in SHE—these are companies with 30 percent women and 70 percent men in senior leadership.

Conversations focus on the excess return component that can come from better decision making. Diversity of perspective allows for active challenge mechanisms. Companies that lack diversity are likely allowing errors into decisions around people—as well as other places. "I have never seen our organization so excited about a product. Gender is intrinsic to who people are—and if you are not a woman, there is certainly a woman you love in your life, daughter, wife, mother—it is such an accessible concept that it ignited a fire within our organization that was palpable," Mitchem says.[6]

For Ailman SHE is good investment and good for the country. It is an "opportunity to make the core work harder, with the added benefit of driving fuller engagement of women in the economy, which may raise the value of our entire portfolio over the long term."[7]

Other strategies expand beyond criteria for diversity in executives and look at a firm's commitment, and record, of working with women across the value chain. For instance, U.S. Trust collaborated with the Women's Foundation of California to design its Women and Girls Equality Strategy (WGES), a U.S. equity and corporate fixed-income strategy designed to look holistically at how companies engage women—as consumers, employees, and agents of global change WGES examines quantitative criteria to compare companies with sector peers on factors such as pay equity; recruiting, retaining, and promoting women; supply chain and subcontractor relationships; gender impact of goods and services; and portrayal of women in media.[8] "We wanted to align our investments with our values, and also to use a gender lens to identify smart investments in companies we're proud to own," says Cathy Schreiber, CFO of the Women's Foundation.[9] WGES was developed as part of U.S. Trust's Socially Innovative Investing Strategy (S2I). As with all the S2I strategies, the social factors are considered in addition to the fundamental research and custom portfolio construction. The strategy considers both policy and practice; for example, specific policies defining inclusive hiring as well as the amount and number of payments for discrimination lawsuits are considerations. Companies that score well in the analysis are likely to have fewer environmental penalties, labor violations, and product safety recalls. A gender lens, as it turns out, provides another important set of metrics for separating high-quality companies from the others.[10]

Pursuing a passive equity strategy (limited buying and selling and long-term holding) while maintaining a commitment to gender equity is another step forward in the evolution of gender lens investing. Aperio Group LLC, a passive investor, offers clients a tax-advantaged ESG indexing strategy. In 2015, it launched a Women's Inclusion Strategy, partnering with a family office. The family office's mission is "to deploy impact investment capital with a gender lens to address society's market failure to fully value women and girls."[11] This led Aperio to focus on "companies with women on boards and in senior management who do not derive significant revenue from adult entertainment." The strategy can track a global, international, or domestic equity market benchmark based on client need.

While new equity offerings are using the growing body of gender data to sharpen their research, and are attracting media attention, it is important to remember that historically strong ESG fund managers, including Calvert Investments, Trillium Asset Management, Dominis Social Investments, and Boston Common Asset Management, among others, have incorporated gender into their ESG frameworks for years. They view gender inclusion as important, although one factor among many.

Newer firms are following these ESG leaders and adding gender criterion to the mix. For example, Nia Global Solutions (Nia in Swahili means intention, goal, or purpose) launched in 2012 and is now part of Green Alpha Advisors. It describes its strategy as an actively managed portfolio designed to harness the innovative social purpose of investment. The public-equity portion of the portfolio consists of thirty to fifty securities selected from Green Alpha's Next Economy universe, spanning the market capitalization spectrum. While gender equality is not a primary focus, Nia weaves a gender lens through portfolio construction, including requiring all holdings have at least one woman in a leadership position.[12]

These firms also have long pursued shareholder engagement. From diversity to pay equity, to supply chains, gender activist investors urge companies to take action in the interest of long-term performance. In 2012, Trillium Capital Resources initiated shareholder proposals aimed at companies in their portfolio with all-male boards and those lagging peers on diversity. After the Rana Plaza collapse in Bangladesh in 2013, members of the Interfaith Center on Corporate Responsibility, representing $3.1 trillion in assets under management, urged all apparel brands and retailers to advocate for implementation of garment industry reforms to protect factory workers, who are disproportionately women.[13] And, increasingly, investors have found success in calling for transparency in pay gaps.

Activist Investors Who Carry a Gender Lens

Shareholder engagement on social issues is one-way investors infuse their identity and responsibility as corporate owners with efforts to influence company decisions. In 1977, The Reverend Leon Sullivan, a clergyman and member of the board of General Motors, forced the automaker—then the largest employer in apartheid South Africa—to divest. Eventually, 100 of the U.S. companies signed the Sullivan Principles and withdrew their operations from South Africa.

The advent of electronic reporting and the growth of social media have enabled shareholders (more equity than debt owners) to be more sophisticated and targeted in their engagement, focusing on areas with strong business cases in addition to the moral high ground. Their actions may result in a proxy resolution shareholders vote on, but just as often, the resolution is resolved as the targeted corporation takes action before the issue becomes public.

Natasha Lamb, director of equity research and shareholder engagement at Arjuna Capital, saw an opportunity to engage companies around pay equity. Given the research base espousing the benefits of pay equity, Lamb appealed to companies' "enlightened self-interest" to address this structural barrier so as to attract and retain more women employees. Arjuna filed a first-of-its kind resolution calling for eBay to close its gender wage gap in November 2014. eBay's Board opposed the proposal, but found itself on the wrong side of the political mood. Calls for equal pay for equal work came from President Obama in his State of the Union just weeks before, while Patricia Arquette's Oscar acceptance speech, given a mere 48 hours after eBay committed to oppose the proposal, went viral as she said "It's our time to have wage equality once and for all and equal rights for women in the United States of America." As the press denounced eBay for opposing the resolution, Salesforce proactively came forward with its own commitment to pay equity. Corporate leaders and the laggards soon became clear and investors took notice. Heightening the stakes, Lamb sent shareholder resolutions to nine tech companies in late 2015 (eBay, Amazon, Google, Expedia, Facebook, Adobe, Microsoft, Apple, and Intel), and in early 2016 she began withdrawing proposals at Intel, Apple, Expedia, and Microsoft based on the companies' public commitments to report gender wage gaps and close them.

Arjuna won a battle with Amazon, who tried to block the proposal at the Securities and Exchange Commission (SEC), and the company released its internal pay data in March 2016. On April 27, 2016, a big shift occurred at eBay as 51.2 percent of shareholders voted for a resolution calling for the tech giant to close the gender pay gap, which included the support of Institutional Shareholder Services. The level of support had grown sixfold from the year before. In response to the vote, the CEO of eBay, Devin Wang, announced the company would publish a report on pay equity in the fall of 2016. In June 2016, the proposal went to a vote at Facebook and Google. Facebook's claim on Equal Pay Day in May 2016 that "men and women earn the same" was not sufficient for Lamb to withdraw her proposal. "If the number is 100 percent, say 100 percent," Lamb said. "Otherwise, you're perpetuating the same black box that women have been dealing with for decades. In August 2016, Adobe issued the requested report on gender pay equity and Apple announced it had closed its gap."[14]

It's taken the fixed-income market longer than the equity markets to incorporate ESG factors. The same has been true for gender lens criteria, but fixed income is catching up to equities, with more sophisticated gender strategies inspired by the progress and results in the public equity products. For example, in 2014, Boston-based Breckinridge Capital Advisors launched the Breckinridge Gender Lens Strategy, a fixed-income fund that overweights companies with above-average performance on issues affecting girls and women, such as gender and racial equality, human rights, and health and safety.

Breckinridge specializes in the management of high-grade fixed-income portfolios for institutions and private clients. Its gender analysis uses eighteen metrics and data from MSCI and Bloomberg, and is informed by the U.N. Women's Empowerment Principles. Breckinridge also equates strong gender practices with sustainable, responsible management.

For corporate bonds, the firm's gender criteria include factors such as women on boards and UN Global Compact signatory status. In the municipal bond market, Breckinridge identifies the proportion of women-owned businesses in its assessment of ESG issues for cities and analyzes the prevalence of mammography screening for the nonprofit hospital sector.

The bond market will likely continue to offer new ways for investors to gain exposure to the upside of the growth of women entrepreneurs. The International Finance Corp (IFC) launched the first-ever women's bond in 2013 in the Japanese market. The five-year triple-A-rated offering raised $165 million supported women-led ventures in emerging markets through loans made by local banks.[15] Following the success of this bond, the IFC partnered with Goldman Sachs to create a $600 million facility for investing in women-led enterprises.[16]

Beyond gender-specific products, fixed-income investment providers offer a variety of vehicles that shine a light on the challenges of low-income women. In the United States, for instance, the poor include a disproportionate number of single mothers. The poverty rate for single-mother families in 2013 was 39.6 percent, nearly five times more than the rate (7.6 percent) for married-couple families.[17] Cheryl Smith, a Chartered Financial Analyst (CFA) and Managing Partner at Trillium, who heads the firm's fixed-income process, suggests gender lens investors consider bonds for capital projects to improve public transportation for women who depend on it to get to their jobs. Smith's suggestion is supported by research that illustrates the paradox of the "grand convergence" for low-income women. Two academics writing about their research on transportation and minority women in New York City cite the rapid entry of women into the paid labor force over the last three decades as "a significant trend" and they show the need for transportation systems designed to meet the needs of these working women. Just having a job is not enough without a reasonable way to get there.[18]

Investors can also impact areas such as affordable housing, health care, education, and child welfare. Community Capital Management, founded in 1999, is a fixed-income impact-investing manager that incorporates the "E" (environmental) and "S" (social) aspects of ESG investing by "proactively screening market-rate bonds" financing community development. Their CRA Qualified Investment Fund Institutional Shares ranked among the top 1 percent of performers in the Morningstar intermediate government category for 2015.[19] Their bonds support multifamily housing, childcare centers, and schools that benefit woman and girls living in low- and moderate-income communities. Although extremely difficult to quantify given data challenges, the disproportionate benefit to women makes intuitive sense given the economic realities of this demographic in many urban and semi-urban areas around the United States. Such gender considerations—the intersection of gender, health, transportation, housing, and more—can enable bond managers to drive deeper social dividends for low-income women and their communities.

Private Markets for Investors Across the Wealth Spectrum

Private market gender lens investing opportunities run the gamut from online crowdfunding loans to exclusive private equity funds available only to accredited investors. Often, large private investors (individuals and fund managers) have access to more information and the opportunity to probe deeper into the data through the due diligence process. They may also exert significant influence, for example, by joining a board. Hence, private investors have an opportunity to upgrade their due diligence using a gender lens. Suzanne Biegel, an experienced gender lens investor, joined with Joy Anderson to draft set of inquiries designed to fit within traditional diligence practices and provide additional material information on the potential risks, returns, and impact of investments. The questions provide additional data, which can be integrated into investment decisions at a level that corresponds to the intensity of one's gender lens.[20]

The size of the capital gaps for women entrepreneurs and founding teams including women provides a wide variety of opportunities for investors. New funds are popping up, established players are jumping in, and even the legal frameworks are changing. In 2014, Nisha Dua, the former general manager of AOL's Millennial website, and Susan Lyne, who was president of entertainment at the American Broadcasting Company (ABC), launched BBG Ventures to invest in visionary women entrepreneurs with market-defining consumer products and services. Every company in the portfolio has at least one founder who is a woman. BBG Ventures is backed by AOL and grew out of AOL's #BUILTBYGIRLS initiative. As an early stage fund, investments typically range from $100,000 to $250,000. Dua and Lyne view what some would see as a "constraint" as an opportunity—in fact, they say "the greatest untapped opportunity for venture capital lies in backing women who are using technology to address common life-challenges and transform daily habits."[21]

Astia Ventures, Cowboy Ventures, and a number of other seed and venture funders are among those who also require gender diversity in the founding team. They look for women in key roles with decision making and equity participation. "The capital table is an essential part of due diligence," says Sharon Vosmek, CEO of Astia. "I want to know that the women are fairly incentivized to grow successful companies."[22]

Other private investors go further, only investing in women-owned companies. Golden Seeds, an active angel group that also manages three funds, was founded by Stephanie Newby, a former J.P. Morgan banker who is a business entrepreneur, too. "I care most about ensuring that there is a female voice involved in the creation of company culture," says Newby. Apparently others do as well, as Golden Seeds now has over 275 investors and two funds with over $37 million, which have outperformed other seed-stage investors. Since 2005, and as of May 2016, the group as a whole has invested over $80 million in 76 companies.[23]

Investing in institutions that "bank" on women is a systemic approach to increasing women's access to capital. Sustainability, Finance, Real Economies, or SFRE (pronounced *Sapphire*), "helps innovative expansion-stage companies to become global category leaders" and provides investors exposure to institutions around the world. The fund invests in equity and subordinated debt in small to medium-size banks around the world who are members of the

Global Alliance for Banking on Values (GABV). In April 2016, SFRE made a $4 million investment in PRASAC, a successful Cambodian microfinance institution.[24] PRASAC's mission is to improve the living standards of Cambodia's rural population and contribute to sustainable economic development by being a financially viable microfinance institution. SFRE's mission is to advance social, environmental, and economic development by providing capital to local banks.

SFRE and the other GABV members have committed to follow core principles of financial inclusion for everyone. These institutions invest in individuals and enterprises in the communities in which they operate. David Korslund, who designed the SFRE scorecard, said, "One of the metrics we will be tracking and reporting is lending to female borrowers, as it is important to emphasize that bank credit for women is a critical product."[25]

Investing in "micro" borrowers and savers can occur through debt or equity, with concessionary or market rates, and in emerging or developed country markets.

It was once assumed *microfinance institutions*—or MFIs—were both an anti-poverty silver bullet and an extremely gendered investment option because stories circulated that around "90 percent" of all MFI borrowers were women. Investors today have a robust set of opportunities in microfinance, and a much greater ability to see how their investments promote actual inclusion and other positive effects on women.

Leaders in inclusive finance, like Bamboo Finance, are moving impact reporting from "outputs to outcomes." Bamboo invests in "innovative companies addressing basic human needs where social and economic progress can be achieved simultaneously." Industry focuses include agribusiness, off-grid energy, health care, and financial services sectors and its $290 million assets under management include companies operating in more than 20 emerging and frontier market countries. Impressively, these investments have provided 29 million clients with access to products and services and created more than 25,000 jobs. But Bamboo's commitment is to go further, to not only report on the number of loans or savings accounts but to quantify the effect these products and services have on their clients' personal lives and their businesses.[26] Through efforts like these, while expensive and time consuming, investors can truly understand the impact of their capital on the lives of women and their families.

The Heart and Impact of Root Capital's Gender Strategy

In 2011, an investor asked Root Capital a seemingly simple question, which started the pioneering social lender on a transformational journey. The question: "What is your impact on women?"

Root knew anecdotally that many of its clients' businesses were playing an essential role in connecting women farmers to markets and in redefining professional pathways for women employees and managers. But the organization did not have the metrics to know how many of these businesses there were, nor did it have the impact analysis to inform the range of ways that a lender like Root could support clients in their efforts to increase their impact on women. So they set out to do so, and to answer that 2011 question.

By 2016, Root Capital had a portfolio including 112 gender-inclusive businesses (40 percent of the entire portfolio) through its Women In Agriculture Initiative. The journey included essential grant funding to research the potential for empowering women working up and down agricultural supply chains through new lending products and targeted advisory services. It involved deep debate about the role of investors in suggesting gender-inclusive practices and on appropriate metrics. Also, it spurred a host of conversations and actions to increase internal practices of gender inclusion, profoundly influencing Root's own cultural evolution.

Root Capital invests in women by investing in agricultural businesses that promote gender inclusive practices. It finances and builds the managerial capacity of rural enterprises, strengthening the agricultural businesses that unlock market opportunities for women to be individual farmers, employees, and leaders. When it launched in 2012, Root's Women in Agriculture Initiative set a goal of reaching 200,000 women producers by 2016. In 2015, the firm accomplished the goal a year early. Catherine Gill, senior vice president, Investor Relations and Operations, shepherded the initiative from the start. "Adding gender-based metrics and combining data in a focused initiative enabled us to be a pioneer for the field," she said. Investors in Root Capital's Women in Agriculture received a rate of between 1 and 3 percent, depending on the term.[27]

Root Capital's journey, starting with an investor question, illustrates the role that investors can play in influencing the development of new products that incorporate a gender lens and thus advancing the understanding of impact in sectors like agriculture.

Most private investments mentioned so far require accredited investors. If Jenn Pryce has her way, in a few years, impact investing will no longer be seen as a privilege of the wealthy. Pryce and the team at Calvert Foundation know the unmet opportunity for retail investors to invest for impact. Over 15,000 investors have currently purchased their Community Investment Notes over the last 20 years, and 100 percent of investors have been repaid. The simple structure enables investors to choose their term (1, 3, 5, 10, or 15 years) and corresponding-interest rate (up to 4 percent—remarkably not everyone chooses the maximum). The capital is lent through social purpose organizations such as community development financial institutions and MFIs. Some geographic targeting has been possible, but with recent launches, investors have specific options, including particular cities, countries, or target areas like the aging, education, and housing.

The Women Investing in Women Initiative (WIN-WIN), launched by Calvert Foundation in 2012, raised capital from investors to invest $20 million in organizations around the world that empower women and girls. WIN-WIN was designed as an inclusive investment portfolio with gender-specific indicators to track the impact generated from the portfolio organizations over time.

Calvert Foundation has expanded its WIN-WIN Note to invest another $20 million to address the intersection of women's empowerment and access to clean energy, thus instilling a gender lens (both from a financial and impact perspective) when scaling this young sector through integrated market-based approaches.[28] These loans to enterprises specifically enable the development and distribution of clean energy technologies such as solar lighting and clean cookstoves. The products vastly improve the lives of villagers in these remote off-the-grid communities, especially the women who are risking their lives by working in the dark, walking miles for water, and cooking meals under unhealthy conditions.

With its extensive distribution network and impressive track record in SRI investing, Calvert has found essential partners for WIN-WIN 2.0 in USAID, the Shell Foundation, and the Global Alliance for Clean Cookstoves. The know-how and capital from strategic partnerships such as these, which intersect the worlds of traditional Development Banks, aid organizations, and Foundations and the next-generation funders of entrepreneurs, bodes well for the economic development field and for local women entrepreneurs in developing countries. As Anne-Marie Slaughter, President and CEO of New America, put it, "The emphasis on entrepreneurship stands the traditional foreign-aid paradigm on its head," especially when local women entrepreneurs have equity in the venture.[29]

Kiva, an online microfinance lending network, has lent over $850 million from individual donors and as little as $25. Through its new partnership with USAID and the Inter-American-Development Bank (IADB), Kiva will double its investments in women entrepreneurs. The Women's Development Fund aims to lend to 1 million women entrepreneurs capital ranging from $450 to $100,000 over the next five years—and will match dollar-for-dollar what citizen lenders loan to women entrepreneurs through the Kiva.org website.

The unique three-way partnership makes the goal of a million entrepreneurs credible. Kiva provides reach to investors, IADB offers the entrepreneurs technical assistance, and the State Department's investment in data collection and analysis will enable ongoing adjustments and improvements to the program. Just as importantly, it may set the stage for broader regulatory impact. Currently, lack of data on entrepreneurship, especially data disaggregated by gender, makes it difficult to make the argument for regulatory changes needed to stimulate more lending and find better ways to finance women entrepreneurs.[30]

The Kiva model of borrowing from the general public is similar to the Capital Sisters teams' securities model of return of principal with no interest. These Sister Bonds have proved to be enormously popular. The inaugural $1.5 million bond offering sold out in less than 18 months. A $1,000 zero-interest bond provides ten $100 micro loans to impoverished women in developing countries and the investor is paid back in one, two, three, or five years.[31]

There are many opportunities and funds for investing in women—from angel funds in the United States to debt funds in Africa, from new technology platforms to notes with a twenty-year track record. What's most important to remember is that no matter how small or big your investment, it has the effect of changing the economic prospects of people and countries that have not been well-served by traditional investment practices, and that the collective activity, together, is quite significant.

Cash, Equivalents, and Guarantees

Many investors are willing to do more with their cash. The Self-Help Credit Union, based in Durham, North Carolina, is one of the nation's largest cooperative Community Development Financial Institution credit unions. It offers a savings product specifically focused on women and children. The Women and Children Term Certificate expands financial opportunities for women who are starting to build their assets by opening their first savings accounts, starting businesses, or buying homes. It supports families through financing childcare and public charter schools facilities. At a $500 minimum deposit with National Credit Union Administration (NCUA) insurance up to $250,000 and terms of one to five years it provides an easy entry point for retail investors. The Self-Help Credit Union promotes it as a "double return: higher interest than traditional savings accounts and a great way to support self-help investments that benefit women and children."[32]

Guarantees

MCE Social Capital (formerly, Micro-Credit Enterprises) mobilizes capital to guarantee loans, but not in a traditional way. Jonathan C. Lewis, MCE's founder, started what he thought was retirement by volunteering at a nonprofit microfinance organization called Freedom from Hunger (which he first assumed was a soup kitchen). He quickly realized how MFIs like Freedom from Hunger change women's lives—especially if they had the capability to obtain expansion capital.

So Lewis set out to mobilize private sector capital to meet that need, and MCE Social Capital (MCE) was born. MCE's unique model involves "Guarantors"—individuals and foundations who pledge $1 million (the money is pledged—but does not leave their accounts). Based on this pledge, MCE borrows $500,000 and lends it to an MFI. The MFI makes $100 to $5,000 six-month loans to local entrepreneurs, 73% of whom are women. Each guarantee backs invaluable capital to more than 3000 people, each supporting, on average, a family of five. Which means that through the initial loan from MCE, each guarantor can positively impact the lives of 15,000 people. MCE targets MFIs that reach poor rural women, and that offer additional services such as business planning and health care delivery.

Guarantors are in one unified risk pool, which means the risk is highly distributed (less than 1 percent per default, if one occurs). In ten years, the organization has experienced only two defaults totaling $12,140 (paid as a tax-deductible donation) per Guarantor. Guarantors are not paid a direct fee and may leave the program with only 18-months' notice. The organization, run in the black for the past nine years, operates on 3 percent overhead. Lewis says, "I have a lot of faith in mothers. I think they make solid business partners." Indeed, the historic repayment rate of MCE borrowers since 2006 is an impressive 99.2 percent.[33]

Crowdfunding

Crowdfunding is term thrown around quite frequently these days. However, contrary to the simplicity conveyed by many headlines, crowdfunding is an umbrella term covering four distinct asset categories, based on the nature of the return to investors: donation-based, rewards-based, debt-based, and equity-based.

The U.S. JOBS Act now allows private businesses to raise money via online intermediaries from retail investors. This change in securities law will give a huge boost to crowdfunding. Before the May 2016 amendments to Reg D, companies were only allowed to raise money from accredited investors through the IPO process or other limited exemptions (and definitely not over the Internet). The new law allows companies to raise money from anyone—family, friends, neighbors, customers, work colleagues, whomever. Lynn Walder, an executive assistant who lives in the Boston area interviewed by *Locavesting,* said she opened an account at WeFunder "to be a part of this early because I could see the long-term effects this business model could have on breaking down the barriers to true innovation." "Hopefully," she added, "it will put some wealth creation back into the hands of the average salaried person." WeFunder, having funded over 114 startups and raised $17 million, announced on its website the long-awaited (since 2012) "Reg Crowdfunding is legal on May 16, 2016."[34]

Crowdfunding's development has been accompanied by a sense that it might provide a new avenue for women historically left outside of the capital funding networks. It is early days, but there is some evidence to support this. New York University and the University of Pennsylvania's business schools published a study showing that all-women teams had a 40 percent better chance of meeting fundraising goals on Kickstarter. And in technology, the success rate for women-led Kickstarter projects almost doubled that of men. The study authors point to more women on Kickstarter who want to support women-led ventures—a rare example of choice homophily, that people relate more with similar individuals—working in favor of women in the investment arena. But it's even more complex than that: There's a particular subgroup of "activist" female backers who make a point of funding other women in industries in which women have been historically underrepresented, including tech. (This is an activist or intentional variant of choice homophily).[35]

Just as important to understand, however, is that the value of crowdfunding lies as much in its ability to build communities of support and validate demand as in capital. Time will tell, but the ecosystem around women entrepreneurs continues to expand rapidly. A set of crowdfunding sites, such as Portfolia and Plum Alley, have emerged specifically for women entrepreneurs, though as the conversation and examples of success grow, women are likely to gain even outside these exclusive sites. As Wharton Professor Ethan Mollick puts it, "Moving from an expert-centered process to a platform approach increases diversity, leads to high-quality results, and generally results in successful outcomes."[36]

Startup success no longer requires a Silicon Valley ZIP code—or even residence in a strong, developed nation. A new report from AlliedCrowds highlights global crowdfunding developments of 2015 and forecasts an increase of more than 50 percent over the next twelve months. The report estimates that crowdfunding in emerging economies raised roughly $430 million in 2015 and that the figure will hit $660 million in 2016. The three top-ranking countries for 2015 were India ($27.8 million), Philippines ($26.9 million), and Nepal ($25.5 million). Rounding out the top ten were Mexico, Kenya, Brazil, Colombia, Cambodia, Peru, and Thailand.

Lars Kroijer, founder and CEO of AlliedCrowds, which released the report said, "When platforms in the developing world move further into debt and equity crowdfunding, the growth can be explosive. Crowdfunding has the potential to transform banks and credit institutions in the developing world." The report authors estimate that $96 billion will be raised through crowdfunding in the developing world in the coming ten years. Crowdfunding also fits well with the

UN's latest Sustainable Development Goals initiative that went into effect in 2016.[37]

Gender Lens Investors Are Not a Secret Society

Gender lens investors are pension fund managers, economic development banking professionals, foundation executives and lenders, angels, friends with a checking account, and family with retirement plans. They don't have pink business cards or a secret handshake.

As we've seen, they are found on Wall Street and Sand Hill Road; they include those from exclusive ZIP codes and individuals just establishing their 401(k)s. The energy and enthusiasm of those leading the way has diverse communities advancing gender lens practices and creating efficiencies in matching investors and opportunities.

The Mutiplier Effect of Women's Networks

For years, Suzanne Biegel, Aspen Fellow, former executive director of Investors Circle, and serial entrepreneur, watched with frustration as potential advocates and users of a gender lens were confused and challenged. In 2010, Biegel presented the idea of a gender lens to Investors Circle, and the network responded by beginning to track sex-disaggregated numbers on deal flow and investments made. At the Women's Donor network, Biegel championed a circle of women investors. After moving to the United Kingdom she successfully recruited women into the angel group Clearly So. In 2015, she presented a group of advisors with the idea that gender lens investors needed a global network to learn and share deal opportunities. Thus, the Women Effect was born.[38] Members of this community are individuals, families, and institutional investors who are deploying at least £1 million in capital.

Impact-focused angel networks, such as Toniic, Investors Circle, and Clearly So, also have internal circles of gender lens investors. These groups serve as referral networks for direct deals as well as sources of support beyond capital for the gender inclusive enterprise. Partnerships, such as one between High Water Women, a network of women in finance, and Investors Circle, have sprung up to provide some initial angel training and invite women into impact investing. PYMWIMIC in the Netherlands provides vetted deals to women investors. Similarly, Beyond Our Borders, a circle of women in Colorado, has been a source of significant support to Dr. Stephanie Gripne of the Impact Finance Center, in her ambitious goal to catalyze $100M of impact investments into Colorado.

These communities all help to move significant capital with a gender lens, and demonstrate such opportunities to others.

Historically, women have not been angel investors. In 2015, only 25 percent of U.S. angel investors were women and only 5 percent were minorities.[39] A number of programs are bridging that gap. The Pipeline Angel's Fellowship in the United States is a six-month training program including education, mentorship, and actual investment practice. In the program, women work together to source and vet deals, culminating in an actual investment in a woman-led for-profit social venture by each program participant. At graduation participants get a T-shirt that says, "This is what an Angel looks like."[40] Golden Seeds has planted a group in Australia, called SCORE, and is considering replicating the group in other countries. The blog *Girl Tank* follows the news on women angels and investment activity globally.[41]

Institutional investors, specifically the multilateral development banks, were among the pioneers of the use of gender and they continue to innovate. Some have anchored impact funds. Others have developed gender policies, which are reinforced when internal value-chain analysis also occurs. For instance, Julie Katzman, the COO of the Inter-American-Development Bank, supported a gender review of consultants, pay equity, and panel speakers. Multilateral development banks are increasingly playing roles in partnerships from accelerators to technical assistance to investment facilities.

Pension funds like the California State Teachers Retirement CalSTRS may play very public roles in the integration of gender into investment analysis. They also have long invested in emerging and minority managers via specialized funds. Although women managers are seldom separated from the emerging and minority class, these programs do grow the assets under management of women managers who often lack the networks to gain early investors. The programs also ensure that the pension funds have access and allocation to smaller funds, contributing to their portfolio diversity.

Ed Powers, managing director at HarbourVest, has developed funds for pension investors for over a decade. He's seen the number of inclusive fund managers (defined as a team including a woman who has more than 15 percent of the economics of the fund) triple in the last five years. The return data on the inclusive teams they have selected, while not statistically significant, demonstrate these teams are performing at the benchmark.[42]

Corporations and corporate foundations have awoken to the win-win of supporting women's economic empowerment. Many support women and girls in some way, and the most sophisticated have linked it to their corporate objectives. The Oak Foundation's 2014 report, "A Business Case for Women's Economic Empowerment: An Integrated Approach," quantified the explosion of companies and corporate foundations launching work in women's economic empowerment.[43]

But it also detailed the failure of most approaches to fully utilize all of a company's potential levers to create impact: people, investments, brand, customers, purchasing power, and partnerships. The field leaders have begun to share learnings and challenges. Many joined the U.S. Chamber of Commerce Foundation "A Path to Empowerment" roundtables on private-sector approaches to economically empowering women. Sessions were set up to foster dialogue among peers responsible for driving impact, and included focuses like supply chains, mentoring, champion cultures, and communications strategies and technology.

Women's foundations, some of the earlier adapters of a gender lens in their endowments, are now publicly leading the charge. Their focuses include sharing the opportunity with their donors, as well as with other foundations and endowments. Although many private gender lens investors to date have stayed private about their investments, it's likely that some will begin to step out. Take the Tara Foundation, founded by Dr. Ruth Shaber, an OBGYN with a passion for evidence-based action and a focus on the intersection of gender and health. Ruth flips the traditional approach. She sees the primary role of her 5 percent grant budget as better understanding how her 95 percent investments have—and could have—impact. She's not waiting for all the answers to invest; her portfolio includes public equity funds with a gender lens, private vehicles like Root Capital, and the Calvert Foundation and direct investments in a firm and a women's health clinic. But what about grants? They include organizations, such as Jacaranda Health, a Kenyan Maternity hospital that seeks to become investable, and a two-year research effort with University of Pennsylvania's Center for High Impact Philanthropy looking at the relationship between gender lens investing and improved social, economic, and health conditions in the communities where gender forward public companies are based—that's right, philanthropists funding research in public equities.

As gender lens investors proliferate—and as they examine gender as one of many lenses—they are less likely to be labeled as such. When Stephanie Cordes, for example, attends the global sustainable fashion conference, she's an apparel investor. When Julie Katzman hosts the IFC transportation week, she is a development investor. But both actively bring a gender lens to their work. The most innovative and disruptive uses of a gender lens may prove to not be under a moniker at all.

Creating Your Own Lens

Some investors review their portfolio looking for opportunities across asset classes. Other ask question that inspire their thinking and ideas follow.

What Is the Purpose of Your Capital?

"Begin with the end in mind" has become an overused phrase, but for good reason. You need to articulate how your investments support broader personal or institutional goals. These goals provide clarity around your requirements for return and liquidity—and your risk tolerance. It is a misconception in gender lens investing that the field is best suited to a particular and limited range of risk profiles: gender lens investing provides a wide range of options to suit diverse risk tolerances. Institutions bring operating requirements, complexities of spending policies, and mission alignment. Families add multi-generational needs and perspectives. But once the traditional purposes are clarified, expand the question to see if there is a non-financial goal for the capital—to support businesses in a region, to advance research in healthcare to encourage principle based entrepreneurs. There may not be, but ask the question—and know that asking the question will encourage others to as well.

Why Will You Use a Gender Lens?

Why gender? Is the objective exclusively to drive better investment decisions, increasing returns and reducing risk? Many institutional investors start here, or at least are clear that returns are their *primary* objective. But if your objective includes creating social change, begin by naming the change you wish to see. The change may be something clearly related to gender, such as "create employment opportunities for young girls as alternatives to child marriage" or it may be less initially obvious, such as "drive the growth of sustainably farmed foods" or "increase the amount of conserved rainforest land." For many, this change flows out of the goal of aligning investments with your personal values or purpose—as some will say, "owning what you own"—or your aligning with your organizational mission to avoid reputational risk.

What Is Your Hypothesis?

What do you believe, based on your experience or research? We see a spectrum from very focused hypotheses, such as those surrounding the value of board diversity or firm ownership, to broader or more comprehensive assessments of the impact on women across a company's recruiting, employment, supply chain, and products. Fund managers, specifically, need to clarify if their investors are clearly seeing this opportunity, or they will need to educate them on its merits.

What Is Your Approach?

Likewise, some investors use gender factors as a primary element while others incorporate the information in a more tertiary way. Still others have a more evolutionary approach, one that starts with asking more gender informed questions in due diligence. Often these choices are influenced by whether the data exist and can be simply added to a process or would need to be gathered or acquired.

How Do You Want to Engage?

There is an emerging ecosystem of gender lens investors. You should think about whom you want to connect with and what you can learn from them. If you consider yourself a leader in the field, you want to also be looking for whom to follow. If you have big ideas, connecting with others is how to scale them. If you are a practicing gender lens investor, share your best practices and lessons learned.

Can You Extend Impact with Philanthropy?

Gender lens investors often strategically employ philanthropic capital to achieve their goals. Some funds have philanthropic sidecar vehicles to support technical assistance. Other funders seek to support research around challenges which disproportionately affect women and lack investable solutions. For instance, an Australian gender lens investor is seeking to catalyze an ecosystem approach to solutions which prevent or cure incontinence. Research grants can lead to new vehicles, such as the Gates Foundation support, which enabled Root Capital to conduct essential analysis before launching Women in Agriculture. Subsidies may also make a vehicle viable, like how philanthropic support from Goldman Sachs incents regional banks to enter the women's market and access loan capital from the IFC. And as those engaged in the field know, ongoing funding for research and convening is critical. Funding from the Wallace Foundation, for instance, enabled Criterion Institute to write a "State of the Field" report, increasing the breadth and depth of understanding. And launching networks like the Women Effect, which then bring new investors to the table, often requires initial philanthropic support.[44]

Notes

1. Ordinary Person's Guide To Empire (2005 edition), Penguin Books India – ISBN: 9780144001606, http://www.goodreads.com/quotes/76282-another-world-is-not-only-possible-she-is-on-her.
2. Claudia Goldin. "A Grand Convergence: Its Last Chapter," *American Economic Review* 104(4) (2014): 1091–1119. dx.doi.org/10.1257/aer.104.4.1091, scholar.harvard.edu/files/goldin/files/goldin_aeapress_2014_1.pdf?m=1401372863.
3. Joy Anderson and Katherine Miles, "The State of the Field of Gender Lens Investing: A Review and a Road Map", Prepared by the Criterion Institute with support from the Wallace Global Fund. October 1, 2015, http://criterioninstitute.org/wp-content/uploads/2012/06/State-of-the-Field-of-Gender-Lens-Investing-11-24-2015.pdf.
4. Joe Keefe, "A Personal Rememberance of Linda Pei", http://www.paxellevate.com/fund/linda-pei-remembrance.
5. Invest in Companies that Invest in Women, BMO, May 19, 2016, https://bmoforwomen.bmo.com/invest-in-companies-that-invest-in-women/.
6. Personal correspondence (Kristi Mitchem, July 15, 2016).

7. Personal correspondence (Chris Ailman, March 10, 2016).

8. *Women and Girls Equality: A Clear Focus for Social Investing*, U.S. Trust, http://www.ustrust.com/ust/Pages/ArticleViewer.aspx?Title=women-and-girls-equality-strategy.

9. Personal correspondence (Cathy Schreiber, March 4, 2016).

10. Sarah Kaplan and Jackie Vanderbrug, The Rise of Gender Capitalism, Stanford Social Innovation Review, Fall 2014, http://ssir.org/articles/entry/the_rise_of_gender_capitalism.

11. Aperio Group, Press Release: May 17, 2015, https://www.aperiogroup.com/resource/431/node/download.

12. Green Alpha Advisors Nia Global Solutions Fact Sheet, June 30, 2016, http://greenalphaadvisors.com/wp-content/uploads/2016/07/Nia-Profile_06302016.pdf.

13. "Two Years After Rana Plaza Collapse, Investors Still Look to Apparell Brands and Retailers for Remediation, Press Release, Interfaith Center on Corporate Responsibility, April 23, 2015, http://www.iccr.org/two-years-after-rana-plaza-collapse-investors-still-look-apparel-brands-and-retailers-remediation.

14. Melissa Wylie, "Meet the Activist Investor Going After the Giants on Gender Pay," *BizJournal* (May 12, 2016). www.bizjournals.com/boston/blog/techflash/2016/05/boston-meet-the-activist-investor-going-after.html.

15. Anna Yukhananov, "First Women's Bond from World Bank Raises $165 Million," Reuters (November 6, 2013). www.reuters.com/article/worldbank-women-bond-idUSL2N0IR1IN20131106.

16. "Goldman Sachs 10,000 Women, IFC to Raise up to $600 Million to Support Women Entrepreneurs," press release (March 5, 2014). www.goldmansachs.com/citizenship/10000women/news-and-events/10000women-ifc.html.

17. National Women's Law Center, Poverty & Income Among Women & Families, 2000-2013.

18. Sara McLafferty and Valerie Preston, "Women's Employment: Insights from New York." www.fhwa.dot.gov/ohim/womens/chap19.pdf http://docplayer.net/9036446-Sara-mclafferty-valerie-preston-hunter-college-city-university-of-new-york-york-university-toronto.html.

19. Robert Kropp, "Community Capital Management a Top Fund Performer in 2015", Sustainability Investment News, January 23, 2016, http://www.socialfunds.com/news/article.cgi?sfArticleId=4193.

20. "How to Upgrade Your Due Diligence with a Gender Lens (3.0)," The Criterion Institute. (February 11, 2016), criterioninstitute.org/resources/2016/02/11/how-to-upgrade-your-due-diligence-with-lens/.

21. http://www.bbgventures.com/about/.
22. Personal interview (Sharon Vosmek, September 23, 2015).
23. www.goldenseeds.com/who-we-are/vision.
24. www.prasac.com.kh/en/about-us/profile/.
25. Personal correspondence (David Korslund, September 5, 2016).
26. Bamboo Finance 2015 Impact Report: "Maintaining Momentum and Building Partnerships." The Impact Report details updates from the October 2014 Clinton Global Initiative, where Bamboo Finance pledged to conduct efforts to move from Output to Outcome.
27. Personal interview (Catherine Gill, March 14, 2016).
28. Calvert Foundation, Press Release, March 11, 2014, http://www.calvert foundation.org/press/releases/472-win-win-surpasses-20-million.
29. Anne-Marie Slaughter, "Entrepreneurship as a Diplomatic Tool," Project-Syndicate, March 23, 2016, https://www.project-syndicate.org/commentary/entrepreneurship-as-a-diplomatic-tool-by-anne-marie-slaughter-and-elmira-bayrasli-2016-03" \l "goceXigDdVcosoLy.99.
30. Catherine Cheney, "A New Fund for Women Is the Next Step for Kiva's Evolution," *DevEx* (February 29, 2016). www.devex.com/news/new-fund-for-women-is-the-next-step-in-kiva-s-evolution-87802.
31. www.capitalsisters.org.
32. Self Help Credit Union Women and Children Term Certificate, as of September 2016, https://www.self-help.org/personal/accounts/certificates/women-children-term-certificate.
33. MCE Social Capital, November 2014, http://www.mcesocap.org/wp-content/uploads/2014/11/MCE-Guarantor-Overview-11.20.14.pdf.
34. Amy Cortese, "From Donuts to Bionic Organs, Entrepreneurs Start Raising Under Regulation Crowd Funding," Locavesting.com (May 16, 2016). www.locavesting.com/crowdfunding/from-doughnuts-to-bionic-organs-entrepreneurs-start-raising-under-regulation-crowdfunding/.
35. Jason Greenberg, Ethan R. Mollick, Leaning In or Leaning On? Gender, Homophily, and Activism in Crowdfunding, July 7, 2016, Administrative Science Quarterly, Forthcoming, http://papers.ssrn.com/sol3/papers.cfm?abstract_id=2462254.
36. Ethan Mollick, "The Unique Value of Crowdfunding Is Not Money— It's Community," *Harvard Business Review* (April 21, 2016). hbr.org/2016/04/the-unique-value-of-crowdfunding-is-not-money-its-community.
37. www.un.org/sustainabledevelopment/poverty/.
38. www.womeneffect.com.
39. Jeffrey Sohl, Center for Venture Research, The Angel Investor Market in 2015: A Buyers Market, http://paulcollege.unh.edu/center-venture-research.
40. http://pipelineangels.com/about-pipeline-angels.

41. blog.girltank.org.
42. Personal Interview (Edward Powers, December 10, 2015).
43. "The Business Case for Women's Economic Empowerment: An Integrated Approach," Oak Foundation, 2014.
44. Joy Anderson and Katherine Miles, "The State of the Field of Gender Lens Investing: A Review and a Road Map," Prepared by the Criterion Institute with support from the Wallace Global Fund, October 1, 2015, http://criterioninstitute.org/wp-content/uploads/2012/06/State-of-the-Field-of-Gender-Lens-Investing-11-24-2015.pdf.

CHAPTER 9

A Start That's Here to Stay

"The future is already here—It's just not evenly distributed yet."[1]

—William Gibson

Financial investment fads and products come and go. The churn is constant. What is hot today can be terribly cold tomorrow. Remember the Goldman Sachs BRIC Fund named for the strategy that put Brazil, Russia, India, and China all in the same basket? While a brilliant marketing label, the BRICs really did not have much in common and did not belong in the same basket. Although the fund was not designed to maximize social impact, as it turned out it didn't have much financial impact, either. In 2015, the fund closed after years of underperforming returns.[2] By contrast, gender lens investing is no such fad.

Gender lens investing is neither a theme nor a product. It is a process conceived at the intersection of capital and culture. It is designed to cultivate financial and social value. And it is here to stay. Because investments have always, and will always, have an impact on gender equality: good, bad, or ugly. Recognizing women as an economic asset, and learning how gender affects our lives, is moving from the periphery to the core of the policies, strategies, and practices of nations, enterprises, and investors with each passing year. Arguably, the world has been on this path for as long as we have been alive, if not longer. One reason is the United States. As we wrote at the beginning of this book:

> The U.S. economy has stood on the shoulders of women through two world wars, the oil shocks of the 1970s, and multiple recessions. Whatever the challenge or crisis, American women have been part of the solution.

The gender-equality growth agenda is gaining acceptance not only among government leaders globally, but also among corporations. In the capital markets, all things gender are being recognized as important metrics in evaluating business risk, value, and returns, as well as assessing megatrends such as climate change and changing workforce demographics.

We don't subscribe to the thesis that capitalism has reached the end of its run.[3] Far from it. In 2008, Gurcharan Das, a former P&G executive in India, reflected on the "Dharma of Wall Street." He wrote: The "successes of capitalism produces over time enervating influences… Ferocious competition is a feature of the free market and it can be corrosive. But competition is also an economic stimulant that promotes human welfare."[4] We see gender capitalism emerging as a socio-economic stimulant to reimagining capitalism. We also see it building the world's capacity for intergenerational sustainable development as it was defined by Gro Harlem Brundtland, the former (and first female) prime minister of Norway, at the first Earth Summit in 1992.

New forms of ownership, lending, legal rights, and protections are defining a business subculture around gender thanks to the ingenuity and tenacity of women and men from many countries. In the end, how we deploy capital shapes where it grows, how it grows and the world we live in. It shapes who has the power to solve problems, which problems are solved, and which are left unexplored. That's something that should appeal to many investors.

On International Women's Day, March 8, 2016, the possibility of finance as a force for gender equality, and combining financial and social returns on investment, was celebrated in financial centers across the globe. Thirty-four stock exchanges joined together "Ringing the Bell for Gender Equality." Over the course of the week, opening and closing bells rang around the earth from Egypt to Australia, from Côte d'Ivoire to Peru, from the United States to the South Pacific. The World Federation of Stock Exchanges, the

Sustainable Stock Exchanges Initiative, the UN Global Compact, UN Women, and Women ETFs joined to underscore the business case for women's economic empowerment and the opportunities for the private sector to advance gender equality and sustainable development together. UN Women and the purveyors of global capitalism celebrating together? Unfathomable a decade ago but indicative of the decades to come.

The Tailwinds and the Trends

Yes, it is still early days for gender lens investors but we believe these are the major developments that will influence the pace, breadth, and quality of adoption of this new investment discipline.

The UN Sustainable Development Goals (SDGs)

At the United Nations Sustainable Development Summit on September 25, 2015, after days of debate and discussion, world leaders came together to adopt the 2030 Agenda for Sustainable Development, which includes a set of 17 Sustainable Development Goals (SDGs) to end poverty, fight inequality and injustice, and tackle climate change.[5] These 17 goals (and 169 targets) now guide the direction of international development—policies, investment, and aid for the entire world. The scale of the investment needed to meet the SDGs is stunning; the World Bank estimates the annual investment required to achieve the 2030 goals at $5 trillion to $7 trillion. Gender equality is both a single overarching goal (SDG goal 5: Achieve gender equality and empower all women and girls) as well as a catalyst for change serving as a crosscutting lens guiding implementation across all 17 SDG goals.

The principal objectives build on the United Nations Millennium Development Goals (MDGs), which committed, in 2000, to dramatically reduce poverty, hunger, disease, and gender inequality, and to increase access to water and sanitation by 2015.[6] The aspiration for SDGs is no less than to end poverty and put in place better systems to promote shared and balanced prosperity worldwide. The SDGs lay out a set of goals applicable to countries at all levels of economic development—not just the very poor. Their "zero goals" approach (e.g. ending poverty and hunger not simply reducing them) says we are shooting for the moon and no one will be left behind. Targeting "finishing the job" demands an unprecedented scaling of markets and the participation of all sectors—for-profit, government, and NGOs. In areas where there has been or could be market failure, some concessionary capital will be needed, but the strategic thrust is market-driven solutions.

In these times of partisan and polarized political debates, the agreement on the SDGs was created in an extraordinarily productive participatory process, including online input from millions of people and face-to-face events in over 100 countries. The commitment to act is real but all these efforts require good data on gender that is either hard to find or does not exist. A recent count yielded 28 policy-relevant global gender data gaps across five domains: health, education, economic opportunities, political participation, and human security.[7] One-third of the minimum set of 52 indicators proposed by the UN Statistics Division to track progress on gender issues cannot be generated internationally because they fall short in conceptual clarity, coverage, regular country production, or international standards.[8] Only three of the proposed indicators for the gender equality and empowerment of women and girls goal are currently widely available.

The UN mandate will affect gender lens investing in three related but different ways. First, as the goals become more embedded and acted upon, companies will have more incentives to participate, as will investors. This flywheel effect can be powerful. For example, as the world looks to tackle human health issues such as sanitation, preventable diseases, hunger, and food security, there will be increased interest to invest in women entrepreneurs or funds and enterprises engaging women who hold the keys to solutions.

Second, initiatives like Data2x, dedicated to improving worldwide access to gender data, will propel efforts to improve available information and data needs. Data2x has already proposed sixteen "ready to measure" indicators focused on women and girls that map to major UN goals. These outcome-oriented measures have agreed-upon definitions and provide wide enough coverage to create solid baselines.[9] These data-and more that is generated as the space evolves will be catalytic to gender lens investors.

Third, while UN funding in the past has come primarily from aid, the SDGs put coordinated capital flows from both the private and public sectors at the center of their strategy. As the 2014 United National Conference on Trade and Development's "World Investment Report" put it, "The role of the public sector is fundamental and pivotal, while the private sector contribution is indispensable. The latter can take two main forms, good governance in business practices and investment in sustainable development."[10] To do this, capital investment from corporations, multilateral banks, and foundations has to be better coordinated than it ever has been.

Impact investors like Sonen Capital, a San Francisco–based investment, have already begun to report how their investments contribute to achieving the UN goals.[11] They and others increasingly have the data to support this work. For instance, MSCI's ESG Research launched a framework that investors can use to measure their current exposure to public companies providing sustainable impact solutions. MSCI categorizes the seventeen SDGs into five actionable investment themes—basic needs, empowerment, climate change, natural capital, and governance—and evaluates revenue for 2500 companies within these themes.[12] The MSCI ACWI Sustainable Impact Index identifies companies with at least 50 percent of their revenues from products and services that address environmental and social challenges as defined by the themes.

FinTech

FinTech—the innovative uses of information technology in financial services—is set to be another driver of gender lens investing.

When viewed through a gender lens, the socially and economically disruptive potential of FinTech solutions that specifically benefit women come into focus. First, 1.1 billion women globally make up a large percentage of the world's unbanked population. Mobile banking through a cell phone was an initial step to their financial inclusion. Now apps are spreading the use of a mobile device to deposit checks, receive wages directly, check balances, or transfer funds. FinTech firms will expand access to capital for women entrepreneurs through unsecured loans and nontraditional credit scoring models. Mary Ellen Iskendarian of Women's World Banking offers examples including AMP Credit Technologies, CAN Capital, and Kabbage, which offer unsecured loans to small and medium size enterprises (SMEs) without a formal credit history by analyzing borrower data such as revenue, monthly sales, and credit card payments. In the Philippines, AMP Credit Technologies has seen 53 percent of its loans originate to women-owned businesses, many of which are service-oriented.[13,14]

These small business owners (beauty salons, childcare, restaurants, and more) often do not hold physical collateral, but can electronically verify cash flows. FinTech firms use this information to automate lender decisions on "character" and "capacity" that are part of managing risk in unsecured working capital loans.

In addition to providing tools where they are culturally accepted, FinTech can also be culturally disruptive and threatening to financial systems in countries where working women are not welcome. "Fintech will not eliminate prejudice or stupidity, but the fact that it relies on data and technology to execute its functions means we can expect fewer cases of sexism and ignorance skewing decision-making," says Toby Triebel, CEO and co-founder of Spotcap, an online lender for SMEs and an investor in corporate and bank credit at a leading emerging-markets hedge fund. The FinTech industry can also drive cultural change as it establishes itself: Triebel cites organizations like KashF in Bangladesh that work with FinTech companies to teach women about financial management and help mentor them to start businesses.[15]

(Big) Data and Gender

We live in a world where every day there are 803 million Tweets; 36 million Amazon purchases; 8.8 billion YouTube videos watched; 186 million Instagram photos posted; 152 million Skype calls placed; 2.3 billion gigabytes of web traffic; and 4.2 billion Google searches. Services industries and knowledge-based activities have driven economic growth in Europe and North America for some time. Now, services businesses in India, Brazil, and even China account for more than half of total output. The Internet and digital technologies are part of the services revolution. Big data is the lubricant of growth, innovation, and competitiveness.

Big data is an umbrella term referring to the massive digital data continually generated as a byproduct of everyday interactions with digital products or services. Big data—often characterized by its great volume, variety, and a high rate of velocity—could have a profound effect on expanding data sets and supporting gender-driven growth policies, especially for developing countries. Counter to what many may believe, the problems with missing information about women and girls go beyond simply having data gaps. Gender data are often erroneous or inaccurate. Data collection methods and measures can systematically misrepresent reality, perpetuating inaccuracies by making women appear to be more dependent and less productive than they are, and so forth. For example, the design of census surveys misreports women's work when women report employment that is secondary (to housework), seasonal, or informal.

Looking at big data in a corporate context, Google is far ahead of most companies with respect to using human resource data for talent management. But investment firms like Morgan Stanley and BlackRock's HR departments are also being transformed by the addition of experts in people analytics who can create actionable (versus administrative) HR data that can be used to develop strategies (including gender) for attracting, retaining, and promoting talented people for the right positions. Matthew Breitfelder, a managing director at BlackRock and the firm's chief talent officer, says that data analytics and behavioral research have been critical to advancing BlackRock's talent & diversity agenda. An important step took place a few years ago when the firm brought Harvard Professor Mahzarin Banaji in to address an executive offsite featuring her social psychology research on unconscious bias. "At the time, we weren't sure how this work would be received," he acknowledged, "but our senior leaders immediately understood the connection between mitigating unconscious bias, robust talent practices and driving better talent decision-making. Since that time, we have significantly increased our focus on data analytics in how we attract, retain, and develop our talent and build a more diverse workforce." As other companies follow leaders like BlackRock, the data will help them to achieve that advantage by better understanding the effectiveness of their management processes and the predictive value of people analytics.[16]

Gender and Workplace Research

Corporations are utilizing the growing body of gender and workplace research by scholars such as Harvard's Iris Bohnet (who is also a nonexecutive director at Credit Suisse) and Robin Ely and Deborah Myerson at the Harvard Business School.

For a well-known case study, Meyerson and Ely spent several weeks on two different oil platforms over a period of nineteen months—living, eating, and working alongside the offshore rig's 100 percent male crew. Meyerson and Ely chose this environment because they thought that in dangerous work settings, the gender norms for men—including taking risks, demonstrating physical prowess, and concealing any incompetence or fears—lead to poor decision making and accidents.

Myerson and Ely studied the behavior of crew members at the same time as the company's management took actions to get the men to tone down their hard-driving, macho behaviors. Over time, the men began to admit to dangerous mistakes in judgment and they explored how their mistakes caused them anxiety and stress, and even to doubt their competence. They began to publicly acknowledge their appreciation of each other and they started to routinely ask for and offer help. "These workers shifted their focus from proving their masculinity to larger, more compelling goals: maximizing the safety and well-being of coworkers and doing their jobs effectively," write Ely and Meyerson.[17]

The results speak loudly. The company's accident rate declined by 84 percent while the number of barrels of oil produced, cost per barrel, and production "uptime" increased beyond the industry's previous benchmark. Meyerson and Ely also concluded, "If men in the hyper-masculine environment of oil rigs can let go of the macho ideal and improve their performance, then men in corporate America might be able to do likewise." Indeed, they posed the question: What can managers in white-collar firms learn from roughnecks and roustabouts on an offshore oil rig? The answer cited numerous studies from several industries to show how macho behavior in corporate workplaces "interfere with the training of recruits, compromise decision quality, marginalize women workers, lead to civil- and human-rights violations, and alienate men from their health, feelings, and relationships with others."[18]

Who are the companies making changes based on these trends and this research? The launch in 2016 of Bloomberg's new Financial Gender-Equality Index includes twenty-six publicly traded companies vetted for gender diversity and women-friendly policies. The index will give investors valuable data on the included companies, allowing investors to better gauge their performance relative to the broader market. This index, along with a small but growing ranks of diversity-related ETFs and Index Funds, "gives me hope that the market is beginning to accept the growing body of research that finds that female leadership and gender diversity help the bottom line," wrote Kristen Bellstrom, the intrepid editor of *Fortune*'s daily e-mail, "The Broad Sheet," on the day of the launch.[19]

Men and Women Standing for Equality

A significant part of the case for caring about gender is that it includes the half of the population previously ignored—or under-valued, at best. With that history, you can believe that the field of gender lens investing isn't about to make the same mistake and ignore the male half of the population. As mentioned previously, this is about using a *gender* lens, not a *women's* lens. Men are as important as, or, arguably, as leadership positions are still largely held by men, perhaps more important than women in understanding and making more gender-informed decisions.

Michael Kimmel, an American sociologist, expert on masculinity in American culture, and a self-described "white, middle-class, middle-aged man," was a member of the class of 1969 at Vassar College, one of the first of the U.S. seven sisters colleges to go co-ed.[20] Kimmel has probably done more in his forty-year career than most men of his age group to advance understanding of gender and gender inequality. In 2013, he founded the Center for the Study of Men and Masculinities at Stony Brook University, dedicated to promoting gender equality through solid empirical research. His advisory board includes three of the most famous and outspoken feminists, Gloria Steinem, Jane Fonda, and Eve Ensler (creator of *The Vagina Monologues*). However, in dialogues about gender with men, Kimmel says when he "omits the "F-word" (*feminism*) he does better.[21] Awareness around language (and especially how the word *feminism* is received) is an example of how an informed gender expert can know how to expertly advance conversations on the topic.

Catalyst, founded in 1962 and one of the oldest and most respected women's advocacy and gender research organizations for corporations, has for years published research on the role of men and the importance of engaging them in leading change initiatives toward gender equality and equity. Initially, their work found little audience, and in 2009 they reported, "Regrettably, in their exclusive focus on women, rather than engaging men, many companies have unwittingly alienated [men], inadvertently jeopardizing the success of their gender initiatives."[22]

But today, thanks to resources like MARC (Men Advocating for Real Change), an online community for men started by Catalyst, change is visible. The MARC website serves as a forum in which its members can engage in candid conversations about the role of gender in the workplace. It also showcases member-generated advice, insights, and best practices to inspire men who wish to expand gender diversity within their organizations. Women are welcome to join MARC, the website says, but "its primary purpose to support and inspire men to seek meaningful change.[23]

Male corporate champions for gender equity are increasingly joined by celebrities and millions of average Joes. The meme of the day has shifted, and supporting the achievement of gender equality and women's rights feels more mainstream than fringe. These days, starting with Millennials and younger cohorts, gender equality is seen as a right, not a point of debate; and the conversation is taking place across all genders, not just among women. Majorities in thirty-seven of the thirty-eight countries surveyed by the Pew Charitable Trust in March 2016 said that gender equality was at least "somewhat important." And a global median of 65 percent believe it is "very important" that women have the same rights as men, ranking second only to support for religious freedom among the six democratic values tested.[24]

The UN Women #HeforShe campaign, grounded in the idea that gender equality is an issue that affects all people—socially, economically, and politically—engaged high-profile male leaders from President Obama to Matt Damon to Farhan Akhtar, a Bollywood superstar. Films like *The Mask You Live In*, which explore the struggles of young men to meet the current narrow definition of masculinity, have spurred on the debate about gender roles and desires for both men and women. Gender differences and biases are a fact of life, but as the negative effects become more visible, there is a growing unity among women and men to find better ways to discuss and deal with unfair and uncivil behavior.

Women with Money

The minuscule number of women managing funds today is troubling, though not surprising. In 2009, the National Council of Research on Women called attention to the issue with a ground-breaking report, "Women in Fund Management." Sadly, little has changed. Despite strong returns from women fund managers, fund management is over 90 percent male.[25] Various initiatives are again raising the issue, including a recent collaboration between the Small Business Association (SBA), National Venture Capital Association (NVCA), CrunchBase, and Square 1 Bank. In the words of SBA administrator Contreras-Sweet, "Empowering women investors isn't some act of charity, it's good business."[26] Some gender lens investors agree, and have begun to actively scan for women fund managers.

Younger individual investors and women who have both earned and inherited money are increasingly actively engaged with their financial portfolios. They bring different perspectives, experiences, and priorities to their process, including a greater interest in gender lens investing. "We need 50 percent of the population who could be investing actively to bring their insights and their expertise to the table, and then we need 50 percent of the people coming up with the inspired solutions, who are not getting access to capital, to get access to capital," says Suzanne Biegel, founder of the Clearly Social Angels network in the United Kingdom, whose membership is indeed half women.[27]

The engagement of individuals will change adviser behavior. Advisors notoriously avoid topics they believe might be controversial or where they feel they might not have all the answers. Gender lens investing can be controversial and raise challenging questions. Given that, advisers avoid the topic, fearing either it is militant feminism (and thus, off-putting), or because they don't want to be asked a question they can't answer. These concerns are warranted and need to be addressed.

With regard to being controversial, advisors need the training and opportunity to explore how to intelligently and authentically discuss gender. Like any other new product or sector, advisors need to build up their vocabularies, stories, and data points to discuss gender lens investing. And with regard to not having all the answers and coming off as incompetent, remember: gender lens investing is actually an opportunity to deepen the client–advisor relationship. Institutional families are seeking advisors who ask questions, listen for interest, and demonstrate willingness to explore options.[28]

Gender Investing Hurdles

Having detailed the significant tailwinds and trends, we turn to acknowledge the very real hurdles. Gender lens investing hit the mainstream through a series of new products. Immediately, skeptics asked about the overall assets under management, or AUM. A good question with a complicated answer: Sizing the market is actually difficult, in part because it is not a market, an asset class, or a product. It is, as we said, a practice or approach. That said, no funds publicly promoting their incorporation of gender factors in investment decisions are over a billion dollars. Most are under a hundred million. Some may dismiss the field upon hearing that. They should not.

With a limited view of AUM, the analysis fails to include the potential linkage of gender to sovereign bond ratings, to global infrastructure projects, or to major mutual funds. It is also misses the momentum and transformative potential of gender lens investing on capital markets. Sure, the AUM on self-identified gender lens funds is relatively small. But the more accurate view of gender lens investing is to think about the impact on financial systems, and arguably, on the evolution and improved functioning of capitalism as a whole. Think about it this way: Every investment has some interplay with gender.

Women's World Banking Asset Management (WWBAM), a $50 million private equity fund, hits few people's radar. But its work with the board of India's Ujjivan Financial Services led to the most successful IPO in the country's history. The Ujjivan IPO broke all records for domestic-only IPOs; it was oversubscribed forty-one times. It was initially valued at over $375 million, but climbed above $425 million once it started trading. Through its board seat, WWBAM supported the firm's entry into a new market of direct loans to women (versus group loans) as well as an application for a Small Bank License so that it could also offer savings products, which are critical to women clients. Having an ally in the boardroom with deep insight on the full potential of the female client base proved invaluable.[29]

Data, mentioned previously as a tailwind, is of course also a hurdle. Even with the efforts underway to eliminate the gender data gap, it will take hard work to fill it. While the increase in companies reporting gender-disaggregated data is encouraging, it's far from universal, and especially missing from smaller firms. With big data there will be a sea of information, but little history to determine what gender data are material. It's likely this will have different patterns by sector, and identifying and understanding these patterns will take time to learn. Technology, for instance, may have stronger returns from diversity in R&D while in other sectors it may be in sales. We will benefit from understanding the relationship of gender to safety records and to software usage, to absenteeism and promotions, to acquiring patents, and to retaining clients.

And finally, myths and generalizations—women like pink, are tender, emotional, and less analytical than men—are not going to go away anytime soon. But they often stand in the way of progress.

Despite evidence to the contrary, gender lens investing can be perceived as "soft"—that is, based on subjective. In the investing world subjective approaches are often quickly dismissed. We need to be clear: This is not "feel-good investing." Nor does adding gender analysis reduce the rigor of traditional investment analysis. In fact, it makes it stronger. The research studies and product track records will change minds as long as we keep our biases and stereotypes in check.

Gender and the Path to Better Investing

Gender lens investing is here to stay because it works. With the additional information and context of a gender analysis, investors can make more informed, more prudent decisions.

The fundamental concepts of seeking alpha and reducing beta remain. It is all in how you define them. It is also about how the questions are framed. How do we use gender to make calls on risk and growth more accurate? In early-stage drug companies, how might investors value the knowledge a company was required to use in sex-disaggregated drug testing? How might sovereign debt ratings be correlated to maternal mortality numbers?

For a gender lens to be seen as advancing an investment strategy and a useful addition or augmentation to traditional methods, it must:

1. Be adopted by mainstream investors.
2. Become increasingly sophisticated.
3. Stay diverse and flexible.

Let's look at each of these as we close out this book.

Be Adopted by Mainstream Investors

The brokers of power have already shown interest and found that there are both investable signals and interested clients. While some worry (understandably) about hastily contrived products for a hot market (aka *pink washing*), we see obvious benefits in the resources such firms bring to analysis and the influence their questions wield. And not only does their investment matter, their inquiries do as well. When a large fund manager inquires about retention of female managers or supply chain stability, it matters. Without this, gender lens investing remains a niche play for social activists.

Become Increasingly Sophisticated

Gender lens investing will fail to deliver its potential without increasingly sophisticated gender analysis. Headcounts don't show you what is in people's heads. We've seen that counting women on the board helpful as a measure of who is in the main board-room. The next step is evaluating the gendered nature of board recruitment processes, board committee structures (and who is on them), and even board is culture. And that's just considering corporate boards. When gender design experts support venture capitalists or when gender-informed anthropologists advise on infrastructure financing, investors' insights multiply and mistakes are avoided. Without this, gender lens investing risks missing the true innovations, remaining on the fringe or, worse, underperforming financially or socially.

Stay Diverse and Flexible

Gender lens investing benefits from diversity in objectives, asset classes and approaches. Without experimentation, we won't know how a gender analysis might change real estate investment profiles, or improve municipal debt ratings or shift equity owners to a longer-term orientation. The "big tent" provides powerful cross pollination. The accelerator and seed stage investor designs a due-diligence process to manage or eliminate gender bias after hearing of work at a peer program. The municipal bond portfolio manager gains an insight from talking with a pay-for-success (social impact bond) architect. There are new approaches to be tried, emerging hypothesis to be considered and additional data to be analyzed. It is far too early to declare narrowly what is (or isn't) gender lens investing.

Gender lens investing presents an opportunity to act on your beliefs and use your investments to shape the world we live in. It holds promise as an innovation on its own and a force for change that goes well beyond the financial markets to benefit future generations. Perhaps most compelling it is the very essence of a sustainable development—meeting the needs of investors today without compromising the needs of investors tomorrow.

Those who take the lead today—internally and externally in gender equality, gender equity, gender lens investing—will be the investment leaders of tomorrow.

Notes

1. William Gibson, The Economist, December 4, 2003.
2. Ye Xie, "Goldman's BRIC Era Fund Folds after Years of Losses," Bloomberg (November 8, 2015). www.bloomberg.com/news/articles/2015-11-08/goldman-s-bric-era-ends-as-fund-closes-after-years-of-losses.
3. Paul Mason, "The End of Capitalism Has Begun," *The Guardian* (July 17, 2015). www.theguardian.com/books/2015/jul/17/postcapitalism-end-of-capitalism-begun.
4. Gurcharan Das, "Dharma Fails on Wall Street," *The Times of India* (March 15, 2009). timesofindia.indiatimes.com/gurcharan-das/men-ideas/Dharma-fails-on-Wall-Street/articleshow/4265522.cms?.
5. "Sustainable Development Goals," UNDP.com (2016). www.undp.org/content/undp/en/home/sdgoverview/post-2015-development-agenda.html.
6. "Millennium Development Goals," UNDP.com (2016). www.undp.org/content/undp/en/home/sdgoverview/mdg_goals.html.
7. Maya Buvinic and Ruth Levine, "What Is Wrong with Data on Women and Girls," Data2X.org (November 2015). data2x.org/wp-content/uploads/2014/08/What-Is-Wrong-with-Data-on-Women-and-Girls_November-2015_WEB_1.pdf.
8. *A World That Counts: Mobilising the Data Revolution for Sustainable Development* (The UN Data Revolution Group, 2014). http://www.undatarevolution.org/wp-content/uploads/2014/12/A-World-That-Counts2.pdf.
9. data2x.org/wp-content/uploads/2014/08/Ready_to_Measure.pdf.
10. http://unctad.org/en/PublicationsLibrary/wir2014_en.pdf.
11. "How One Impact Investing Firm Is Mapping the SDGs," *Devex News* (April 11, 2016). www.southsouthnews.com/civil-society/civil-society-features/102-civil-society-and-ngos/devex-news/94981-how-one-impact-investing-firm-is-mapping-the-sdgs.
12. "A Benchmark to Incorporate Sustainable Impact in Your Investment Process," MSCI.com. www.msci.com/msci-acwi-sustainable-impact-index.
13. AMP Credit Technologies internal analysis as of June 2015.
14. Mary Ellen Iskenderian, president and CEO of Women's World Banking, "Unlocking the Potential of Women-Owned SMEs Through FinTech," Global Agenda Council on the Future of Financing & Capital 2016.
15. SpotTheBlindSpot.com.
16. Personal interview (Matthew Breitfelder, May 11, 2016).
17. Robin J. Ely and Debra Meyerson, "Unmasking Manly Men," *Harvard Business Review* (July–August 2008). hbr.org/2008/07/unmasking-manly-men.
18. Ibid.

19. Valentina Zarya, "Bloomberg's New Gender Equality Index Shows Who's Investing in Women," *Fortune* (May 3, 2016). fortune.com/2016/05/03/bloomberg-gender-equality-index/.

20. Michael Kimmel, "Openings: Why Gender Equality Is One for the Boys," *Financial Times* (March 4, 2016). www.ft.com/intl/cms/s/0/947331d8-e062-11e5-8d9b-e88a2a889797.html#axzz4ALArUUmt.

21. Libby Copeland, "Michael Kimmel Is Out to Show Why Feminism Is Good for Men," *Washington Post* (March 8, 2015). www.washingtonpost.com/lifestyle/style/michael-kimmel-is-out-to-show-why-feminism-is-good-for-men/2015/03/08/bedd603e-c50f-11e4-9271-610273846239_story.html.

22. Jean Prime and Corinne Moss-Racusin, "Engaging Men in Gender Initiatives, What Change Agents Need to Know," *Catalyst* (2009). www.catalyst.org/system/files/Engaging_Men_In_Gender_Initiatives_What_Change_Agents_Need_To_Know.pdf.

23. Men Advocating for Real Change. onthemarc.org/about.

24. Hani Zainulbhai, "Strong Global Support for Gender Equality, Especially Among Women," Pew Research Center (March 8, 2016). www.pewresearch.org/fact-tank/2016/03/08/strong-global-support-for-gender-equality-especially-among-women/.

25. Laura Pavlenko Lutton and Erin Davis, Morningstar Research Report, *Fund Managers by Gender*, June 2015. http://corporate.morningstar.com/US/documents/ResearchPapers/Fund-Managers-by-Gender.pdf.

26. Erin Andrew, "Bridging the Venture Capital Gender Gap," SBA (May 13, 2016). www.sba.gov/blogs/bridging-venture-capital-gender-gap.

27. David Bank, *Women Are Hot…Investments*, January 23, 2014. http://www.huffingtonpost.com/david-bank/women-are-hotinvestments_b_4151632.html.

28. Julia Balandina Jaquier, *Catalyzing Wealth for Change: Guide to Impact Investing For High Net Worth Individuals, Family Offices, Foundations, and Businesses*, 2016.

29. *Behind the Most Successful Microfinance IPO in India's History: What does gender lens investing have to do with it?*, May 17, 2016. http://nextbillion.net/behind-the-most-successful-microfinance-ipo-in-indias-history-what-does-gender-lens-investing-have-to-do-with-it/CJJuhasz.

Index

Note: Page references followed by f and t indicate an illustrated figure and table, respectively.